THE MAN

BRAM STOKER

TRUE SIGN
PUBLISHING HOUSE

Published by True Sign Publishing House
Address: SY. No. 21/2 & 21/3, Sonnenahalli,
Krishnarajapura, Bengaluru,
Karnataka - 560049 India
E-mail: truesignbooks@gmail.com
Website: www.truesign.in

The Man
Author: Bram Stoker

ISBN: 978-93-5584-100-1

First Edition: 2022

Contents

Fore-Glimpse

'I would rather be an angel than God!'

The voice of the speaker sounded clearly through the hawthorn tree. The young man and the young girl who sat together on the low tombstone looked at each other. They had heard the voices of the two children talking, but had not noticed what they said; it was the sentiment, not the sound, which roused their attention.

The girl put her finger to her lips to impress silence, and the man nodded; they sat as still as mice whilst the two children went on talking.

* * * * *

The scene would have gladdened a painter's heart. An old churchyard. The church low and square-towered, with long mullioned windows, the yellow-grey stone roughened by age and tender-hued with lichens. Round it clustered many tombstones tilted in all directions. Behind the church a line of gnarled and twisted yews.

The churchyard was full of fine trees. On one side a magnificent cedar; on the other a great copper beech. Here and there among the tombs and headstones many beautiful blossoming trees rose from the long green grass. The laburnum glowed in the June afternoon sunlight; the lilac, the hawthorn and the clustering meadowsweet which fringed the edge of the lazy stream mingled their heavy sweetness in sleepy fragrance. The yellow-grey crumbling walls were green in places with wrinkled harts-tongues, and were topped with sweet-williams and spreading house-leek and stone-crop and wild-flowers whose delicious sweetness made for the drowsy repose of perfect summer.

But amid all that mass of glowing colour the two young figures seated on the grey old tomb stood out conspicuously. The man was in conventional hunting-dress: red coat, white stock, black hat, white breeches, and top-boots. The girl was one of the richest, most glowing, and yet withal daintiest figures the eye of man could linger on. She was in riding-habit of hunting scarlet cloth; her black hat was tipped forward by piled-up masses red-golden hair. Round her neck was a white lawn scarf in the fashion of a man's hunting-stock, close fitting, and sinking into a gold-buttoned waistcoat of snowy twill. As she sat with the long skirt across her left arm her tiny black top-boots appeared underneath. Her gauntleted gloves were of white buckskin; her riding-whip was plaited of white leather, topped with ivory and banded with gold.

Even in her fourteenth year Miss Stephen Norman gave promise of striking beauty; beauty of a rarely composite character. In her the various elements of her race seemed to have cropped out. The firm-set jaw, with chin broader and more square than is usual in a woman, and the wide fine forehead and aquiline nose marked the high descent from Saxon through Norman. The glorious mass of red hair, of the true flame colour, showed the blood of another ancient ancestor of Northern race, and suited well with the voluptuous curves of the full, crimson lips. The purple-black eyes, the raven eyebrows and eyelashes, and the fine curve of the nostrils spoke of the Eastern blood of the far-back wife of the Crusader. Already she was tall for her age, with something of that lankiness which marks the early development of a really fine figure. Long-legged, long-necked, as straight as a lance, with head poised on the proud neck like a lily on its stem.

Stephen Norman certainly gave promise of a splendid womanhood. Pride, self-reliance and dominance were marked in every feature; in her bearing and in her lightest movement.

Her companion, Harold An Wolf, was some five years her senior, and by means of those five years and certain qualities had long stood in the position of her mentor. He was more than six feet two in height, deep-chested, broad-shouldered, lean-flanked, long-armed and big-handed. He had that appearance strength, with well-poised neck and forward set of the head, which marks the successful athlete.

The two sat quiet, listening. Through the quiet hum of afternoon came the voices of the two children. Outside the lich-gate, under the shade of the spreading cedar, the horses stamped occasionally as the flies troubled them. The grooms were mounted; one held the delicate-limbed white Arab, the other the great black horse.

'I would rather be an angel than God!'

The little girl who made the remark was an ideal specimen of the village Sunday-school child. Blue-eyed, rosy-cheeked, thick-legged, with her straight brown hair tied into a hard bunch with a much-creased, cherry-coloured ribbon. A glance at the girl would have satisfied the most sceptical as to her goodness. Without being in any way smug she was radiant with self-satisfaction and well-doing. A child of the people; an early riser; a help to her mother; a good angel to her father; a little mother to her brothers and sisters; cleanly in mind and body; self-reliant, full of faith, cheerful.

The other little girl was prettier, but of a more stubborn type; more passionate, less organised, and infinitely more assertive. Black-haired, black-eyed, swarthy, large-mouthed, snub-nosed; the very type and essence of unrestrained, impulsive, emotional, sensual nature. A seeing eye would have noted inevitable danger for the early years of her womanhood. She seemed amazed by the self-abnegation implied by her companion's statement; after a pause she replied:

'I wouldn't! I'd rather be up at the top of everything and give orders to the angels if I chose. I can't think, Marjorie, why you'd rather take orders than give them.'

'That's just it, Susan. I don't want to give orders; I'd rather obey them. It must be very terrible to have to think of things so much, that you want everything done your own way. And besides, I shouldn't like to have to be just!'

'Why not?' the voice was truculent, though there was wistfulness in it also.

'Oh Susan. Just fancy having to punish; for of course justice needs punishing as well as praising. Now an angel has such a nice time, helping people and comforting them, and bringing sunshine into dark places. Putting down fresh dew every morning; making the flowers grow, and bringing babies and taking care of them till their mothers find them. Of course God is very good and very sweet and very merciful, but oh, He must be very terrible.'

'All the same I would rather be God and able to do things!'

Then the children moved off out of earshot. The two seated on the tombstone looked after them. The first to speak was the girl, who said:

'That's very sweet and good of Marjorie; but do you know, Harold, I like Susie's idea better.'

'Which idea was that, Stephen?'

'Why, didn't you notice what she said: "I'd like to be God and be able to do things"?'

'Yes,' he said after a moment's reflection. 'That's a fine idea in the abstract; but I doubt of its happiness in the long-run.'

'Doubt of its happiness? Come now? what could there be better, after all? Isn't it good enough to be God? What more do you want?'

The girl's tone was quizzical, but her great black eyes blazed with some thought of sincerity which lay behind the fun. The young man shook his head with a smile of kindly tolerance as he answered:

'It isn't that—surely you must know it. I'm ambitious enough, goodness knows; but there are bounds to satisfy even me. But I'm not sure that the good little thing isn't right. She seemed, somehow, to hit a bigger truth than she knew: "fancy having to be just."'

'I don't see much difficulty in that. Anyone can be just!'

'Pardon me,' he answered, 'there is perhaps nothing so difficult in the whole range of a man's work.' There was distinct defiance in the girl's eyes as she asked:

'A man's work! Why a man's work? Isn't it a woman's work also?'

'Well, I suppose it ought to be, theoretically; practically it isn't.'

'And why not, pray?' The mere suggestion of any disability of woman as such aroused immediate antagonism. Her companion suppressed a smile as he answered deliberately:

'Because, my dear Stephen, the Almighty has ordained that justice is not a virtue women can practise. Mind, I do not say women are unjust. Far from it, where there are no interests of those dear to them they can be of a sincerity of justice that can make a man's blood run cold. But justice in the abstract is not an ordinary virtue: it has to be considerate as well as stern, and above all interest of all kinds and of every one—' The girl interrupted hotly:

'I don't agree with you at all. You can't give an instance where women are unjust. I don't mean of course individual instances, but classes of cases where injustice is habitual.' The suppressed smile cropped out now unconsciously round the man's lips in a way which was intensely aggravating to the girl.

'I'll give you a few,' he said. 'Did you ever know a mother just to a boy who beat her own boy at school?' The girl replied quietly:

'Ill-treatment and bullying are subjects for punishment, not justice.'

'Oh, I don't mean that kind of beating. I mean getting the prizes their own boys contended for; getting above them in class; showing superior powers in running or cricket or swimming, or in any of the forms of effort in which boys vie with each other.' The girl reflected, then she spoke:

'Well, you may be right. I don't altogether admit it, but I accept it as not on my side. But this is only one case.'

'A pretty common one. Do you think that Sheriff of Galway, who in default of a hangman hanged his son with his own hands, would have done so if he had been a woman?' The girl answered at once:

'Frankly, no. I don't suppose the mother was ever born who would do such a thing. But that is not a common case, is it? Have you any other?' The young man paused before he spoke:

'There is another, but I don't think I can go into it fairly with you.'

'Why not?'

'Well, because after all you know, Stephen, you are only a girl and you can't be expected to know.' The girl laughed:

'Well, if it's anything about women surely a girl, even of my tender age, must know something more of it, or be able to guess at, than any young man can. However, say what you think and I'll tell you frankly if I agree—that is if a woman can be just, in such a matter.'

'Shortly the point is this: Can a woman be just to another woman, or to a man for the matter of that, where either her own affection or a fault of the other is concerned?'

'I don't see any reason to the contrary. Surely pride alone should ensure justice in the former case, and the consciousness of superiority in the other.' The young man shook his head:

'Pride and the consciousness of superiority! Are they not much the same thing. But whether or no, if either of them has to be relied on, I'm afraid the scales of Justice would want regulating, and her sword should be blunted in case its edge should be turned back on herself. I have an idea that although pride might be a guiding principle with you individually, it would be a failure with the average. However, as it would be in any case a rule subject to many exceptions I must let it go.'

Harold looked at his watch and rose. Stephen followed him; transferring her whip into the hand which held up the skirt, she took his arm with her right hand in the pretty way in which a young girl clings to her elders. Together they went out at the lich-gate. The groom drew over with the horses. Stephen patted hers and gave her a lump of sugar. Then putting her foot into Harold's ready hand she sprang lightly into the saddle. Harold swung himself into his saddle with the dexterity of an accomplished rider.

As the two rode up the road, keeping on the shady side under the trees, Stephen said quietly, half to herself, as if the sentence had impressed itself on her mind:

'To be God and able to do things!'

Harold rode on in silence. The chill of some vague fear was upon him.

CHAPTER-1
Stephen

Stephen Norman of Normanstand had remained a bachelor until close on middle age, when the fact took hold of him that there was no immediate heir to his great estate. Whereupon, with his wonted decision, he set about looking for a wife.

He had been a close friend of his next neighbour, Squire Rowly, ever since their college days. They had, of course, been often in each other's houses, and Rowly's young sister—almost a generation younger than himself, and the sole fruit of his father's second marriage—had been like a little sister to him too. She had, in the twenty years which had elapsed, grown to be a sweet and beautiful young woman. In all the past years, with the constant opportunity which friendship gave of close companionship, the feeling never altered. Squire Norman would have been surprised had he been asked to describe Margaret Rowly and found himself compelled to present the picture of a woman, not a child.

Now, however, when his thoughts went womanward and wifeward, he awoke to the fact that Margaret came within the category of those he sought. His usual decision ran its course. Semi-brotherly feeling gave place to a stronger and perhaps more selfish feeling. Before he even knew it, he was head over ears in love with his pretty neighbour.

Norman was a fine man, stalwart and handsome; his forty years sat so lightly on him that his age never seemed to come into question in a woman's mind. Margaret had always liked him and trusted him; he was the big brother who had no duty in the way of scolding to do. His presence had always been a gladness; and the sex of the girl, first unconsciously then consciously, answered to the man's overtures, and her consent was soon obtained.

When in the fulness of time it was known that an heir was expected, Squire Norman took for granted that the child would be a boy, and held the idea so tenaciously that his wife, who loved him deeply, gave up warning and remonstrance after she had once tried to caution him against too fond a hope. She saw how bitterly he would be disappointed in case it should prove to be a girl. He was, however, so fixed on the point that she determined to say no more. After all, it might be a boy; the chances were equal. The Squire would not listen to any one else at all; so as the time went on his idea was more firmly fixed than ever. His arrangements were made on the base that he would have a son. The name was of course decided. Stephen had been the name of all the Squires of Normanstand for ages—as far back as the records went; and Stephen the new heir of course would be.

Like all middle-aged men with young wives he was supremely anxious as the time drew near. In his anxiety for his wife his belief in the son became passive rather than active. Indeed, the idea of a son was so deeply fixed in his mind that it was not disturbed even by his anxiety for the young wife he idolised.

When instead of a son a daughter was born, the Doctor and the nurse, who knew his views on the subject, held back from the mother for a little the knowledge of the sex. Dame Norman was so weak that the Doctor feared lest anxiety as to how her husband would bear the disappointment, might militate against her. Therefore the Doctor sought the Squire in his study, and went resolutely at his task.

'Well, Squire, I congratulate you on the birth of your child!' Norman was of course struck with the use of the word 'child'; but the cause of his anxiety was manifested by his first question:

'How is she, Doctor? Is she safe?' The child was after all of secondary importance! The Doctor breathed more freely; the question had lightened his task. There was, therefore, more assurance in his voice as he answered:

'She is safely through the worst of her trouble, but I am greatly anxious yet. She is very weak. I fear anything that might upset her.'

The Squire's voice came quick and strong:

'There must be no upset! And now tell me about my son?' He spoke the last word half with pride, half bashfully.

'Your son is a daughter!' There was silence for so long that the Doctor began to be anxious. Squire Norman sat quite still; his right hand resting on the writing-table before him became clenched so hard that the knuckles looked white and the veins red. After a long slow breath he spoke:

'She, my daughter, is well?' The Doctor answered with cheerful alacrity:

'Splendid!—I never saw a finer child in my life. She will be a comfort and an honour to you!' The Squire spoke again:

'What does her mother think? I suppose she's very proud of her?'

'She does not know yet that it is a girl. I thought it better not to let her know till I had told you.'

'Why?'

'Because—because—Norman, old friend, you know why! Because you had set your heart on a son; and I know how it would grieve that sweet young wife and mother to feel your disappointment. I want your lips to be the first to tell her; so that on may assure her of your happiness in that a daughter has been born to you.'

The Squire put out his great hand and laid it on the other's shoulder. There was almost a break in his voice as he said:

'Thank you, my old friend, my true friend, for your thought. When may I see her?'

'By right, not yet. But, as knowing your views, she may fret herself till she knows, I think you had better come at once.'

All Norman's love and strength combined for his task. As he leant over and kissed his young wife there was real fervour in his voice as he said:

'Where is my dear daughter that you may place her in my arms?' For an instant there came a chill to the mother's heart that her hopes had been so far disappointed; but then came the reaction of her joy that her husband, her baby's father, was pleased. There was a heavenly dawn of red on her pale face as she drew her husband's head down and kissed him.

'Oh, my dear,' she said, 'I am so happy that you are pleased!' The nurse took the mother's hand gently and held it to the baby as she laid it in the father's arms.

He held the mother's hand as he kissed the baby's brow.

The Doctor touched him gently on the arm and beckoned him away. He went with careful footsteps, looking behind as he went.

After dinner he talked with the Doctor on various matters; but presently he asked:

'I suppose, Doctor, it is no sort of rule that the first child regulates the sex of a family?'

'No, of course not. Otherwise how should we see boys and girls mixed in one family, as is nearly always the case. But, my friend,' he went on, 'you must not build hopes so far away. I have to tell you that your wife is far from strong. Even now she is not so well as I could wish, and there yet may be change.' The Squire leaped impetuously to his feet as he spoke quickly:

'Then why are we waiting here? Can nothing be done? Let us have the best help, the best advice in the world.' The Doctor raised his hand.

'Nothing can be done as yet. I have only fear.'

'Then let us be ready in case your fears should be justified! Who are the best men in London to help in such a case?' The Doctor mentioned two names; and within a few minutes a mounted messenger was galloping to Norcester, the nearest telegraph centre. The messenger was to arrange for a special train if necessary. Shortly afterwards the Doctor went again to see his patient. After a long absence he came back, pale and agitated. Norman felt his heart sink when he saw him; a groan broke from him as the Doctor spoke:

'She is much worse! I am in great fear that she may pass away before the morning!' The Squire's strong voice was clouded, with a hoarse veil as he asked:

'May I see her?'

'Not yet; at present she is sleeping. She may wake strengthened; in which case you may see her. But if not—'

'If not?'—the voice was not like his own.

'Then I shall send for you at once!' The Doctor returned to his vigil. The Squire, left alone, sank on his knees, his face in his hands; his great shoulders shook with the intensity of his grief.

An hour or more passed before he heard hurried steps. He sprang to the door:

'Well?'

'You had better come now.'

'Is she better?'

'Alas! no. I fear her minutes are numbered. School yourself, my dear old friend! God will help you in this bitter hour. All you can do now is to make her last moments happy.'

'I know! I know!' he answered in a voice so calm that his companion wondered.

When they came into the room Margaret was dozing. When her eyes opened and she found her husband beside her bed there spread over her face a glad look; which, alas! soon changed to one of pain. She motioned to him to bend down. He knelt and put his head beside her on the pillow; his arms went tenderly round her as though by his iron devotion and strength he would shield her from all harm. Her voice came very low and in broken gasps; she was summoning all her strength that she might speak:

'My dear, dear husband, I am so sad at leaving you! You have made me so happy, and I love you so! Forgive me, dear, for the pain I know you will suffer when I am gone! And oh, Stephen, I know you will cherish our little one—yours and mine—when I am gone. She will have no mother; you will have to be father and mother too.'

'I will hold her in my very heart's core, my darling, as I hold you!' He could hardly speak from emotion. She went on:

'And oh, my dear, you will not grieve that she is not a son to carry on your name?' And then a sudden light came into her eyes; and there was exultation in her weak voice as she said:

'She is to be our only one; let her be indeed our son! Call her the name we both love!' For answer he rose and laid his hand very, very tenderly on the babe as he said:

'This dear one, my sweet wife, who will carry your soul in her breast, will be my son; the only son I shall ever have. All my life long I shall, please Almighty God, so love her—our little Stephen—as you and I love each other!'

She laid her hand on his so that it touched at once her husband and her child. Then she raised the other weak arm, and placed it round his neck, and their lips met. Her soul went out in this last kiss.

CHAPTER-2

The Heart of A Child

For some weeks after his wife's death Squire Norman was overwhelmed with grief. He made a brave effort, however, to go through the routine of his life; and succeeded so far that he preserved an external appearance of bearing his loss with resignation. But within, all was desolation.

Little Stephen had winning ways which sent deep roots into her father's heart. The little bundle of nerves which the father took into his arms must have realised with all its senses that, in all that it saw and heard and touched, there was nothing but love and help and protection. Gradually the trust was followed by expectation. If by some chance the father was late in coming to the nursery the child would grow impatient and cast persistent, longing glances at the door. When he came all was joy.

Time went quickly by, and Norman was only recalled to its passing by the growth of his child. Seedtime and harvest, the many comings of nature's growth were such commonplaces to him, and had been for so many years, that they made on him no impressions of comparison. But his baby was one and one only. Any change in it was not only in itself a new experience, but brought into juxtaposition what is with what was. The changes that began to mark the divergence of sex were positive shocks to him, for they were unexpected. In the very dawn of babyhood dress had no special import; to his masculine eyes sex was lost in youth. But, little by little, came the tiny changes which convention has established. And with each change came to Squire Norman the growing realisation that his child was a woman. A tiny woman, it is true, and requiring more care and protection and devotion than a bigger one; but still a woman. The pretty little ways, the eager caresses, the graspings and holdings of the childish hands, the little roguish smiles and pantings and flirtings were all but repetitions in little of the dalliance of long ago. The father, after all, reads in the same book in which the lover found his knowledge.

At first there was through all his love for his child a certain resentment of her sex. His old hope of a son had been rooted too deeply to give way easily. But when the conviction came, and with it the habit of its acknowledgment, there came also a certain resignation, which is the halting-place for satisfaction. But he never, not then nor afterwards, quite lost the old belief that Stephen was indeed a son. Could there ever have been a doubt, the remembrance of his wife's eyes and of her faint voice, of her hope and her faith, as she placed her baby in his arms would have refused it a resting-place. This belief tinged all his after-life and moulded his policy with regard to his girl's upbringing. If she was to be indeed his son as well as his daughter, she must from the first be accustomed to boyish as well as to girlish ways. This, in that she was an only child, was not a difficult matter to accomplish. Had she had brothers and sisters, matters of her sex would soon have found their own level.

There was one person who objected strongly to any deviation from the conventional rule of a girl's education. This was Miss Laetitia Rowly, who took after a time, in so far as such a place could be taken, that of the child's mother. Laetitia Rowly was a young aunt of Squire Rowly of Norwood; the younger sister of his father and some sixteen years his own senior. When the old Squire's second wife had died, Laetitia, then a conceded spinster of thirty-six, had taken possession of the young Margaret. When Margaret had married Squire Norman, Miss Rowly was well satisfied; for she had known Stephen Norman all her life. Though she could have wished a younger bridegroom for her darling, she knew it would be hard to get a better man or one of more suitable station in life. Also she knew that Margaret loved him, and the woman who had never found the happiness of mutual love in her own life found a pleasure in the romance of true love, even when the wooer was middle-aged. She had been travelling in the Far East when the belated news of Margaret's death came to her. When she had arrived home she announced her intention of taking care of Margaret's child, just as she had taken care of Margaret. For several reasons this could not be done in the same way. She was not old enough to go and live at Normanstand without exciting comment; and the Squire absolutely refused to allow that his daughter should live anywhere except in his own house. Educational supervision, exercised at such distance and so intermittently, could neither be complete nor exact.

Though Stephen was a sweet child she was a wilful one, and very early in life manifested a dominant nature. This was a secret pleasure to her father, who, never losing sight of his old idea that she was both son and daughter, took pleasure as well as pride out of each manifestation of her imperial will. The keen instinct of childhood, which reasons in feminine fashion, and is therefore doubly effective in a woman-child, early grasped the possibilities of her own will. She learned the measure of her nurse's foot and then of her father's; and so, knowing where lay the bounds of possibility of the achievement of her wishes, she at once avoided trouble and learned how to make the most of the space within the limit of her tether.

It is not those who 'cry for the Moon' who go furthest or get most in this limited world of ours. Stephen's pretty ways and unfailing good temper were a perpetual joy to her father; and when he found that as a rule her desires were reasonable, his wish to yield to them became a habit.

Miss Rowly seldom saw any individual thing to disapprove of. She it was who selected the governesses and who interviewed them from time to time as to the child's progress. Not often was there any complaint, for the little thing had such a pretty way of showing affection, and such a manifest sense of justified trust in all whom she encountered, that it would have been hard to name a specific fault.

But though all went in tears of affectionate regret, and with eminently satisfactory emoluments and references, there came an irregularly timed succession of governesses.

Stephen's affection for her 'Auntie' was never affected by any of the changes. Others might come and go, but there no change came. The child's little hand would steal into one of the old lady's strong ones, or would clasp a finger and hold it tight. And then the woman who had never had a child of her own would feel, afresh each time, as though the child's hand was gripping her heart.

With her father she was sweetest of all. And as he seemed to be pleased when she did anything like a little boy, the habit of being like one insensibly grew on her.

An only child has certain educational difficulties. The true learning is not that which we are taught, but that which we take in for ourselves from experience and observation, and children's experiences and observation, especially of things other than repressive, are mainly of children. The little ones teach each other. Brothers and sisters are more with each other than are ordinary playmates, and in the familiarity of their constant intercourse some of the great lessons, so useful in after-life, are learned. Little Stephen had no means of learning the wisdom of give-and-take. To her everything was given, given bountifully and gracefully. Graceful acceptance of good things came to her naturally, as it does to one who is born to be a great lady.

The children of the farmers in the neighbourhood, with whom at times she played, were in such habitual awe of the great house, that they were seldom sufficiently at ease to play naturally. Children cannot be on equal terms on special occasions with a person to whom they have been taught to bow or courtesy as a public habit. The children of neighbouring landowners, who were few and far between, and of the professional people in Norcester, were at such times as Stephen met them, generally so much on their good behaviour, that the spontaneity of play, through which it is that sharp corners of individuality are knocked off or worn down, did not exist.

And so Stephen learned to read in the Book of Life; though only on one side of it. At the age of six she had, though surrounded with loving care and instructed by skilled teachers, learned only the accepting side of life. Giving of course there was in plenty, for the traditions of Normanstand were royally benevolent; many a blessing followed the little maid's footsteps as she accompanied some timely aid to the sick and needy sent from the Squire's house. Moreover, her Aunt tried to inculcate certain maxims founded on that noble one that it is more blessed to give than to receive. But of giving in its true sense: the giving that which we want for ourselves, the giving that is as a temple built on the rock of self-sacrifice, she knew nothing. Her sweet and spontaneous nature, which gave its love and sympathy so readily, was almost a bar to education: it blinded the eyes that would have otherwise seen any defect that wanted altering, any evil trait that needed repression, any lagging virtue that required encouragement—or the spur.

CHAPTER-3
Harold

Squire Norman had a clerical friend whose rectory of Carstone lay some thirty miles from Normanstand. Thirty miles is not a great distance for railway travel; but it is a long drive. The days had not come, nor were they ever likely to come, for the making of a railway between the two places. For a good many years the two men had met in renewal of their old University days. Squire Norman and Dr. An Wolf had been chums at Trinity, Cambridge, and the boyish friendship had ripened and lasted. When Harold An Wolf had put in his novitiate in a teeming Midland manufacturing town, it was Norman's influence which obtained the rectorship for his friend. It was not often that they could meet, for An Wolf's work, which, though not very exacting, had to be done single-handed, kept him to his post. Besides, he was a good scholar and eked out a small income by preparing a few pupils for public school. An occasional mid-week visit to Normanstand in the slack time of school work on the Doctor's part, and now and again a drive by Norman over to the rectory, returning the next day, had been for a good many years the measure of their meeting. Then An Wolf's marriage and the birth of a son had kept him closer to home. Mrs. An Wolf had been killed in a railway accident a couple of years after her only child had been born; and at the time Norman had gone over to render any assistance in his power to the afflicted man, and to give him what was under the circumstances his best gift, sympathy. After an interval of a few years the Squire's courtship and marriage, at which his old friend had assisted, had confined his activities to a narrower circle. The last time they had met was when An Wolf had come over to Norcester to aid in the burial of his friend's wife. In the process of years, however, the shadow over Norman's life had begun to soften; when his baby had grown to be something of a companion, they met again. Norman, 'who had never since his wife's death been able to tear himself, even for a night, away from Normanstand and Stephen, wrote to his old friend asking him to come to him. An Wolf gladly promised, and for a week of growing expectation the Squire looked forward to their meeting. Each found the other somewhat changed, in all but their old affection.

An Wolf was delighted with the little Stephen. Her dainty beauty seemed to charm him; and the child, seeming to realise what pleasure she was giving, exercised all her little winning ways. The rector, who knew more of children than did his, friend, told her as she sat on his knee of a very interesting person: his own son. The child listened, interested at first, then enraptured. She asked all kinds of questions; and the father's eyes brightened as he gladly answered the pretty sympathetic child, already deep in his heart for her father's sake. He told her about the boy who was so big and strong, and who could run and leap and swim and play cricket and football better than any other boy with whom he played. When, warmed himself by the keen interest of the little girl, and seeing her beautiful black eyes beginning to glow, he too woke to the glory of the time; and all the treasured moments of the father's lonely heart gave out their store. And the other father, thrilled with delight because of his baby's joy with, underlying all, an added pleasure that the little Stephen's interest was in sports that were for boys, looked on approvingly, now and again asking questions himself in furtherance of the child's wishes.

All the afternoon they sat in the garden, close to the stream that came out of the rock, and An Wolf told father's tales of his only son. Of the great cricket match with Castra Puerorum when he had made a hundred not out. Of the school races when he had won so many prizes. Of the swimming match in the Islam River when, after he had won the race and had dressed himself, he went into the water in his clothes to help some children who had upset a boat. How when Widow Norton's only son could not be found, he dived into the deep hole of the intake of the milldam of the great Carstone mills where Wingate the farrier had been drowned. And how, after diving twice without success, he had insisted on going down the third time though people had tried to hold him back; and how he had brought up in his arms the child all white and so near death that they had to put him in the ashes of the baker's oven before he could be brought back to life.

When her nurse came to take her to bed, she slid down from her father's knee and coming over to Dr. An Wolf, gravely held out her hand and said: 'Good-bye!' Then she kissed him and said:

'Thank you so much, Mr. Harold's daddy. Won't you come soon again, and tell us more?' Then she jumped again upon her father's knee and hugged him round the neck and kissed him, and whispered in his ear:

'Daddy, please make Mr. Harold's daddy when he comes again, bring Harold with him!'

After all it is natural for women to put the essence of the letter in the postscript!

Two weeks afterwards Dr. An Wolf came again and brought Harold with him. The time had gone heavily with little Stephen when she knew that Harold was coming with his father. Stephen had been all afire to see the big boy whose feats had so much interested her, and for a whole week had flooded Mrs. Jarrold with questions which she was unable to answer. At last the time came and she went out to the hall door with her father to welcome the guests. At the top of the great granite steps, down which in time of bad weather the white awning ran, she stood holding her father's hand and waving a welcome.

'Good morning, Harold! Good morning, Mr. Harold's daddy!'

The meeting was a great pleasure to both the children, and resulted in an immediate friendship. The small girl at once conceived a great admiration for the big, strong boy nearly twice her age and more than twice her size. At her time of life the convenances are not, and love is a thing to be spoken out at once and in the open. Mrs. Jarrold, from the moment she set eyes on him, liked the big kindly-faced boy who treated her like a lady, and who stood awkwardly blushing and silent in the middle of the nursery listening to the tiny child's proffers of affection. For whatever kind of love it is that boys are capable of, Harold had fallen into it. 'Calf-love' is a thing habitually treated with contempt. It may be ridiculous; but all the same it is a serious reality—to the calf.

Harold's new-found affection was as deep as his nature. An only child who had in his memory nothing of a mother's love, his naturally affectionate nature had in his childish days found no means of expression. A man child can hardly pour out his full heart to a man, even a father or a comrade; and this child had not, in a way, the consolations of other children. His father's secondary occupation of teaching brought other boys to the house and necessitated a domestic routine which had to be exact. There was no place for little girls in a boys' school; and though many of Dr. An Wolf's friends who were mothers made much of the pretty, quiet boy, and took him to play with their children, he never seemed to get really intimate with them. The equality of companionship was wanting. Boys he knew, and with them he could hold his own and yet be on affectionate terms. But girls were strange to him, and in their presence he was shy. With this lack of understanding of the other sex, grew up a sort of awe of it. His opportunities of this kind of study were so few that the view never could become rectified.

And so it was that from his boyhood up to his twelfth year, Harold's knowledge of girlhood never increased nor did his awe diminish. When his father had told him all about his visit to Normanstand and of the invitation which had been extended to him there came first awe, then doubt, then expectation. Between Harold and his father there was love and trust and sympathy. The father's married love so soon cut short found expression towards his child; and between them there had never been even the shadow of a cloud. When his father told him how pretty the little Stephen was, how dainty, how sweet, he began to picture her in his mind's eye and to be bashfully excited over meeting her.

His first glimpse of Stephen was, he felt, one that he never could forget. She had made up her mind that she would let Harold see what she could do. Harold could fly kites and swim and play cricket; she could not do any of these, but she could ride. Harold should see her pony, and see her riding him all by herself. And there would be another pony for Harold, a big, big, big one—she had spoken about its size herself to Topham, the stud-groom. She had coaxed her daddy into promising that after lunch she should take Harold riding. To this end she had made ready early. She had insisted on putting on the red riding habit which Daddy had given her for her birthday, and now she stood on the top of the steps all glorious in hunting pink, with the habit held over her arms, with the tiny hunting-hoots all shiny underneath. She had no hat on, and her beautiful hair of golden red shone in its glory. But even it was almost outshone by the joyous flush on her cheeks as she stood waving the little hand that did not hold Daddy's. She was certainly a picture to dream of! Her father's eyes lost nothing of her dainty beauty. He was so proud of her that he almost forgot to wish that she had been a boy. The pleasure he felt in her appearance was increased by the fact that her dress was his own idea.

During luncheon Stephen was fairly silent; she usually chattered all through as freely as a bird sings. Stephen was silent because the occasion was important. Besides, Daddy wasn't all alone, and therefore had not to be cheered up. Also—this in postscript form—Harold was silent! In her present frame of mind Harold could do no wrong, and what Harold did was right. She was unconsciously learning already a lesson from his presence.

That evening when going to bed she came to say good-night to Daddy. After she had kissed him she also kissed 'old Mr. Harold,' as she now called him, and as a matter of course kissed Harold also. He coloured up at once. It was the first time a girl had ever kissed him.

The next day from early morning until bed-time was one long joy to Stephen, and there were few things of interest that Harold had not been shown; there were few of the little secrets which had not been shared with him as they went about hand in hand. Like all manly boys Harold was good to little children and patient with them. He was content to follow Stephen about and obey all her behests. He had fallen in love with her to the very bottom of his boyish heart.

When the guests were going, Stephen stood with her father on the steps to see them off. When the carriage had swept behind the farthest point in the long avenue, and when Harold's cap waving from the window could no longer be seen, Squire Norman turned to go in, but paused in obedience to the unconscious restraint of Stephen's hand. He waited patiently till with a long sigh she turned to him and they went in together.

That night before she went to bed Stephen came and sat on her father's knee, and after sundry pattings and kissings whispered in his ear:

'Daddy, wouldn't it be nice if Harold could come here altogether? Couldn't you ask him to? And old Mr. Harold could come too. Oh, I wish he was here!'

CHAPTER-4
Harold At Normanstand

Two years afterwards a great blow fell upon Harold. His father, who had been suffering from repeated attacks of influenza, was, when in the low condition following this, seized with pneumonia, to which in a few days he succumbed. Harold was heart-broken. The affection which had been between him and his father had been so consistent that he had never known a time when it was not.

When Squire Norman had returned to the house with him after the funeral, he sat in silence holding the boy's hand till he had wept his heart out. By this time the two were old friends, and the boy was not afraid or too shy to break down before him. There was sufficient of the love of the old generation to begin with trust in the new.

Presently, when the storm was past and Harold had become his own man again, Norman said:

'And now, Harold, I want you to listen to me. You know, my dear boy, that I am your father's oldest friend, and right sure I am that he would approve of what I say. You must come home with me to live. I know that in his last hours the great concern of your dear father's heart would have been for the future of his boy. And I know, too, that it was a comfort to him to feel that you and I are such friends, and that the son of my dearest old friend would be as a son to me. We have been friends, you and I, a long time, Harold; and we have learned to trust, and I hope to love, one another. And you and my little Stephen are such friends already that your coming into the house will be a joy to us all. Why, long ago, when first you came, she said to me the night you went away: "Daddy, wouldn't it be nice if Harold could come here altogether?"'

And so Harold An Wolf came back with the Squire to Normanstand, and from that day on became a member of his house, and as a son to him. Stephen's delight at his coming was of course largely qualified by her sympathy with his grief; but it would have been hard to give him more comfort than she did in her own pretty way. Putting her lips to his she kissed him, and holding his big hand in both of her little ones, she whispered softly:

'Poor Harold! You and I should love each other, for we have both lost our mother. And now you have lost your father. But you must let my dear daddy be yours too!'

At this time Harold was between fourteen and fifteen years old. He was well educated in so far as private teaching went. His father had devoted much care to him, so that he was well grounded in all the Academic branches of learning. He was also, for his years, an expert in most manly exercises. He could ride anything, shoot straight, fence, run, jump or swim with any boy more than his age and size.

In Normanstand his education was continued by the rector. The Squire used often to take him with him when he went to ride, or fish, or shoot; frankly telling him that as his daughter was, as yet, too young to be his companion in these matters, he would act as her locum tenens. His living in the house and his helping as he did in Stephen's studies made familiarity perpetual. He was just enough her senior to command her childish obedience; and there were certain qualities in his nature which were eminently calculated to win and keep the respect of women as well as of men. He was the very incarnation of sincerity, and had now and again, in certain ways, a sublime self-negation which, at times, seemed in startling contrast to a manifestly militant nature. When at school he had often been involved in fights which were nearly always on matters of principle, and by a sort of unconscious chivalry he was generally found fighting on the weaker side. Harold's father had been very proud of his ancestry, which was Gothic through the Dutch, as the manifestly corrupted prefix of the original name implied, and he had gathered from a constant study of the Sagas something of the philosophy which lay behind the ideas of the Vikings.

This new stage of Harold's life made for quicker development than any which had gone before. Hitherto he had not the same sense of responsibility. To obey is in itself a relief; and as it is an actual consolation to weak natures, so it is only a retarding of the strong. Now he had another individuality to think of. There was in his own nature a vein of anxiety of which the subconsciousness of his own strength threw up the outcrop.

Little Stephen with the instinct of her sex discovered before long this weakness. For it is a weakness when any quality can be assailed or used.

The using of a man's weakness is not always coquetry; but it is something very like it. Many a time the little girl, who looked up to and admired the big boy who could compel her to anything when he was so minded, would, for her own ends, work on his sense of responsibility, taking an elfin delight in his discomfiture.

The result of Stephen's harmless little coquetries was that Harold had occasionally either to thwart some little plan of daring, or else cover up its results. In either case her confidence in him grew, so that before long he became an established fact in her life, a being in whose power and discretion and loyalty she had absolute, blind faith. And this feeling seemed to grow with her own growth. Indeed at one time it came to be more than an ordinary faith. It happened thus:

The old Church of St. Stephen, which was the parish church of Normanstand, had a peculiar interest for the Norman family. There, either within the existing walls or those which had preceded them when the church was rebuilt by that Sir Stephen who was standard-bearer to Henry VI., were buried all the direct members of the line. It was an unbroken record of the inheritors since the first Sir Stephen, who had his place in the Domesday Book. Without, in the churchyard close to the church, were buried all such of the collaterals as had died within hail of Norcester. Some there were of course who, having achieved distinction in various walks of life, were further honoured by a resting-place within the chancel. The whole interior was full of records of the family. Squire Norman was fond of coming to the place; and often from the very beginning had taken Stephen with him. One of her earliest recollections was kneeling down with her father, who held her hand in his, whilst with the other he wiped the tears from his eyes, before a tomb sculptured beautifully in snowy marble. She never forgot the words he had said to her:

'You will always remember, darling, that your dear mother rests in this sacred place. When I am gone, if you are ever in any trouble come here. Come alone and open out your heart. You need never fear to ask God for help at the grave of your mother!' The child had been impressed, as had been many and many another of her race. For seven hundred years each child of the house of Norman had been brought alone by either parent and had heard some such words. The custom had come to be almost a family ritual, and it never failed to leave its impress in greater or lesser degree.

Whenever Harold had in the early days paid a visit to Normanstand, the church had generally been an objective of their excursions. He was always delighted to go. His love for his own ancestry made him admire and respect that of others; so that Stephen's enthusiasm in the matter was but another cord to bind him to her.

In one of their excursions they found the door into the crypt open; and nothing would do Stephen but that they should enter it. To-day, however, they had no light; but they arranged that on the morrow they would bring candles with them and explore the place thoroughly. The afternoon of the next day saw them at the door of the crypt with a candle, which Harold proceeded to light. Stephen looked on admiringly, and said in a half-conscious way, the half-consciousness being shown in the implication:

'You are not afraid of the crypt?'

'Not a bit! In my father's church there was a crypt, and I was in it several times.' As he spoke the memory of the last time he had been there swept over him. He seemed to see again the many lights, held in hands that were never still, making a grim gloom where the black shadows were not; to hear again the stamp and hurried shuffle of the many feet, as the great oak coffin was borne by the struggling mass of men down the steep stairway and in through the narrow door . . . And then the hush when voices faded away; and the silence seemed a real thing, as for a while he stood alone close to the dead father who had been all in all to him. And once again he seemed to feel the recall to the living world of sorrow and of light, when his inert hand was taken in the strong loving one of Squire Norman.

He paused and drew back.

'Why don't you go on?' she asked, surprised.

He did not like to tell her then. Somehow, it seemed out of place. He had often spoken to her of his father, and she had always been a sympathetic listener; but here, at the entrance of the grim vault, he did not wish to pain her with his own thoughts of sorrow and all the terrible memories which the similarity of the place evoked. And even whilst he hesitated there came to him a thought so laden with pain and fear that he rejoiced at the pause which gave it to him in time. It was in that very crypt that Stephen's mother had been buried, and had they two gone in, as they had intended, the girl might have seen her mother's coffin as he had seen his father's, but under circumstances which made him shiver. He had been, as he said, often in the crypt at Carstone; and well he knew the sordidness of the chamber of death. His imagination was alive as well as his memory; he shuddered, not for himself, but for Stephen. How could he allow the girl to suffer in such a way as she might, as she infallibly would, if it were made apparent to her in such a brutal way? How pitiful, how meanly pitiful, is the aftermath of death. Well he remembered how many a night he woke in an agony, thinking of how his father lay in that cold, silent, dust-strewn vault, in the silence and the dark, with never a ray of light or hope or love! Gone, abandoned, forgotten by all, save perhaps one heart which bled . . . He would save little Stephen, if he could, from such a memory. He would not give any reason for refusing to go in.

He blew out the candle, and turned the key in the lock, took it out, and put it in his pocket.

'Come, Stephen!' he said, 'let us go somewhere else. We will not go into the crypt to-day!'

'Why not?' The lips that spoke were pouted mutinously and the face was flushed. The imperious little lady was not at all satisfied to give up the cherished project. For a whole day and night she had, whilst waking, thought of the coming adventure; the thrill of it was not now to be turned to cold disappointment without even an explanation. She did not think that Harold was afraid; that would be ridiculous. But she wondered; and mysteries always annoyed her. She did not like to be at fault, more especially when other people knew. All the pride in her revolted.

'Why not?' she repeated more imperiously still.

Harold said kindly:

'Because, Stephen, there is really a good reason. Don't ask me, for I can't tell you. You must take it from me that I am right. You know, dear, that I wouldn't willingly disappoint you; and I know that you had set your heart on this. But indeed, indeed I have a good reason.'

Stephen was really angry now. She was amenable to reason, though she did not consciously know what reason was; but to accept some one else's reason blindfold was repugnant to her nature, even at her then age. She was about to speak angrily, but looking up she saw that Harold's mouth was set with marble firmness. So, after her manner, she acquiesced in the inevitable and said:

'All right! Harold.'

But in the inner recesses of her firm-set mind was a distinct intention to visit the vault when more favourable circumstances would permit.

CHAPTER-5

The Crypt

It was some weeks before Stephen got the chance she wanted. She knew it would be difficult to evade Harold's observation, for the big boy's acuteness as to facts had impressed itself on her. It was strange that out of her very trust in Harold came a form of distrust in others. In the little matter of evading him she inclined to any one in whom there was his opposite, in whose reliability she instinctively mistrusted. 'There is nothing bad or good but thinking makes it so!' To enter that crypt, which had seemed so small a matter at first, had now in process of thinking and wishing and scheming become a thing to be much desired. Harold saw, or rather felt, that something was in the girl's mind, and took for granted that it had something to do with the crypt. But he thought it better not to say anything lest he should keep awake a desire which he hoped would die naturally.

One day it was arranged that Harold should go over to Carstone to see the solicitor who had wound up his father's business. He was to stay the night and ride back next day. Stephen, on hearing of the arrangement, so contrived matters that Master Everard, the son of a banker who had recently purchased an estate in the neighbourhood, was asked to come to play with her on the day when Harold left. It was holiday time at Eton, and he was at home. Stephen did not mention to Harold the fact of his coming; it was only from a chance allusion of Mrs. Jarrold before he went that he inferred it. He did not think the matter of sufficient importance to wonder why Stephen, who generally told him everything, had not mentioned this.

During their play, Stephen, after pledging him to secrecy, told Leonard of her intention of visiting the crypt, and asked him to help her in it. This was an adventure, and as such commended itself to the schoolboy heart. He entered at once into the scheme con amore; and the two discussed ways and means. Leonard's only regret was that he was associated with a little girl in such a project. It was something of a blow to his personal vanity, which was a large item in his moral equipment, that such a project should have been initiated by the girl and not by himself. He was to get possession of the key and in the forenoon of the next day he was to be waiting in the churchyard, when Stephen would join him as soon as she could evade her nurse. She was now more than eleven, and had less need of being watched than in her earlier years. It was possible, with strategy, to get away undiscovered for an hour.

* * * * *

At Carstone Harold got though what he had to do that same afternoon and arranged to start early in the morning for Normanstand. After an early breakfast he set out on his thirty-mile journey at eight o'clock. Littlejohn, his horse, was in excellent form, notwithstanding his long journey of the day before, and with his nose pointed for home, put his best foot foremost. Harold felt in great spirits. The long ride the day before had braced him physically, though there were on his journey times of great sadness when the thought of his father came back to him and the sense of loss was renewed with each thought of his old home. But youth is naturally buoyant. His visit to the church, the first thing on his arrival at Carstone, and his kneeling before the stone made sacred to his father's memory, though it entailed a silent gush of tears, did him good, and even seemed to place his sorrow farther away. When he came again in the morning before leaving Carstone there were no tears. There was only a holy memory which seemed to sanctify loss; and his father seemed nearer to him than ever.

As he drew near Normanstand he looked forward eagerly to seeing Stephen, and the sight of the old church lying far below him as he came down the steep road over Alt Hill, which was the short-cut from Norcester, set his mind working. His visit to the tomb of his own father made him think of the day when he kept Stephen from entering the crypt.

The keenest thought is not always conscious. It was without definite intention that when he came to the bridle-path Harold turned his horse's head and rode down to the churchyard. As he pushed open the door of the church he half expected to see Stephen; and there was a vague possibility that Leonard Everard might be with her.

The church was cool and dim. Coming from the hot glare the August sunshine it seemed, at the first glance, dark. He looked around, and a sense of relief came over him. The place was empty.

But even as he stood, there came a sound which made his heart grow cold. A cry, muffled, far away and full of anguish; a sobbing cry, which suddenly ceased.

It was the voice of Stephen. He instinctively knew where it came from; the crypt. Only for the experience he had had of her desire to enter the place, he would never have suspected that it was so close to him. He ran towards the corner where commenced the steps leading downward. As he reached the spot a figure came rushing up the steps. A boy in Eton jacket and wide collar, careless, pale, and agitated. It was Leonard Everard. Harold seized him as he came.

'Where is Stephen?' he cried in a quick, low voice.

'In the vault below there. She dropped her light and then took mine, and she dropped it too. Let me go! Let me go!' He struggled to get away; but Harold held him tight.

'Where are the matches?'

'In my pocket. Let me go! Let me go!'

'Give me them—this instant!' He was examining the frightened boy's waistcoat pockets as he spoke. When he had got the matches he let the boy go, and ran down the steps and through the open door into the crypt, calling out as he came:

'Stephen! Stephen dear, where are you? It is I—Harold!' There was no response; his heart seemed to grow cold and his knees to weaken. The match spluttered and flashed, and in the momentary glare he saw across the vault, which was not a large place, a white mass on the ground. He had to go carefully, lest the match should be blown out by the wind of his passage; but on coming close he saw that it was Stephen lying senseless in front of a great coffin which rested on a built-out pile of masonry. Then the match went out. In the flare of the next one he lit he saw a piece of candle lying on top of the coffin. He seized and lit it. He was able to think coolly despite his agitation, and knew that light was the first necessity. The bruised wick was slow to catch; he had to light another match, his last one, before it flamed. The couple of seconds that the light went down till the grease melted and the flame leaped again seemed of considerable length. When the lit candle was placed steadily on top of the coffin, and a light, dim, though strong enough to see with, spread around, he stooped and lifted Stephen in his arms. She was quite senseless, and so limp that a great fear came upon him that she might be dead. He did not waste time, but carried her across the vault where the door to the church steps stood out sharp against the darkness, and bore her up into the church. Holding her in one arm, with the other hand he dragged some long cushions from one of the pews and spread them on the floor; on these he laid her. His heart was smitten with love and pity as he looked. She was so helpless; so pitifully helpless! Her arms and legs were doubled up as though broken, disjointed; the white frock was smeared with patches of thick dust. Instinctively he stooped and pulled the frock down and straightened out the arms and feet. He knelt beside her, and felt if her heart was still beating, a great fear over him, a sick apprehension. A gush of thankful prayer came from his heart. Thank God! she was alive; he could feel her heart beat, though faintly underneath his hand. He started to his feet and ran towards the door, seizing his hat, which lay on a seat. He wanted it to bring back some water. As he passed out of the door he saw Leonard a little distance off, but took no notice of him. He ran to the stream, filled his hat with water, and brought it back. When he came into the church he saw Stephen, already partially restored, sitting up on the cushions with Leonard supporting her.

He was rejoiced; but somehow disappointed. He would rather Leonard had not been there. He remembered—he could not forget—the white face of the boy who fled out of the crypt leaving Stephen in a faint within, and who had lingered outside the church door whilst he ran for water. Harold came forward quickly and raised Stephen, intending to bring her into the fresh air. He had a shrewd idea that the sight of the sky and God's greenery would be the best medicine for her after her fright. He lifted her in his strong arms as he used to do when she was a very little child and had got tired in their walks together; and carried her to the door. She lent herself unconsciously to the movement, holding fast with her arm round his neck as she used to do. In her clinging was the expression of her trust in him. The little sigh with which she laid her head on his shoulder was the tribute to his masculine power, and her belief in it. Every instant her senses were coming back to her more and more. The veil of oblivion was passing from her half-closed eyes, as the tide of full remembrance swept in upon her. Her inner nature was expressed in the sequence of her emotions. Her first feeling was one of her own fault. The sight of Harold and his proximity recalled to her vividly how he had refused to go into the crypt, and how she had intentionally deceived him, negatively, as to her intention of doing that of which he disapproved. Her second feeling was one of justice; and was perhaps partially evoked by the sight of Leonard, who followed close as Harold brought her to the door. She did not wish to speak of herself or Harold before him; but she did not hesitate to speak of him to Harold:

'You must not blame Leonard. It was all my fault. I made him come!' Her generosity appealed to Harold. He was angry with the boy for being there at all; but more for his desertion of the girl in her trouble.

'I'm not blaming him for being with you!' he said simply. Leonard spoke at once. He had been waiting to defend himself, for that was what first concerned that young gentleman; next to his pleasure, his safety most appealed to him.

'I went to get help. You had let the candle drop; and how could I see in the dark? You would insist on looking at the plate on the coffin!'

A low moan broke from Stephen, a long, low, trembling moan which went to Harold's heart. Her head drooped over again on his shoulder; and she clung close to him as the memory of her shock came back to her. Harold spoke to Leonard over his shoulder in a low, fierce whisper, which Stephen did not seem to hear:

'There! that will do. Go away! You have done enough already. Go! Go!' he added more sternly, as the boy seemed disposed to argue. Leonard ran a few steps, then walked to the lich-gate, where he waited.

Stephen clung close to Harold in a state of agitation which was almost hysterical. She buried her face in his shoulder, sobbing brokenly:

'Oh, Harold! It was too awful. I never thought, never for a moment, that my poor dear mother was buried in the crypt. And when I went to look at the name on the coffin that was nearest to where I was, I knocked away the dust, and then I saw her name: "Margaret Norman, aetat 22." I couldn't bear it. She was only a girl herself, only just twice my age—lying there in that terrible dark place with all the thick dust and the spiders' webs. Oh, Harold, Harold! How shall I ever bear to think of her lying there, and that I shall never see her dear face? Never! Never!'

He tried to soothe her by patting and holding her hands. For a good while the resolution of the girl faltered, and she was but as a little child. Then her habitual strength of mind asserted itself. She did not ask Harold how she came to be out in the church instead of in the crypt when she recovered her senses. She seemed to take it for granted that Leonard had carried her out; and when she said how brave it had been of him, Harold, with his customary generosity, allowed her to preserve the belief. When they had made their way to the gate Leonard came up to them; but before he could speak Stephen had begun to thank him. He allowed her to do so, though the sight of Harold's mouth set in scorn, and his commanding eyes firmly fixed on him, made him grow hot and cold alternately. He withdrew without speaking; and took his way home with a heart full of bitterness and revengeful feelings.

In the park Stephen tried to dust herself, and then Harold tried to assist her. But her white dress was incurably soiled, the fine dust of the vault seemed to have got ingrained in the muslin. When she got to the house she stole upstairs, so that no one might notice her till she had made herself tidy.

The next day but one she took Harold for a walk in the afternoon. When they were quite alone and out of earshot she said:

'I have been thinking all night about poor mother. Of course I know she cannot be moved from the crypt. She must remain there. But there needn't be all that dust. I want you to come there with me some time soon. I fear I am afraid to go alone. I want to bring some flowers and to tidy up the place. Won't you come with me this time? I know now, Harold, why you didn't let me go in before. But now it is different. This is not curiosity. It is Duty and Love. Won't you come with me, Harold?'

Harold leaped from the edge of the ha-ha where he had been sitting and held up his hand. She took it and leaped down lightly beside him.

'Come,' he said, 'let us go there now!' She took his arm when they got on the path again, and clinging to him in her pretty girlish way they went together to the piece of garden which she called her own; there they picked a great bunch of beautiful white flowers. Then they walked to the old church. The door was open and they passed in. Harold took from his pocket a tiny key. This surprised her, and heightened the agitation which she naturally suffered from revisiting the place. She said nothing whilst he opened the door to the crypt. Within, on a bracket, stood some candles in glass shades and boxes of matches. Harold lit three candles, and leaving one of them on the shelf, and placing his cap beside it, took the other two in his hands. Stephen, holding her flowers tightly to her breast with her right hand, took Harold's arm with the left, and with beating heart entered the crypt.

For several minutes Harold kept her engaged, telling her about the crypt in his father's church, and how he went down at his last visit to see the coffin of his dear father, and how he knelt before it. Stephen was much moved, and held tight to his arm, her heart beating. But in the time she was getting accustomed to the place. Her eyes, useless at first on coming out of the bright sunlight, and not able to distinguish anything, began to take in the shape of the place and to see the rows of great coffins that stood out along the far wall. She also saw with surprise that the newest coffin, on which for several reasons her eyes rested, was no longer dusty but was scrupulously clean. Following with her eyes as well as she could see into the further corners she saw that there the same reform had been effected. Even the walls and ceiling had been swept of the hanging cobwebs, and the floor was clean with the cleanliness of ablution. Still holding Harold's arm, she moved over towards her mother's coffin and knelt before it. Harold knelt with her; for a little while she remained still and silent, praying inwardly. Then she rose, and taking her great bunch of flowers placed them lovingly on the lid of the coffin above where she thought her mother's heart would be. Then she turned to Harold, her eyes flowing and her cheeks wet with tears, and laid her head against his breast. Her arms could not go round his neck till he had bent his head, for with his great height he simply towered above her. Presently she was quiet; the paroxysm of her grief had passed. She took Harold's hand in both hers, and together they went to the door. With his disengaged hand, for he would not have disturbed the other for worlds, Harold put out the lights and locked the door behind them.

In the church she held him away from her, and looked him fairly in the face. She said slowly:

'Harold, was it you who had the crypt cleaned?' He answered in a low voice:

'I knew you would want to go again!'

She took the great hand which she held between hers, and before he knew what she was doing and could prevent her, raised it to her lips and kissed it, saying lovingly:

'Oh, Harold! No brother in all the wide world could be kinder. And—and—' this with a sob, 'we both thank you; mother and I!'

CHAPTER-6

A Visit To Oxford

The next important move in the household was Harold's going to Cambridge. His father had always intended this, and Squire Norman had borne his wishes in mind. Harold joined Trinity, the college which had been his father's, and took up his residence in due course.

Stephen was now nearly twelve. Her range of friendships, naturally limited by her circumstances in life, was enlarged to the full; and if she had not many close friends there were at least of them all that was numerically possible. She still kept up to certain degree the little gatherings which in her childhood were got together for her amusement, and in the various games then instituted she still took a part. She never lost sight of the fact that her father took a certain pleasure in her bodily vigour. And though with her growing years and the conscious acceptance of her womanhood, she lost sight of the old childish fancy of being a boy instead of a girl, she could not lose sight of the fact that strength and alertness are sources of feminine as well as of masculine power.

Amongst the young friends who came from time to time during his holidays was Leonard Everard, now a tall, handsome boy. He was one of those boys who develop young, and who seem never to have any of that gawky stage so noticeable in the youth of men made in a large pattern. He was always well-poised, trim-set, alert; fleet of foot, and springy all over. In games he was *facile princeps*, seeming to make his effort always in the right way and without exertion, as if by an instinct of physical masterdom. His universal success in such matters helped to give him an easy debonair manner which was in itself winning. So physically complete a youth has always a charm. In its very presence there is a sort of sympathetic expression, such as comes with the sunshine.

Stephen always in Leonard's presence showed something of the common attitude. His youth and beauty and sex all had their influence on her. The influence of sex, as it is understood with regard to a later period of life, did not in her case exist; Cupid's darts are barbed and winged for more adult victims. But in her case Leonard's masculine superiority, emphasised by the few years between their age, his sublime self-belief, and, above all, his absolute disregard for herself or her wishes or her feelings, put him on a level at which she had to look up to him. The first step in the ladder of pre-eminence had been achieved when she realised that he was not on her level; the second when she experienced rather than thought that he had more influence on her than she had on him. Here again was a little morsel of hero worship, which, though based on a misconception of fact, was still of influence. In that episode of the crypt she had always believed that it was Leonard who had carried her out and laid her on the church floor in light and safety. He had been strong enough and resolute enough to do this, whilst she had fainted! Harold's generous forbearance had really worked to a false end.

It was not strange, therefore, that she found occasional companionship with the handsome, wilful, domineering boy somewhat of luxury. She did not see him often enough to get tired of him; to find out the weakness of his character; to realise his deep-seated, remorseless selfishness. But after all he was only an episode in a young life which was full of interests. Term after term came and went; the holidays had their seasonable pleasures, occasionally shared in common. That was all.

Harold's attitude was the same as ever. He was of a constant nature; and now that manhood was within hail the love of his boyhood was ripening to a man's love. That was all. He was with regard to Stephen the same devoted, worshipping protector, without thought of self; without hope of reward. Whatever Stephen wished Harold did; and Stephen, knowing their old wishes and their old pleasures, was content with their renewal. Each holiday between the terms became mainly a repetition of the days of the old life. They lived in the past.

Amongst the things that did not change was Stephen's riding dress. The scarlet habit had never been a thing for everyday wear, but had from the first been kept for special occasions. Stephen herself knew that it was not a conventional costume; but she rather preferred it, if on that account alone. In a certain way she felt justified in using it; for a red habit was a sort of tradition in the family.

It was on one of these occasions that she had gone with Harold into the churchyard where they had heard the discussion regarding God and the Angels.

* * * * *

When Stephen was about sixteen she went for a short visit to Oxford. She stayed at Somerville with Mrs. Egerton, an old friend of her mother's, who was a professor at the college. She sent back her maid who had travelled with her, as she knew that the college girls did not have servants of their own. The visit was prolonged by mutual consent into a duration of some weeks. Stephen fell in love with the place and the life, and had serious thoughts of joining the college herself. Indeed she had made up her mind to ask her father to allow her, knowing well that he would consent to that or to any other wholesome wish of hers. But then came the thought that he would be all alone at home; and following that came another thought, and one of more poignant feeling. He was alone now! Already, for many days, she had left him, for the first time in her life! Stephen was quick to act; well she knew that at home there would be no fault found with her for a speedy return. Within a few hours she had brought her visit to an end, and was by herself, despite Mrs. Egerton's protest, in the train on the way back to Norcester.

In the train she began to review, for the first time, her visit to the university. All had been so strange and new and delightful to her that she had never stopped for retrospect. Life in the new and enchanting place had been in the moving present. The mind had been receptive only, gathering data for later thought. During her visit she had had no one to direct her thought, and so it had been all personal, with the freedom of individuality at large. Of course her mother's friend, skilled in the mind-workings of average girls, and able to pick her way through intellectual and moral quagmires, had taken good care to point out to her certain intellectual movements and certain moral lessons; just as she had in their various walks and drives pointed out matters of interest—architectural beauties and spots of historic import. And she had taken in, loyally accepted, and thoroughly assimilated all that she had been told. But there were other lessons which were for her young eyes; facts which the older eyes had ceased to notice, if they had ever noticed them at all. The self-content, the sex-content in the endless tide of young men that thronged the streets and quads and parks; the all-sufficing nature of sport or study, to whichever their inclinations tended. The small part which womankind seemed to have in their lives. Stephen had had, as we know, a peculiar training; whatever her instincts were, her habits were largely boy habits. Here she was amongst boys, a glorious tide of them; it made now and again her heart beat to look at them. And yet amongst them all she was only an outsider. She could not do anything better than any of them. Of course, each time she went out, she became conscious of admiring glances; she could not be woman without such consciousness. But it was as a girl that men looked at her, not as an equal. As well as personal experience and the lessons of eyes and ears and intelligence, there were other things to classify and adjust; things which were entirely from the outside of her own life. The fragments of common-room gossip, which it had been her fortune to hear accidentally now and again. The half confidences of scandals, borne on whispered breaths. The whole confidences of dormitory and study which she had been privileged to share. All were parts of the new and strange world, the great world which had swum into her ken.

As she sat now in the train, with some formulation of memory already accomplished in the two hours of solitude, her first comment, spoken half audibly, would have surprised her teachers as much as it would have surprised herself, if she had been conscious of it; for as yet her thinking was not self-conscious:

'Surely, I am not like that!'

It was of the women she had been thinking, not of the men. The glimpse which she had had of her own sex had been an awakening to her; and the awakening had not been to a pleasant world. All at once she seemed to realise that her sex had defects—littlenesses, meannesses, cowardices, falsenesses. That their occupations were apt to be trivial or narrow or selfish; that their desires were earthly, and their tastes coarse; that what she held to be goodness was apt to be realised only as fear. That innocence was but ignorance, or at least baffled curiosity. That . . .

A flood of shame swept over her, and instinctively she put her hands before her burning face. As usual, she was running all at once into extremes.

And above all these was borne upon her, and for the first time in her life, that she was herself a woman!

For a long time she sat quite still. The train thrilled and roared on its way. Crowded stations took and gave their quantum of living freight; but the young girl sat abstracted, unmoved, seemingly unconscious. All the dominance and energy of her nature were at work.

If, indeed, she was a woman, and had to abide by the exigencies of her own sex, she would at least not be ruled and limited by woman's weakness. She would plan and act and manage things for herself, in her own way.

Whatever her thoughts might be, she could at least control her acts. And those acts should be based not on woman's weakness, but on man's strength!

CHAPTER-7

The Need of Knowing

When Stephen announced her intention of going with her father to the Petty Sessions Court, there was consternation amongst the female population of Normanstand and Norwood. Such a thing had not been heard of in the experiences of any of them. Courts of Justice were places for men; and the lower courts dealt with a class of cases . . . It was quite impossible to imagine where any young lady could get such an idea . . .

Miss Laetitia Rowly recognised that she had a difficult task before her, for she was by now accustomed to Stephen's quiet method of having her own way.

She made a careful toilet before driving over to Normanstand. Her wearing her best bonnet was a circumstance not unattended with dread for some one. Behold her then, sailing into the great drawing-room at Normanstand with her mind so firmly fixed on the task before her as to be oblivious of minor considerations. She was so fond of Stephen, and admired so truly her many beauties and fine qualities, that she was secure and without flaw in her purpose. Stephen was in danger, and though she doubted if she would be able to effect any change, she was determined that at least she should not go into danger with her eyes unopened.

Stephen entered hastily and ran to her. She loved her great-aunt; really and truly loved her. And indeed it would have been strange if she had not, for from the earliest hour which she could recollect she had received from her nothing but the truest, fondest affection. Moreover she deeply respected the old lady, her truth, her resolution, her kindliness, her genuine common-sense ability. Stephen always felt safe with her aunt. In the presence of others she might now and again have a qualm or a doubt; but not with her. There was an abiding calm in her love, answering love realised and respected. Her long and intimate knowledge of Laetitia made her aware of her moods. She could read the signs of them. She knew well the meaning of the bonnet which actually seemed to quiver as though it had a sentience of its own. She knew well the cause of her aunt's perturbation; the pain which must be caused to her was perhaps the point of most resistance in herself—she having made up her mind to her new experience. All she could do would be to try to reconcile her by the assurance of good intention; by reason, and by sweetness of manner. When she had kissed her and sat beside her, holding her hand after her pretty way, she, seeing the elder woman somewhat at a loss, opened the subject herself:

'You look troubled, auntie! I hope it is nothing serious?'

'It is, my dear! Very serious! Everything is serious to me which touches you.'

'Me, Auntie!' Hypocrisy is a fine art.

'Yes! yes, Stephen. Oh! my dear child, what is this I hear about your going to Petty Sessions with your father?'

'Oh, that! Why, Auntie dear, you must not let that trouble you. It is all right. That is necessary!'

'Necessary!' the old lady's figure grew rigid and her voice was loud and high. 'Necessary for a young lady to go to a court house. To hear low people speaking of low crimes. To listen to cases of the most shocking kind; cases of low immorality; cases of a kind, of a nature of a—a—class that you are not supposed to know anything about. Really, Stephen! . . . ' She was drawing away her hand in indignation. But Stephen held it tight, as she said very sweetly:

'That is just it, Auntie. I am so ignorant that I feel I should know more of the lives of those very people!' Miss Laetitia interrupted:

'Ignorant! Of course you are ignorant. That is what you ought to be. Isn't it what we have all been devoting ourselves to effect ever since you were born? Read your third chapter of Genesis and remember what came of eating of the fruit of the Tree of Knowledge.'

'I think the Tree of Knowledge must have been an orange tree.' The old lady looked up, her interest aroused:

'Why?'

'Because ever since Eden other brides have worn its blossom!' Her tone was demure. Miss Rowly looked sharply at her, but her sharpness softened off into a smile.

'H'm!' she said, and was silent. Stephen seized the opportunity to put her own case:

'Auntie dear, you must forgive me! You really must, for my heart is set on this. I assure you I am not doing it merely to please myself. I have thought over the whole matter. Father has always wished me to be in a position—a position of knowledge and experience—to manage Normanstand if I should ever succeed him. From the earliest time I can remember he has always kept this before me, and though of course I did not at first understand what it meant, I have seemed in the last few years to know better. Accordingly I learned all sorts of things under his care, and sometimes even without his help. I have studied the estate map, and I have been over the estate books and read some of the leases and all such matters which they deal with in the estate office. This only told me the bones of the thing. I wanted to know more of our people; and so I made a point of going now and again to each house that we own. Of seeing the people and talking with them familiarly; as familiarly as they would let me, and indeed so far as was possible considering my position. For, Auntie dear, I soon began to learn—to learn in a way there was no mistaking—what my position is. And so I want to get to know more of their ordinary lives; the darker as well as the lighter side. I would like to do them good. I can see how my dear daddy has always been a sort of power to help them, and I would like to carry on his work; to carry it further if I may. But I must know.'

Her aunt had been listening with growing interest, and with growing respect too, for she realised the intense earnestness which lay behind the girl's words and her immediate purpose. Her voice and manner were both softened:

'But, my dear, surely it is not necessary to go into the Court to know these things. The results of each case become known.'

'That is just it, Auntie,' she answered quickly. 'The magistrates have to hear the two sides of the case before even they can make up their minds. I want to hear both sides, too! If people are guilty, I want to know the cause of their guilt. If they are innocent, I want to know what the circumstances can be which make innocence look like guilt. In my own daily life I may be in the way of just such judgments; and surely it is only right that judgment should be just!'

Again she paused; there rose before her mind that conversation in the churchyard when Harold had said that it was difficult for women to be just.

Miss Rowly reflected too. She was becoming convinced that in principle the girl was right. But the details were repugnant as ever to her; concentrating her mind on the point where she felt the ground firm under her, she made her objection:

'But, Stephen dear, there are so many cases that are sordid and painful!'

'The more need to know of sordid things; if sordidness plays so important a part in the tragedy of their lives!'

'But there are cases which are not within a woman's province. Cases that touch sin . . . '

'What kind of sin do you mean? Surely all wrong-doing is sin!' The old lady was embarrassed. Not by the fact, for she had been for too many years the mistress of a great household not to know something of the subject on which she spoke, but that she had to speak of such a matter to the young girl whom she so loved.

'The sin, my dear, of . . . of woman's wrong-doing . . . as woman . . . of motherhood, without marriage!' All Stephen's nature seemed to rise in revolt.

'Why, Auntie,' she spoke out at once, 'you yourself show the want of the very experience I look for!'

'How? what?' asked the old lady amazed and bristling. Stephen took her hand and held it affectionately as she spoke:

'You speak of a woman's wrong-doing, when surely it is a man's as well. There does not seem to be blame for him who is the more guilty. Only for poor women! . . . And, Auntie dear, it is such poor women that I should like to help . . . Not when it is too late, but before! But how can I help unless I know? Good girls cannot tell me, and good women won't! You yourself, Auntie, didn't want to speak on the subject; even to me!'

'But, my dear child, these are not things for unmarried women. I never speak of them myself except with matrons.' Stephen's answer flashed out like a sword; and cut like one:

'And yet you are unmarried! Oh, Auntie dear, I did not and I do not mean to be offensive, or to hurt you in any way. I know, dear, your goodness and your kindness to all. But you limit yourself to one side!' The elder lady interrupted:

'How do you mean? one side! which side?'

'The punishment side. I want to know the cause of that which brings the punishment. There surely is some cross road in a girl's life where the ways part. I want to stand there if I can, with warning in one hand and help in the other. Oh! Auntie, Auntie, can't you see that my heart is in this . . . These are our people; Daddy says they are to be my people; and I want to know their lives right through; to understand their wants, and their temptations, and their weakness. Bad and good, whatever it be, I must know it all; or I shall be working in the dark, and may injure or crush where I had looked to help and raise.'

As she spoke she looked glorified. The afternoon autumn sun shone full through the great window and lighted her up till she looked like a spirit. Lighted her white diaphanous dress till it seemed to take shape as an ethereal robe; lighted her red hair till it looked like a celestial crown; lighted her great dark eyes till their black beauty became swept in the tide of glory.

The heart of the old woman who loved her best heaved, and her bosom swelled with pride. Instinctively she spoke:

'Oh, you noble, beautiful creature! Of course you are right, and your way is God's way!' With tears that rained down her furrowed cheeks, she put her arms round the girl and kissed her fondly. Still holding her in her arms she gave her the gentle counsel which was the aftermath of her moment of inspiration.

'But Stephen dear, do be careful! Knowledge is a two-edged sword, and it is apt to side with pride. Remember what was the last temptation of the serpent to Eve: "Your eyes shall be opened, and ye shall be as gods, knowing good and evil."'

'I shall be very careful,' she said gravely; and then added as if by an afterthought, 'of course you understand that my motive is the acquisition of knowledge?'

'Yes?' the answer was given interrogatively.

'Don't you think, dear, that Eve's object was not so much the acquisition of knowledge as the gratification of curiosity.'

'That may be,' said the elder lady in a doubtful tone; 'but my dear, who is to enlighten us as to which is which? We are apt in such matters to deceive ourselves. The more we know, the better are we able to deceive others; and the better we are able to deceive others the better we are able to deceive ourselves. As I tell you, dear, knowledge is two-edged and needs extra carefulness in its use!'

'True!' said Stephen reflectively. Long after her aunt had gone she sat thinking.

* * * * *

Once again did Miss Rowly try to restrain Stephen from a project. This was when a little later she wished to go for a few days to the University Mission House in the East end of London. Ever since her visit to Oxford she had kept up a correspondence with her mother's old friend. It was this lady's habit to spend a part of vacation in the Mission; and Stephen had had much correspondence with her regarding the work. At last she wrote that if she might, she would like to come and see for herself. The answer was a cordial invitation, armed with which she asked her father to allow her to go. He at once assented. He had been watching keenly the development of her character, and had seen with pride and satisfaction that as time went on she seemed to acquire greater resolution, larger self-dependence. She was becoming more and more of his ideal. Without losing any of her womanhood, she was beginning to look at things more from a man's point of view than is usually done by, or possible to, women.

When she returned at the end of a week she was full of new gravity. After a while this so far changed that her old lighter moods began to have their place, but it seemed that she never lost, and that she never would lose, the effect of that week of bitter experience amongst the 'submerged tenth.'

The effect of the mental working was shown by a remark made by Harold when home on his next college vacation. He had been entering with her on a discussion of an episode on the estate:

'Stephen, you are learning to be just!'

At the moment she was chagrined by the remark, though she accepted it in silence; but later, when she had thought the matter over, she took from it infinite pleasure. This was indeed to share man's ideas and to think with the workings of man's mind. It encouraged her to further and larger ideas, and to a greater toleration than she had hitherto dreamed of.

Of all those who loved her, none seemed to understand so fully as Laetitia Rowly the change in her mental attitude, or rather the development of it. Now and again she tried to deflect or modify certain coming forces, so that the educational process in which she had always had a part would continue in the right direction. But she generally found that the girl had been over the ground so thoroughly that she was able to defend her position. Once, when she had ventured to remonstrate with her regarding her attitude of woman's equality with man, she felt as if Stephen's barque was indeed entering on dangerous seas. The occasion had arisen thus: Stephen had been what her aunt had stigmatised as 'laying down the law' with regard to the position a married woman, and Miss Rowly, seeing a good argumentative opening, remarked:

'But what if a woman does not get the opportunity of being married?' Stephen looked at her a moment before saying with conviction:

'It is a woman's fault if she does not get the opportunity!' The old lady smiled as she answered:

'Her fault? My dear, what if no man asks her?' This seemed to her own mind a poser.

'Still her own fault! Why doesn't she ask him?' Her aunt's lorgnon was dropped in horrified amazement.

Stephen went on impassively.

'Certainly! Why shouldn't she? Marriage is a union. As it is in the eye of the law a civil contract, either party to it should be at liberty to originate the matter. If a woman is not free to think of a man in all ways, how is she to judge of the suitability of their union? And if she is free in theory, why not free to undertake if necessary the initiative in a matter so momentous to herself?' The old lady actually groaned and wrung her hands; she was horrified at such sentiments. They were daring enough to think; but to put them in words! . . .

'Oh, my dear, my dear!' she moaned, 'be careful what you say. Some one might hear you who would not understand, as I do, that you are talking theory.' Stephen's habit of thought stood to her here. She saw that her aunt was distressed, and as she did not wish to pain her unduly, was willing to divert the immediate channel of her fear. She took the hand which lay in her lap and held it firmly whilst she smiled in the loving old eyes.

'Of course, Auntie dear, it is theory. But still it is a theory which I hold very strongly!' . . . Here a thought struck her and she said suddenly:

'Did you ever . . . How many proposals did you have, Auntie?' The old lady smiled; her thoughts were already diverted.

'Several, my dear! It is so long ago that I don't remember!'

'Oh yes, you do, Auntie! No woman ever forgets that, no matter what else she may or may not remember! Tell me, won't you?' The old lady blushed slightly as she answered:

'There is no need to specify, my dear. Let it be at this, that there were more than you could count on your right hand!'

'And why did you refuse them?' The tone was wheedling, and the elder woman loved to hear it. Wheedling is the courtship, by the young of the old.

'Because, my dear, I didn't love them.'

'But tell me, Auntie, was there never any one that you did love?'

'Ah! my dear, that is a different matter. That is the real tragedy of a woman's life.' In flooding reminiscent thought she forgot her remonstrating; her voice became full of natural pathos:

'To love; and be helpless! To wait, and wait, and wait; with your heart all aflame! To hope, and hope; till time seems to have passed away, and all the world to stand still on your hopeless misery! To know that a word might open up Heaven; and yet to have to remain mute! To keep back the glances that could enlighten; to modulate the tones that might betray! To see all you hoped for passing away . . . to another! . . . '

Stephen bent over and kissed her, then standing up said:

'I understand! Isn't it wrong, Auntie, that there should be such tragedies? Should not that glance be given? Why should that tone be checked? Why should one be mute when a single word might, would, avert the tragedy? Is it not possible, Auntie, that there is something wrong in our social system when such things can happen; and can happen so often?'

She looked remorseless as well as irresistible in the pride of her youthful strength as with eyes that blazed, not flashing as in passion but with a steady light that seemed to burn, she continued:

'Some day women must learn their own strength, as well as they have learned their own weakness. They are taught this latter from their cradles up; but no one ever seems to teach them wherein their power lies. They have to learn this for themselves; and the process and the result of the self-teaching are not good. In the University Settlement I learned much that made my heart ache; but out of it there seemed some lesson for good.' She paused; and her aunt, wishing to keep the subject towards higher things, asked:

'And that lesson, Stephen dear?' The blazing eyes turned to her so that she was stirred by them as the answer came:

'It is bad women who seem to know men best, and to be able to influence them most. They can make men come and go at will. They can turn and twist and mould them as they choose. And *they* never hesitate to speak their own wishes; to ask for what they want. There are no tragedies, of the negative kind, in *their* lives. Their tragedies have come and gone already; and their power remains. Why should good women leave power to such as they? Why should good women's lives be wrecked for a convention? Why in the blind following of some society fetish should life lose its charm, its possibilities? Why should love eat its heart out, in vain? The time will come when women will not be afraid to speak to men, as they should speak, as free and equal. Surely if a woman is to be the equal and lifelong companion of a man, the closest to him—nay, the only one really close to him: the mother of his children—she should be free at the very outset to show her inclination to him just as he would to her. Don't be frightened, Auntie dear; your eyes are paining me! . . . There! perhaps I said too much. But after all it is only theory. Take for your comfort, Auntie dear, that I am free an heart-whole. You need not fear for me; I can see what your dear eyes tell me. Yes! I am very young; perhaps too young to think such things. But I have thought of them. Thought them all over in every way and phase I can imagine.'

She stopped suddenly; bending over, she took the old lady in her arms and kissed her fondly several times, holding her tight. Then, as suddenly releasing her, she ran away before she could say a word.

CHAPTER-8
The T-Cart

When Harold took his degree, Stephen's father took her to Cambridge. She enjoyed the trip very much; indeed, it seemed under conditions that were absolutely happy.

When they had returned to Normanstand, the Squire took an early opportunity of bringing Harold alone into his study. He spoke to him with what in a very young man would have seemed diffidence:

'I have been thinking, Harold, that the time has come when you should be altogether your own master. I am more than pleased, my boy, with the way you have gone through college; it is, I am sure, just as your dear father would have wished it, and as it would have pleased him best.' He paused, and Harold said in a low voice:

'I tried hard, sir, to do what I thought he would like; and what you would.' The Squire went on more cheerfully:

'I know that, my boy! I know that well. And I can tell you that it is not the least of the pleasures we have all had in your success, how you have justified yourself. You have won many honours in the schools, and you have kept the reputation as an athlete which your father was so proud of. Well, I suppose in the natural order of things you would go into a profession; and of course if you so desire you can do that. But if you can see your way to it I would rather that you stayed here. My house is your home as long as I live; but I don't wish you to feel in any way dependent. I want you to stay here if you will; but to do it just because you wish to. To this end I have made over to you the estate at Camp which was my father's gift to me when I came of age. It is not a very large one; but it will give you a nice position of your own, and a comfortable income. And with it goes my blessing, my dear boy. Take it as a gift from your father and myself!'

Harold was much moved, not only by the act itself but by the gracious way of doing it. There were tears in his eyes as he wrung the Squire's hand; his voice thrilled with feeling as he said:

'Your many goodnesses to my father's son, sir, will, I hope, be justified by his love and loyalty. If I don't say much it is because I do not feel quite master of myself. I shall try to show in time, as I cannot say it all at once, all that I feel.'

Harold continued to live at Normanstand. The house at Camp was in reality a charming cottage. A couple of servants were installed, and now and again he stayed there for a few days as he wished to get accustomed to the place. In a couple of months every one accepted the order of things; and life at Normanstand went on much as it had done before Harold had gone to college. There was a man in the house now instead of a boy: that was all. Stephen too was beginning to be a young woman, but the relative positions were the same as they had been. Her growth did not seem to make an ostensible difference to any one. The one who might have noticed it most, Mrs. Jarrold, had died during the last year of Harold's life at college.

When the day came for the quarterly meeting of the magistrates of the county of Norcester, Squire Rowly arranged as usual to drive Squire Norman. This had been their habit for good many years. The two men usually liked to talk over the meeting as they returned home together. It was a beautiful morning for a drive, and when Rowly came flying up the avenue in his T-cart with three magnificent bays, Stephen ran out on the top of the steps to see him draw up. Rowly was a fine whip, and his horses felt it. Squire Norman was ready, and, after a kiss from Stephen, climbed into the high cart. The men raised their hats and waved good-bye. A word from Rowly; with a bound the horses were off. Stephen stood looking at them delighted; all was so sunny, so bright, so happy. The world was so full of life and happiness to-day that it seemed as if it would never end; that nothing except good could befall.

Harold, later on that morning, was to go into Norcester also; so Stephen with a lonely day before her set herself to take up loose-ends of all sorts of little personal matters. They would all meet at dinner as Rowly was to stop the night at Normanstand.

Harold left the club in good time to ride home to dinner. As he passed the County Hotel he stopped to ask if Squire Norman had left; and was told that he had started only a short time before with Squire Rowly in his T-cart. He rode on fast, thinking that perhaps he might overtake them and ride on with them. But the bays knew their work, and did it. They kept their start; it was only at the top of the North hill, five miles out of Norcester, that he saw them in the distance, flying along the level road. He knew he would not now overtake them, and so rode on somewhat more leisurely.

The Norcester highroad, when it has passed the village of Brackling, turns away to the right behind the great clump of oaks. From this the road twists to the left again, making a double curve, and then runs to Norling Parva in a clear stretch of some miles before reaching the sharp turn down the hill which is marked 'Dangerous to Cyclists.' From the latter village branches the by-road over the hill which is the short cut to Normanstand.

When Harold turned the corner under the shadow of the oaks he saw a belated road-mender, surrounded by some gaping peasants, pointing excitedly in the distance. The man, who of course knew him, called to him to stop.

'What is it?' he asked, reining up.

'It be Squire Rowly's bays which have run away with him. Three on 'em, all in a row and comin' like the wind. Squire he had his reins all right, but they 'osses didn't seem to mind 'un. They was fair mad and bolted. The leader he had got frightened at the heap o' stones theer, an' the others took scare from him.'

Without a word Harold shook his reins and touched the horse with his whip. The animal seemed to understand and sprang forward, covering the ground at a terrific pace. Harold was not given to alarms, but here might be serious danger. Three spirited horses in a light cart made for pace, all bolting in fright, might end any moment in calamity. Never in his life did he ride faster than on the road to Norling Parva. Far ahead of him he could see at the turn, now and again, a figure running. Something had happened. His heart grew cold: he knew as well as though he had seen it, the high cart swaying on one wheel round the corner as the maddened horses tore on their way; the one jerk too much, and the momentary reaction in the crash! . . .

With beating heart and eyes aflame in his white face he dashed on.

It was all too true. By the side of the roadway on the inner curve lay the cart on its side with broken shafts. The horses were prancing and stamping about along the roadway not recovered from their fright. Each was held by several men.

And on the grass two figures were still lying where they had been thrown out. Rowly, who had of course been on the off-side, had been thrown furthest. His head had struck the milestone that stood back on the waste ground before the ditch. There was no need for any one to tell that his neck had been broken. The way his head lay on one side, and the twisted, inert limbs, all told their story plainly enough.

Squire Norman lay on his back stretched out. Some one had raised him to a sitting posture and then lowered him again, straightening his limbs. He did not therefore look so dreadful as Rowly, but there were signs of coming death in the stertorous breathing, the ooze of blood from nostrils and ears as well as mouth. Harold knelt down by him at once and examined him. Those who were round all knew him and stood back. He felt the ribs and limbs; so far as he could ascertain by touch no bone was broken.

Just then the local doctor, for whom some one had run, arrived in his gig. He, too, knelt beside the injured man, a quick glance having satisfied him that there was only one patient requiring his care. Harold stood up and waited. The doctor looked up, shaking his head. Harold could hardly suppress the groan which was rising in his throat. He asked:

'Is it immediate? Should his daughter be brought here?'

'How long would it take her to arrive?'

'Perhaps half an hour; she would not lose an instant.'

'Then you had better send for her.'

'I shall go at once!' answered Harold, turning to jump on his horse, which was held on the road.

'No, no!' said the doctor, 'send some one else. You had better stay here yourself. He may become conscious just before the end; and he may want to say something!' It seemed to Harold that a great bell was sounding in his ears.—'Before the end! Good God! Poor Stephen!' . . . But this was no time for sorrow, or for thinking of it. That would come later. All that was possible must be done; and to do it required a cool head. He called to one of the lads he knew could ride and said to him:

'Get on my horse and ride as fast as you can to Normanstand. Send at once to Miss Norman and tell her that she is wanted instantly. Tell her that there has been an accident; that her father is alive, but that she must come at once without a moment's delay. She had better ride my horse back as it will save time. She will understand from that the importance of time. Quick!'

The lad sprang to the saddle, and was off in a flash. Whilst Harold was speaking, the doctor had told the men, who, accustomed to hunting accidents, had taken a gate from its hinges and held it in readiness, to bring it closer. Then under his direction the Squire was placed on the gate. The nearest house was only about a hundred yards away; and thither they bore him. He was lifted on a bed, and then the doctor made fuller examination. When he stood up he looked very grave and said to Harold:

'I greatly fear she cannot arrive in time. That bleeding from the ears means rupture of the brain. It is relieving the pressure, however, and he may recover consciousness before he dies. You had better be close to him. There is at present nothing that can be done. If he becomes conscious at all it will be suddenly. He will relapse and probably die as quickly.'

All at once Norman opened his eyes, and seeing him said quietly, as he looked around:

'What place is this, Harold?'

'Martin's—James Martin's, sir. You were brought here after the accident.'

'Yes, I remember! Am I badly hurt? I can feel nothing!'

'I fear so, sir! I have sent for Stephen.'

'Sent for Stephen! Am I about to die?' His voice, though feeble, was grave and even.

'Alas! sir, I fear so!' He sank on his knees as he spoke and took him, his second father, in his arms.

'Is it close?'

'Yes.'

'Then listen to me! If I don't see Stephen, give her my love and blessing! Say that with my last breath I prayed God to keep her and make her happy! You will tell her this?'

'I will! I will!' He could hardly speak for the emotion which was choking him. Then the voice went on, but slower and weaker:

'And Harold, my dear boy, you will look after her, will you not? Guard her and cherish her, as if you were indeed my son and she your sister!'

'I will. So help me God!' There was a pause of a few seconds which seemed an interminable time. Then in a feebler voice Squire Norman spoke again:

'And Harold—bend down—I must whisper! If it should be that in time you and Stephen should find that there is another affection between you, remember that I sanction it—with my dying breath. But give her time! I trust that to you! She is young, and the world is all before her. Let her choose . . . and be loyal to her if it is another! It may be a hard task, but I trust you, Harold. God bless you, my other son!' He rose slightly and listened. Harold's heart leaped. The swift hoof-strokes of a galloping horse were heard . . . The father spoke joyously:

'There she is! That is my brave girl! God grant that she may be in time. I know what it will mean to her hereafter!'

The horse stopped suddenly.

A quick patter of feet along the passage and then Stephen half dressed with a peignoir thrown over her, swept into the room. With the soft agility of a leopard she threw herself on her knees beside her father and put her arms round him. The dying man motioned to Harold to raise him. When this had been done he laid his hand tenderly on his daughter's head, saying:

'Let now, O Lord, Thy servant depart in peace! God bless and keep you, my dear child! You have been all your life a joy and a delight to me! I shall tell your mother when I meet her all that you have been to me! Harold, be good to her! Good-bye—Stephen! . . . Margaret! . . .'

His head fell over, and Harold, laying him gently down, knelt beside Stephen. He put his arm round her; and she, turning to him, laid her hand on his breast and sobbed as though her heart would break.

* * * * *

The bodies of the two squires were brought to Normanstand. Rowly had long ago said that if he died unmarried he would like to lie beside his half-sister, and that it was fitting that, as Stephen would be the new Squire of Norwood, her dust should in time lie by his. When the terrible news of her nephew's and of Norman's death came to Norwood, Miss Laetitia hurried off to Normanstand as fast as the horses could bring her.

Her coming was an inexpressible comfort to Stephen. After the first overwhelming burst of grief she had settled into an acute despair. Of course she had been helped by the fact that Harold had been with her, and she was grateful for that too. But it did not live in her memory of gratitude in the same way. Of course Harold was with her in trouble! He had always been; would always be.

But the comfort which Aunt Laetitia could give was of a more positive kind.

From that hour Miss Rowly stayed at Normanstand. Stephen wanted her; and she wanted to be with Stephen.

After the funeral Harold, with an instinctive delicacy of feeling, had gone to live in his own house; but he came to Normanstand every day. Stephen had so long been accustomed to consulting him about everything that there was no perceptible change in their relations. Even necessary business to be done did not come as a new thing.

And so things went on outwardly at Normanstand very much as they had done before the coming of the tragedy. But for a long time Stephen had occasional bursts of grief which to witness was positive anguish to those who loved her.

Then her duty towards her neighbours became a sort of passion. She did not spare herself by day or by night. With swift intuition she grasped the needs of any ill case which came before her, and with swift movement she took the remedy in hand.

Her aunt saw and approved. Stephen, she felt, was in this way truly fulfilling her duty as a woman. The old lady began to secretly hope, and almost to believe, that she had laid aside those theories whose carrying into action she so dreaded.

But theories do not die so easily. It is from theory that practice takes its real strength, as well as its direction. And did the older woman whose life had been bound under more orderly restraint but know, Stephen was following out her theories, remorselessly and to the end.

CHAPTER-9
In The Spring

The months since her father's death spread into the second year before Stephen began to realise the loneliness of her life. She had no companion now but her aunt; and though the old lady adored her, and she returned her love in full, the mere years between them made impossible the companionship that youth craves. Miss Rowly's life was in the past. Stephen's was in the future. And loneliness is a feeling which comes unbidden to a heart.

Stephen felt her loneliness all round. In old days Harold was always within hail, and companionship of equal age and understanding was available. But now his very reticence in her own interest, and by her father's wishes, made for her pain. Harold had put his strongest restraint on himself, and in his own way suffered a sort of silent martyrdom. He loved Stephen with every fibre of his being. Day by day he came toward her with eager step; day by day he left her with a pang that made his heart ache and seemed to turn the brightness of the day to gloom. Night by night he tossed for hours thinking, thinking, wondering if the time would ever come when her kisses would be his . . . But the tortures and terrors of the night had their effect on his days. It seemed as if the mere act of thinking, of longing, gave him ever renewed self-control, so that he was able in his bearing to carry out the task he had undertaken: to give Stephen time to choose a mate for herself. Herein lay his weakness—a weakness coming from his want of knowledge of the world of women. Had he ever had a love affair, be it never so mild a one, he would have known that love requires a positive expression. It is not sufficient to sigh, and wish, and hope, and long, all to oneself. Stephen felt instinctively that his guarded speech and manner were due to the coldness—or rather the trusting abated worship—of the brotherhood to which she had been always accustomed. At the time when new forces were manifesting and expanding themselves within her; when her growing instincts, cultivated by the senses and the passions of young nature, made her aware of other forces, new and old, expanding themselves outside her; at the time when the heart of a girl is eager for new impressions and new expansions, and the calls of sex are working within her all unconsciously, Harold, to whom her heart would probably have been the first to turn, made himself in his effort to best show his love, a *quantité negligeable*.

Thus Stephen, whilst feeling that the vague desires of budding womanhood were trembling within her, had neither thought nor knowledge of their character or their ultimate tendency. She would have been shocked, horrified, had that logical process, which she applied so freely to less personal matters, been used upon her own intimate nature. In her case logic would of course act within a certain range; and as logic is a conscious intellectual process, she became aware that her objective was man. Man—in the abstract. 'Man,' not 'a man.' Beyond that, she could not go. It is not too much to say that she did not ever, even in her most errant thought, apply her reasoning, or even dream of its following out either the duties, the responsibilities, or the consequences of having a husband. She had a vague longing for younger companionship, and of the kind naturally most interesting to her. There thought stopped.

One only of her male acquaintances did not at this time appear. Leonard Everard, who had some time ago finished his course at college, was living partly in London and partly on the Continent. His very absence made him of added interest to his old play-fellow. The image of his grace and comeliness, of his dominance and masculine force, early impressed on her mind, began to compare favourably with the actualities of her other friends; those of them at least who were within the circle of her personal interest. 'Absence makes the heart grow fonder.' In Stephen's mind had been but a very mustard-seed of fondness. But new lights were breaking for her; and all of them, in greater or lesser degree, shone in turn on the memory of the pretty self-willed dominant boy, who now grew larger and more masculine in stature under the instance of each successive light. Stephen knew the others fairly well through and through. The usual mixture of good and evil, of strength and weakness, of purpose and vacillation, was quite within the scope of her own feeling and of her observation. But this man was something of a problem to her; and, as such, had a prominence in her thoughts quite beyond his own worthiness.

In movement of some form is life; and even ideas grow when the pulses beat and thought quickens. Stephen had long had in her mind the idea of sexual equality. For a long time, in deference to her aunt's feelings, she had not spoken of it; for the old lady winced in general under any suggestion of a breach of convention. But though her outward expression being thus curbed had helped to suppress or minimise the opportunities of inward thought, the idea had never left her. Now, when sex was, consciously or unconsciously, a dominating factor in her thoughts, the dormant idea woke to new life. She had held that if men and women were equal the woman should have equal rights and opportunities as the man. It had been, she believed, an absurd conventional rule that such a thing as a proposal of marriage should be entirely the prerogative of man.

And then came to her, as it ever does to woman, opportunity. Opportunity, the cruelest, most remorseless, most unsparing, subtlest foe that womanhood has. Here was an opportunity for her to test her own theory; to prove to herself, and others, that she was right. They—'they' being the impersonal opponents of, or unbelievers in, her theory—would see that a woman could propose as well as a man; and that the result would be good.

It is a part of self-satisfaction, and perhaps not the least dangerous part of it, that it has an increasing or multiplying power of its own. The desire to do increases the power to do; and desire and power united find new ways for the exercise of strength. Up to now Stephen's inclination towards Leonard had been vague, nebulous; but now that theory showed a way to its utilisation it forthwith began to become, first definite, then concrete, then substantial. When once the idea had become a possibility, the mere passing of time did the rest.

Her aunt saw—and misunderstood. The lesson of her own youth had not been applied; not even of those long hours and days and weeks at which she hinted when she had spoken of the tragedy of life which by inference was her own tragedy: 'to love and to be helpless. To wait, and wait, and wait, with your heart all aflame!'

Stephen recognised her aunt's concern for her health in time to protect herself from the curiosity of her loving-kindness. Her youth and readiness and adaptability, and that power of play-acting which we all have within us and of which she had her share, stood to her. With but little effort, based on a seeming acquiescence in her aunt's views, she succeeded in convincing the old lady that her incipient feverish cold had already reached its crisis and was passing away. But she had gained certain knowledge in the playing of her little part. All this self-protective instinct was new; for good or ill she had advanced one more step in not only the knowledge but the power of duplicity which is so necessary in the conventional life of a woman.

Oh! did we but see! Could we but see! Here was a woman, dowered in her youth with all the goods and graces in the power of the gods to bestow, who fought against convention; and who yet found in convention the strongest as well as the readiest weapon of defence.

For nearly two weeks Stephen's resolution was held motionless, neither advancing nor receding; it was veritably the slack water of her resolution. She was afraid to go on. Not afraid in sense of fear as it is usually understood, but with the opposition of virginal instincts; those instincts which are natural, but whose uses as well as whose powers are unknown to us.

CHAPTER-10
The Resolve

The next few days saw Stephen abnormally restless. She had fairly well made up her mind to test her theory of equality of the sexes by asking Leonard Everard to marry her; but her difficulty was as to the doing it. She knew well that it would not do to depend on a chance meeting for an opportunity. After all, the matter was too serious to allow of the possibility of levity. There were times when she thought she would write to him and make her proffer of affection in this way; but on every occasion when such thought recurred it was forthwith instantly abandoned. During the last few days, however, she became more reconciled to even this method of procedure. The fever of growth was unabated. At last came an evening which she had all to herself. Miss Laetitia was going over to Norwood to look after matters there, and would remain the night. Stephen saw in her absence an opportunity for thought and action, and said that, having a headache, she would remain at home. Her aunt offered to postpone her visit. But she would not hear of it; and so she had the evening to herself.

After dinner in her boudoir she set herself to the composition of a letter to Leonard which would convey at least something of her feelings and wishes towards him. In the depths of her heart, which now and again beat furiously, she had a secret hope that when once the idea was broached Leonard would do the rest. And as she thought of that 'rest' a languorous dreaminess came upon her. She thought how he would come to her full of love, of yearning passion; how she would try to keep towards him, at first, an independent front which would preserve her secret anxiety until the time should come when she might yield herself to his arms and tell him all. For hours she wrote letter after letter, destroying them as quickly as she wrote, as she found that she had but swayed pendulum fashion between overtness and coldness. Some of the letters were so chilly in tone that she felt they would defeat their own object. Others were so frankly warm in the expression of—regard she called it, that with burning blushes she destroyed them at once at the candle before her.

At last she made up her mind. Just as she had done when a baby she realised that the opposing forces were too strong for her; she gave in gracefully. It would not do to deal directly in a letter with the matter in hand. She would write to Leonard merely asking him to see her. Then, when they were together without fear of interruption, she would tell him her views.

She got as far as 'Dear Mr. Leonard,' when she stood up, saying to herself:

'I shall not be in a hurry. I must sleep on it before I write!' She took up the novel she had been reading in the afternoon, and read on at it steadily till her bedtime.

That night she did not sleep. It was not that she was agitated. Indeed, she was more at ease than she had been for days; she had after much anxious thought made up her mind to a definite course of action. Therefore her sleeplessness was not painful. It was rather that she did not want to sleep, than that she could not. She lay still, thinking, thinking; dreaming such dreams as are the occasions of sanctified privacy to her age and sex.

In the morning she was no worse for her vigil. When at luncheon-time Aunt Laetitia had returned she went into all the little matters of which she had to report. It was after tea-time when she found herself alone, and with leisure to attend to what was, she felt, directly her own affair. During the night she had made up her mind exactly what to say to Leonard; and as her specific resolution bore the test of daylight she was satisfied. The opening words had in their inception caused her some concern; but after hours of thought she had come to the conclusion that to address, under the circumstance, the recipient of the letter as 'Dear Mr. Everard' would hardly do. The only possible justification of her unconventional act was that there existed already a friendship, an intimacy of years, since childhood; that there were already between them knowledge and understanding of each other; that what she was doing, and about to do, was but a further step in a series of events long ago undertaken.

She thought it better to send by post rather than messenger, as the latter did away with all privacy with regard to the act.

The letter was as follows:

> 'DEAR LEONARD,—Would it be convenient for you to meet me to-morrow, Tuesday, at half-past twelve o'clock on the top of Caester Hill? I want to speak about a matter that may have some interest to you, and it will be more private there than in the house. Also it will be cooler in the shade on the hilltop.—
>
> Yours sincerely, STEPHEN NORMAN.'

Having posted the letter she went about the usual routine of her life at Normanstand, and no occasion of suspicion or remark regarding her came to her aunt.

In her room that night when she had sent away her maid, she sat down to think, and all the misgivings of the day came back. One by one they were conquered by one protective argument:

'I am free to do as I like. I am my own mistress; and I am doing nothing that is wrong. Even if it is unconventional, what of that? God knows there are enough conventions in the world that are wrong, hopelessly, unalterably wrong. After all, who are the people who are most bound by convention? Those who call themselves "smart!" If Convention is the god of the smart set, then it is about time that honest people chose another!'

* * * * *

Leonard received the letter at breakfast-time. He did not give it any special attention, as he had other letters at the same time, some of which were, if less pleasant, of more immediate importance. He had of late been bombarded with dunning letters from tradesmen; for during his University life, and ever since, he had run into debt. The moderate allowance his father made him he had treated as cash for incidental expenses, but everything else had been on credit. Indeed he was beginning to get seriously alarmed about the future, for his father, who had paid his debts once, and at a time when they were by comparison inconsiderable, had said that he would not under any circumstances pay others. He was not sorry, therefore, for an opportunity of getting away for a few hours from home; from himself—from anxieties, possibilities. The morning was a sweltering one, and he grumbled to himself as he set out on his journey through the woods.

* * * * *

Stephen rose fresh and in good spirits, despite her sleepless night. When youth and strength are to the fore, a night's sleep is not of much account, for the system once braced up is not allowed to slacken. It was a notable sign of her strong nature that she was not even impatient, but waited with calm fixity the hour at which she had asked Leonard Everard to meet her. It is true that as the time grew closer her nerve was less marked. And just before it she was a girl—and nothing more; with all girl's diffidence, a girl's self-distrust, a girl's abnegation, a girl's plasticity.

In the more purely personal aspect of her enterprise Stephen's effort was more conscious. It is hardly possible for a pretty woman to seek in her study of perfection the aid of her mirror and to be unconscious of her aims.

There must certainly be at least one dominant purpose: the achievement of success. Stephen did not attempt to deny her own beauty; on the contrary she gave it the fullest scope. There was a certain triumph in her glance as she took her last look in her mirror; a gratification of her wish to show herself in the best way possible. It was a very charming picture which the mirror reflected.

It may be that there is a companionship in a mirror, especially to a woman; that the reflection of oneself is an emboldening presence, a personality which is better than the actuality of an unvalued stranger. Certainly, when Stephen closed the door and stood in the wainscoted passage, which was only dimly lit by the high window at either end, her courage seemed at once to ooze away.

Probably for the first time in her life, as she left the shade of the long passage and came out on the staircase flooded with the light of the noonday sun, Stephen felt that she was a girl—'girl' standing as some sort of synonym for weakness, pretended or actual. Fear, in whatever form or degree it may come, is a vital quality and must move. It cannot stand at a fixed point; if it be not sent backward it must progress. Stephen felt this, and, though her whole nature was repugnant to the task, forced herself to the effort of repression. It would, she felt, have been to her a delicious pleasure to have abandoned all effort; to have sunk in the lassitude of self-surrender.

The woman in her was working; her sex had found her out!

She turned and looked around her, as though conscious of being watched. Then, seeing that she was alone, she went her way with settled purpose; with flashing eyes and glowing cheeks—and a beating heart. A heart all woman's since it throbbed the most with apprehension when the enemy, Man, was the objective of her most resolute attack. She knew that she must keep moving; that she must not stop or pause; or her whole resolution must collapse. And so she hurried on, fearful lest a chance meeting with any one might imperil her purpose.

On she went through the faint moss-green paths; through meadows rich with flowering grasses and the many reds of the summer wild-flowers. And so up through the path cut in the natural dipping of the rock that rose over Caester Hill and formed a strong base for the clump of great trees that made a landmark for many a mile around. During the first part of her journey between the house and the hilltop, she tried to hold her purpose at arm's length; it would be sufficient to face its terrors when the time had come. In the meantime the matter was of such overwhelming importance that nothing else could take its place; all she could do was to suspend the active part of the thinking faculties and leave the mind only receptive.

But when she had passed through the thin belt of stunted oak and beech which hedged in the last of the lush meadows, and caught sight of the clump of trees on the hilltop, she unconsciously braced herself as a young regiment loses its tremors when the sight of the enemy breaks upon it. No longer her eyes fell earthward; they were raised, and raised proudly. Stephen Norman was fixed in her intention. Like the woman of old, her feet were on the ploughshares and she would not hesitate.

As she drew near the appointed place her pace grew slower and slower; the woman in her was unconsciously manifesting itself. She would not be first in her tryst with a man. Unconsciousness, however, is not a working quality which can be relied upon for staying power; the approach to the trysting-place brought once more home to her the strange nature of her enterprise. She had made up her mind to it; there was no use in deceiving herself. What she had undertaken to do was much more unconventional than being first at a meeting. It was foolish and weak to delay. The last thought braced her up; and it was with a hurried gait, which alone would have betrayed her to an intelligent observer, that she entered the grove.

CHAPTER-11

The Meeting

Had Stephen been better acquainted with men and women, she would have been more satisfied with herself for being the first at the tryst. The conventional idea, in the minds of most women and of all men, is that a woman should never be the first. But real women, those in whom the heart beats strong, and whose blood can leap, know better. These are the commanders of men. In them sex calls to sex, all unconsciously at first; and men answer to their call, as they to men's.

Two opposite feelings strove for dominance as Stephen found herself on the hilltop, alone. One a feeling natural enough to any one, and especially to a girl, of relief that a dreaded hour had been postponed; the other of chagrin that she was the first.

After a few moments, however, one of the two militant thoughts became dominant: the feeling of chagrin. With a pang she thought if she had been a man and summoned for such a purpose, how she would have hurried to the trysting-place; how the flying of her feet would have vied with the quick rapturous beating of her heart! With a little sigh and a blush, she remembered that Leonard did not know the purpose of the meeting; that he was a friend almost brought up with her since boy and girl times; that he had often been summoned in similar terms and for the most trivial of social purposes.

For nearly half an hour Stephen sat on the rustic seat under the shadow of the great oak, looking, half unconscious of its beauty and yet influenced by it, over the wide landscape stretched at her feet.

In spite of her disregard of conventions, she was no fool; the instinct of wisdom was strong within her, so strong that in many ways it ruled her conscious efforts. Had any one told her that her preparations for this interview were made deliberately with some of the astuteness that dominated the Devil when he took Jesus to the top of a high mountain and showed him all the kingdoms of the earth at His feet, she would have, and with truth, denied it with indignation. Nevertheless it was a fact that she had, in all unconsciousness, chosen for the meeting a spot which would evidence to a man, consciously or unconsciously, the desirability for his own sake of acquiescence in her views and wishes. For all this spreading landscape was her possession, which her husband would share. As far as the eye could reach was within the estate which she had inherited from her father and her uncle.

The half-hour passed in waiting had in one way its advantages to the girl: though she was still as high strung as ever, she acquired a larger measure of control over herself. The nervous tension, however, was so complete physically that all her faculties were acutely awake; very early she became conscious of a distant footstep.

To Stephen's straining ears the footsteps seemed wondrous slow, and more wondrous regular; she felt instinctively that she would have liked to have listened to a more hurried succession of less evenly-marked sounds. But notwithstanding these thoughts, and the qualms which came in their turn, the sound of the coming feet brought great joy. For, after all, they were coming; and coming just in time to prevent the sense of disappointment at their delay gaining firm foothold. It was only when the coming was assured that she felt how strong had been the undercurrent of her apprehension lest they should not come at all.

Very sweet and tender and beautiful Stephen looked at this moment. The strong lines of her face were softened by the dark fire in her eyes and the feeling which glowed in the deep blushes which mantled her cheeks. The proudness of her bearing was no less marked than ever, but in the willowy sway of her body there was a yielding of mere sorry pride. In all the many moods which the gods allow to good women there is none so dear or so alluring, consciously as well as instinctively, to true men as this self-surrender. As Leonard drew near, Stephen sank softly into a seat, doing so with a guilty feeling of acting a part. When he actually came into the grove he found her seemingly lost in a reverie as she gazed out over the wide expanse in front of her. He was hot after his walk, and with something very like petulance threw himself into a cane armchair, exclaiming as he did so with the easy insolence of old familiarity:

'What a girl you are, Stephen! dragging a fellow all the way up here. Couldn't you have fixed it down below somewhere if you wanted to see me?'

Strangely enough, as it seemed to her, Stephen did not dislike his tone of mastery. There was something in it which satisfied her. The unconscious recognition of his manhood, as opposed to her womanhood, soothed her in a peaceful way. It was easy to yield to a dominant man. She was never more womanly than when she answered him softly:

'It was rather unfair; but I thought you would not mind coming so far. It is so cool and delightful here; and we can talk without being disturbed.' Leonard was lying back in his chair fanning himself with his wide-brimmed straw hat, with outstretched legs wide apart and resting on the back of his heels. He replied with grudging condescension:

'Yes, it's cool enough after the hot tramp over the fields and through the wood. It's not so good as the house, though, in one way: a man can't get a drink here. I say, Stephen, it wouldn't be half bad if there were a shanty put up here like those at the Grands Mulets or on the Matterhorn. There could be a tap laid on where a fellow could quench his thirst on a day like this!'

Before Stephen's eyes floated a momentary vision of a romantic châlet with wide verandah and big windows looking over the landscape; a great wide stone hearth; quaint furniture made from the gnarled branches of trees; skins on the floor; and the walls adorned with antlers, great horns, and various trophies of the chase. And amongst them Leonard, in a picturesque suit, lolling back just as at present and smiling with a loving look in his eyes as she handed him a great blue-and-white Munich beer mug topped with cool foam. There was a soft mystery in her voice as she answered:

'Perhaps, Leonard, there will some day be such a place here!' He seemed to grumble as he replied:

'I wish it was here now. Some day seems a long way off!'

This seemed a good opening for Stephen; for the fear of the situation was again beginning to assail her, and she felt that if she did not enter on her task at once, its difficulty might overwhelm her. She felt angry with herself that there was a change in her voice as she said:

'Some day may mean—can mean everything. Things needn't be a longer way off than we choose ourselves, sometimes!'

'I say, that's a good one! Do you mean to say that because I am some day to own Brindehow I can do as I like with it at once, whilst the governor's all there, and a better life than I am any day? Unless you want me to shoot the old man by accident when we go out on the First.' He laughed a short, unmeaning masculine laugh which jarred somewhat on her. She did not, however, mean to be diverted from her main purpose, so she went on quickly:

'You know quite well, Leonard, that I don't mean anything of the kind. But there was something I wanted to say to you, and I wished that we should be alone. Can you not guess what it is?'

'No, I'll be hanged if I can!' was his response, lazily given.

Despite her resolution she turned her head; she could not meet his eyes. It cut her with a sharp pain to notice when she turned again that he was not looking at her. He continued fanning himself with his hat as he gazed out at the view. She felt that the critical moment of her life had come, that it was now or never as to her fulfilling her settled intention. So with a rush she went on her way:

'Leonard, you and I have been friends a long time. You know my views on some points, and that I think a woman should be as free to act as a man!' She paused; words and ideas did not seem to flow with the readiness she expected. Leonard's arrogant assurance completed the dragging her back to earth which her own self-consciousness began:

'Drive on, old girl! I know you're a crank from Crankville on some subjects. Let us have it for all you're worth. I'm on the grass and listening.'

Stephen paused. 'A crank from Crankville!'—this after her nights of sleepless anxiety; after the making of the resolution which had cost her so much, and which was now actually in process of realisation. Was it all worth so much? why not abandon it now? . . . Abandon it! Abandon a resolution! All the obstinacy of her nature—she classed it herself as firmness—rose in revolt. She shook her head angrily, pulled herself together, and went on:

'That may be! though it's not what I call myself, or what I am usually called, so far as I know. At any rate my convictions are honest, and I am sure you will respect them as such, even if you do not share them.' She did not see the ready response in his face which she expected, and so hurried on:

'It has always seemed to me that a—when a woman has to speak to a man she should do so as frankly as she would like him to speak to her, and as freely. Leonard, I—I,' as she halted, a sudden idea, winged with possibilities of rescuing procrastination came to her. She went on more easily:

'I know you are in trouble about money matters. Why not let me help you?' He sat up and looked at her and said genially:

'Well, Stephen, you are a good old sort! No mistake about it. Do you mean to say you would help me to pay my debts, when the governor has refused to do so any more?'

'It would be a great pleasure to me, Leonard, to do anything for your good or your pleasure.'

There was a long pause; they both sat looking down at the ground. The woman's heart beat loud; she feared that the man must hear it. She was consumed with anxiety, and with a desolating wish to be relieved from the strain of saying more. Surely, surely Leonard could not be so blind as not to see the state of things! . . . He would surely seize the occasion; throw aside his diffidence and relieve her! . . . His words made a momentary music in her ears as he spoke:

'And is this what you asked me to come here for?'

The words filled her with a great shame. She felt herself a dilemma. It had been no part of her purpose to allude his debts. Viewed in the light of what was to follow, it would seem to him that she was trying to foreclose his affection. That could not be allowed to pass; the error must be rectified. And yet! . . . And yet this very error must be cleared up before she could make her full wish apparent. She seemed to find herself compelled by inexorable circumstances into an unlooked-for bluntness. In any case she must face the situation. Her pluck did not fail her; it was with a very noble and graceful simplicity that she turned to her companion and said:

'Leonard, I did not quite mean that. It would be a pleasure to me to be of that or any other service to you, if I might be so happy! But I never meant to allude to your debts. Oh! Leonard, can't you understand! If you were my husband—or—or going to be, all such little troubles would fall away from you. But I would not for the world have you think . . . '

Her very voice failed her. She could not speak what was in her mind; she turned away, hiding in her hands her face which fairly seemed to burn. This, she thought, was the time for a true lover's opportunity! Oh, if she had been a man, and a woman had so appealed, how he would have sprung to her side and taken her in his arms, and in a wild rapture of declared affection have swept away all the pain of her shame!

But she remained alone. There was no springing to her side; no rapture of declared affection; no obliteration of her shame. She had to bear it all alone. There, in the open; under the eyes that she would fain have seen any other phase of her distress. Her heart beat loud and fast; she waited to gain her self-control.

Leonard Everard had his faults, plenty of them, and he was in truth composed of an amalgam of far baser metals than Stephen thought; but he had been born of gentle blood and reared amongst gentlefolk. He did not quite understand the cause or the amount of his companion's concern; but he could not but recognise her distress. He realised that it had followed hard upon her most generous intention towards himself. He could not, therefore, do less than try to comfort her, and he began his task in a conventional way, but with a blundering awkwardness which was all manlike. He took her hand and held it in his; this much at any rate he had learned in sitting on stairs or in conservatories after extra dances. He said as tenderly as he could, but with an impatient gesture unseen by her:

'Forgive me, Stephen! I suppose I have said or done something which I shouldn't. But I don't know what it is; upon my honour I don't. Anyhow, I am truly sorry for it. Cheer up, old girl! I'm not your husband, you know; so you needn't be distressed.'

Stephen took her courage *à deux mains*. If Leonard would not speak she must. It was manifestly impossible that the matter could be left in its present state.

'Leonard,' she said softly and solemnly, 'might not that some day be?'

Leonard, in addition to being an egotist and the very incarnation of selfishness, was a prig of the first water. He had been reared altogether in convention. Home life and Eton and Christchurch had taught him many things, wise as well as foolish; but had tended to fix his conviction that affairs of the heart should proceed on adamantine lines of conventional decorum. It never even occurred to him that a lady could so far step from the confines of convention as to take the initiative in a matter of affection. In his blind ignorance he blundered brutally. He struck better than he knew, as, meaning only to pass safely by an awkward conversational corner, he replied:

'No jolly fear of that! You're too much of a boss for me!' The words and the levity with which they were spoken struck the girl as with a whip. She turned for an instant as pale as ashes; then the red blood rushed from her heart, and face and neck were dyed crimson. It was not a blush, it was a suffusion. In his ignorance Leonard thought it was the former, and went on with what he considered his teasing.

'Oh yes! You know you always want to engineer a chap your own way and make him do just as you wish. The man who has the happiness of marrying you, Stephen, will have a hard row to hoe!' His 'chaff' with its utter want of refinement seemed to her, in her high-strung earnest condition, nothing short of brutal, and for a few seconds produced a feeling of repellence. But it is in the nature of things that opposition of any kind arouses the fighting instinct of a naturally dominant nature. She lost sight of her femininity in the pursuit of her purpose; and as this was to win the man to her way of thinking, she took the logical course of answering his argument. If Leonard Everard had purposely set himself to stimulate her efforts in this direction he could hardly have chosen a better way. It came somewhat as a surprise to Stephen, when she heard her own words:

'I would make a good wife, Leonard! A husband whom I loved and honoured would, I think, not be unhappy!' The sound of her own voice speaking these words, though the tone was low and tender and more self-suppressing by far than was her wont, seemed to peal like thunder in her own ears. Her last bolt seemed to have sped. The blood rushed to her head, and she had to hold on to the arms of the rustic chair or she would have fallen forward.

The time seemed long before Leonard spoke again; every second seemed an age. She seemed to have grown tired of waiting for the sound of his voice; it was with a kind of surprise that she heard him say:

'You limit yourself wisely, Stephen!'

'How do you mean?' she asked, making a great effort to speak.

'You would promise to love and honour; but there isn't anything about obeying.'

As he spoke Leonard stretched himself again luxuriously, and laughed with the intellectual arrogance of a man who is satisfied with a joke, however inferior, of his own manufacture. Stephen looked at him with a long look which began in anger—that anger which comes from an unwonted sense of impotence, and ends in tolerance, the intermediate step being admiration. It is the primeval curse that a woman's choice is to her husband; and it is an important part of the teaching of a British gentlewoman, knit in the very fibres of her being by the remorseless etiquette of a thousand years, that she be true to him. The man who has in his person the necessary powers or graces to evoke admiration in his wife, even for a passing moment, has a stronghold unconquerable as a rule by all the deadliest arts of mankind.

Leonard Everard was certainly good to look upon as he lolled at his ease on that summer morning. Tall, straight, supple; a typical British gentleman of the educated class, with all parts of the body properly developed and held in some kind of suitable poise.

As Stephen looked, the anxiety and chagrin which tormented her seemed to pass. She realised that here was a nature different from her own, and which should be dealt with in a way unsuitable to herself; and the conviction seemed to make the action which it necessitated more easy as well as more natural to her. Perhaps for the first time in her life Stephen understood that it may be necessary to apply to individuals a standard of criticism unsuitable to self-judgment. Her recognition might have been summed up in the thought which ran through her mind:

'One must be a little lenient with a man one loves!'

Stephen, when once she had allowed the spirit of toleration to work within her, felt immediately its calming influence. It was with brighter thoughts and better humour that she went on with her task. A task only, it seemed now; a means to an end which she desired.

'Leonard, tell me seriously, why do you think I gave you the trouble of coming out here?'

'Upon my soul, Stephen, I don't know.'

'You don't seem to care either, lolling like that when I am serious!' The words were acid, but the tone was soft and friendly, familiar and genuine, putting quite a meaning of its own on them. Leonard looked at her indolently:

'I like to loll.'

'But can't you even guess, or try to guess, what I ask you?'

'I can't guess. The day's too hot, and that shanty with the drinks is not built yet.'

'Or may never be!' Again he looked at her sleepily.

'Never be! Why not?'

'Because, Leonard, it may depend on you.'

'All right then. Drive on! Hurry up the architect and the jerry-builder!'

A quick blush leaped to Stephen's cheeks. The words were full of meaning, though the tone lacked something; but the news was too good. She could not accept it at once; she decided to herself to wait a short time. Ere many seconds had passed she rejoiced that she had done so as he went on:

'I hope you'll give me a say before that husband of yours comes along. He might be a blue-ribbonite; and it wouldn't do to start such a shanty for rot-gut!'

Again a cold wave swept over her. The absolute difference of feeling between the man and herself; his levity against her earnestness, his callous blindness to her purpose, even the commonness of his words chilled her. For a few seconds she wavered again in her intention; but once again his comeliness and her own obstinacy joined hands and took her back to her path. With chagrin she felt that her words almost stuck in her throat, as summoning up all her resolution she went on:

'It would be for you I would have it built, Leonard!' The man sat up quickly.

'For me?' he asked in a sort of wonderment.

'Yes, Leonard, for you and me!' She turned away; her blushes so overcame her that she could not look at him. When she faced round again he was standing up, his back towards her.

She stood up also. He was silent for a while; so long that the silence became intolerable, and she spoke:

'Leonard, I am waiting!' He turned round and said slowly, the absence of all emotion from his face chilling her till her face blanched:

'I don't think I would worry about it!'

Stephen Norman was plucky, and when she was face to face with any difficulty she was all herself. Leonard did not look pleasant; his face was hard and there was just a suspicion of anger. Strangely enough, this last made the next step easier to the girl; she said slowly:

'All right! I think I understand!'

He turned from her and stood looking out on the distant prospect. Then she felt that the blow which she had all along secretly feared had fallen on her. But her pride as well as her obstinacy now rebelled. She would not accept a silent answer. There must be no doubt left to torture her afterwards. She would take care that there was no mistake. Schooling herself to her task, and pressing one hand for a moment to her side as though to repress the beating of her heart, she came behind him and touched him tenderly on the arm.

'Leonard,' she said softly, 'are you sure there is no mistake? Do you not see that I am asking you,' she intended to say 'to be my husband,' but she could not utter the words, they seemed to stick in her mouth, so she finished the sentence: 'that I be your wife?'

The moment the words were spoken—the bare, hard, naked, shameless words—the revulsion came. As a lightning flash shows up the blackness of the night the appalling truth of what she had done was forced upon her. The blood rushed to her head till cheeks and shoulders and neck seemed to burn. Covering her face with her hands she sank back on the seat crying silently bitter tears that seemed to scald her eyes and her cheeks as they ran.

Leonard was angry. When it began to dawn upon him what was the purpose of Stephen's speech, he had been shocked. Young men are so easily shocked by breaches of convention made by women they respect! And his pride was hurt. Why should he have been placed in such a ridiculous position! He did not love Stephen in that way; and she should have known it. He liked her and all that sort of thing; but what right had she to assume that he loved her? All the weakness of his moral nature came out in his petulance. It was boyish that his eyes filled with tears. He knew it, and that made him more angry than ever. Stephen might well have been at a loss to understand his anger, as, with manifest intention to wound, he answered her:

'What a girl you are, Stephen. You are always doing something or other to put a chap in the wrong and make him ridiculous. I thought you were joking—not a good joke either! Upon my soul, I don't know what I've done that you should fix on me! I wish to goodness—'

If Stephen had suffered the red terror before, she suffered the white terror now. It was not injured pride, it was not humiliation, it was not fear; it was something vague and terrible that lay far deeper than any of these. Under ordinary circumstances she would have liked to have spoken out her mind and given back as good as she got; and even as the thoughts whirled through her brain they came in a torrent of vague vituperative eloquence. But now her tongue was tied. Instinctively she knew that she had put it out of her power to revenge, or even to defend herself. She was tied to the stake, and must suffer without effort and in silence.

Most humiliating of all was the thought that she must propitiate the man who had so wounded her. All love for him had in the instant passed from her; or rather she realised fully the blank, bare truth that she had never really loved him at all. Had she really loved him, even a blow at his hands would have been acceptable; but now . . .

She shook the feelings and thoughts from her as a bird does the water from its wings; and, with the courage and strength and adaptability of her nature, addressed herself to the hard task which faced her in the immediate present. With eloquent, womanly gesture she arrested the torrent of Leonard's indignation; and, as he paused in surprised obedience, she said:

'That will do, Leonard! It is not necessary to say any more; and I am sure you will see, later on, that at least there was no cause for your indignation! I have done an unconventional thing, I know; and I dare say I shall have to pay for it in humiliating bitterness of thought later on! But please remember we are all alone! This is a secret between us; no one else need ever know or suspect it!'

She rose as she concluded. The quiet dignity of her speech and bearing brought back Leonard in some way to his sense of duty as a gentleman. He began, in a sheepish way, to make an apology:

'I'm sure I beg your pardon, Stephen.' But again she held the warning hand:

'There is no need for pardon; the fault, if there were any, was mine alone. It was I, remember, who asked you to come here and who introduced and conducted this melancholy business. I have asked you several things, Leonard, and one more I will add—'tis only one: that you will forget!'

As she moved away, her dismissal of the subject was that of an empress to a serf. Leonard would have liked to answer her; to have given vent to his indignation that, even when he had refused her offer, she should have the power to treat him if he was the one refused, and to make him feel small and ridiculous in his own eyes. But somehow he felt constrained to silence; her simple dignity outclassed him.

There was another factor too, in his forming his conclusion of silence. He had never seen Stephen look so well, or so attractive. He had never respected her so much as when her playfulness had turned to majestic gravity. All the boy and girl strife of the years that had gone seemed to have passed away. The girl whom he had played with, and bullied, and treated as frankly as though she had been a boy, had in an instant become a woman—and such a woman as demanded respect and admiration even from such a man.

CHAPTER-12

On The Road Home

When Leonard Everard parted from Stephen he did so with a feeling of dissatisfaction: firstly, with Stephen; secondly, with things in general; thirdly, with himself. The first was definite, concrete, and immediate; he could give himself chapter and verse for all the girl's misdoing. Everything she had said or done had touched some nerve painfully, or had offended his feelings; and to a man of his temperament his feelings are very sacred things, to himself.

'Why had she put him in such a ridiculous position? That was the worst of women. They were always wanting him to do something he didn't want to do, or crying . . . there was that girl at Oxford.'

Here he turned his head slowly, and looked round in a furtive way, which was getting almost a habit with him. 'A fellow should go away so that he wouldn't have to swear lies. Women were always wanting money; or worse: to be married! Confound women; they all seemed to want him to marry them! There was the Oxford girl, and then the Spaniard, and now Stephen!' This put his thoughts in a new channel. He wanted money himself. Why, Stephen had spoken of it herself; had offered to pay his debts. Gad! it was a good idea that every one round the countryside seemed to know his affairs. What a flat he had been not to accept her offer then and there before matters had gone further. Stephen had lots of money, more than any girl could want. But she didn't give him time to get the thing fixed . . . If he had only known beforehand what she wanted he could have come prepared . . . that was the way with women! Always thinking of themselves! And now? Of course she wouldn't stump up after his refusing her. What would his father say if he came to hear of it? And he must speak to him soon, for these chaps were threatening to County Court him if he didn't pay. Those harpies in Vere Street were quite nasty . . . ' He wondered if he could work Stephen for a loan.

He walked on through the woodland path, his pace slower than before. 'How pretty she had looked!' Here he touched his little moustache. 'Gad!

Stephen was a fine girl anyhow! If it wasn't for all that red hair . . . I like 'em dark better! . . . And her being such an infernal boss!'. . . Then he said unconsciously aloud:

'If I was her husband I'd keep her to rights!'

Poor Stephen!

'So that's what the governor meant by telling me that fortune was to be had, and had easily, if a man wasn't a blind fool. The governor is a starchy old party. He wouldn't speak out straight and say, "Here's Stephen Norman, the richest girl you are ever likely to meet; why don't you make up to her and marry her?" But that would be encouraging his son to be a fortune-hunter! Rot! . . . And now, just because she didn't tell me what she wanted to speak about, or the governor didn't give me a hint so that I might be prepared, I have gone and thrown away the chance. After all it mightn't be so bad. Stephen is a fine girl! . . . But she mustn't ever look at me as she did when I spoke about her not obeying. I mean to be master in my own house anyhow!

'A man mustn't be tied down too tight, even if he is married. And if there's plenty of loose cash about it isn't hard to cover up your tracks . . . I think I'd better think this thing over calmly and be ready when Stephen comes at me again. That's the way with women. When a woman like Stephen fixes her cold grey on a man she does not mean to go asleep over it. I daresay my best plan will be to sit tight, and let her work herself up a bit. There's nothing like a little wholesome neglect for bringing a girl to her bearings!' . . .

For a while he walked on in satisfied self-complacency.

'Confound her! why couldn't she have let me know that she was fond of me in some decent way, without all that formal theatrical proposing? It's a deuced annoying thing in the long run the way the women get fond of me. Though it's nice enough in some ways while it lasts!' he added, as if in unwilling recognition of fact. As the path debouched on the highroad he said to himself half aloud:

'Well, she's a mighty fine girl, anyhow! And if she is red I've had about enough of the black! . . . That Spanish girl is beginning to kick too! I wish I had never come across . . . '

'Shut up, you fool!' he said to himself as he walked on.

When he got home he found a letter from his father. He took it to his room before breaking the seal. It was at least concise and to the point:

'The enclosed has been sent to me. You will have to deal with it yourself. You know my opinion and also my intention. The items which I have marked have been incurred since I spoke to you last about your debts. I shall not pay another farthing for you. So take your own course!

'JASPER EVERARD.'

The enclosed was a jeweller's bill, the length and the total of which lengthened his face and drew from him a low whistle. He held it in his hand for a long time, standing quite still and silent. Then drawing a deep breath he said aloud:

'That settles it! The halter is on me! It's no use squealing. If it's to be a red head on my pillow! . . . All right! I must only make the best of it. Anyhow I'll have a good time to-day, even if it must be the last!'

That day Harold was in Norcester on business. It was late when he went to the club to dine. Whilst waiting for dinner he met Leonard Everard, flushed and somewhat at uncertain in his speech. It was something of a shock to Harold to see him in such a state.

Leonard was, however, an old friend, and man is as a rule faithful to friends in this form of distress. So in his kindly feeling Harold offered to drive him home, for he knew that he could thus keep him out of further harm. Leonard thanked him in uncertain speech, and said he would be ready. In the meantime he would go and play billiards with the marker whilst Harold was having his dinner.

At ten o'clock Harold's dogcart was ready and he went to look for Leonard, who had not since come near him. He found him half asleep in the smoking-room, much drunker than he had been earlier in the evening.

The drive was fairly long, so Harold made up his mind for a prolonged term of uneasiness and anxiety. The cool night-air, whose effect was increased by the rapid motion, soon increased Leonard's somnolence and for a while he slept soundly, his companion watching carefully lest he should sway over and fall out of the trap. He even held him up as they swung round sharp corners.

After a time he woke up, and woke in a nasty temper. He began to find fault in an incoherent way with everything. Harold said little, just enough to prevent any cause for further grievance. Then Leonard changed and became affectionate. This mood was a greater bore than the other, but Harold managed to bear it with stolid indifference. Leonard was this by time making promises to do things for him, that as he was what he called a 'goo' fell',' he might count on his help and support in the future. As Harold knew him to be a wastrel, over head and ears in debt and with only the succession to a small estate, he did not take much heed to his maunderings. At last the drunken man said something which startled him so much that he instinctively drew himself together with such suddenness as to frighten the horse and almost make him rear up straight.

'Woa! Woa! Steady, boy. Gently!' he said, quieting him. Then turning to his companion said in a voice hollow with emotion and vibrant with suppressed passion:

'What was it you said?'

Leonard, half awake, and not half of that half master of himself, answered:

'I said I will make you agent of Normanstand when I marry Stephen.'

Harold grew cold. To hear of any one marrying Stephen was to him like plunging him in a glacier stream; but to hear her name so lightly spoken, and by such a man, was a bewildering shock which within a second set his blood on fire.

'What do you mean?' he thundered. 'You marry Ste . . . Miss Norman! You're not worthy to untie her shoe! You indeed! She wouldn't look on the same side of the street with a drunken brute like you! How dare you speak of her in such a way!'

'Brute!' said Leonard angrily, his vanity reaching inward to heart and brain through all the numbing obstacle of his drunken flesh. 'Who's brute? Brute yourself! Tell you goin' to marry Stephen, 'cos Stephen wants it. Stephen loves me. Loves me with all her red head! Wha're you doin'! Wha!!'

His words merged in a lessening gurgle, for Harold had now got him by the throat.

'Take care what you say about that lady! damn you!' he said, putting his face close the other's with eyes that blazed. 'Don't you dare to mention her name in such a way, or you will regret it longer than you can think. Loves you, you swine!'

The struggle and the fierce grip on his throat sobered Leonard somewhat. Momentarily sobbed him to that point when he could be coherent and vindictive, though not to the point where he could think ahead. Caution, wisdom, discretion, taste, were not for him at such a moment. Guarding his throat with both hands in an instinctive and spasmodic manner he answered the challenge:

'Who are you calling swine? I tell you she loves me. She ought to know. Didn't she tell me so this very day!' Harold drew back his arm to strike him in the face, his anger too great for words. But the other, seeing the motion and in the sobering recognition of danger, spoke hastily:

'Keep your hair on! You know so jolly much more than I do. I tell you that she told me this and a lot more this morning when she asked me to marry her.'

Harold's heart grew cold as ice. There is something in the sound of a voice speaking truthfully which a true man can recognise. Through all Leonard's half-drunken utterings came such a ring of truth; and Harold recognised it. He felt that his voice was weak and hollow as he spoke, thinking it necessary to give at first a sort of official denial to such a monstrous statement:

'Liar!'

'I'm no liar!' answered Leonard. He would like to have struck him in answer to such a word had he felt equal to it. 'She asked me to marry her to-day on the hill above the house, where I went to meet her by appointment. Here! I'll prove it to you. Read this!' Whilst he was speaking he had opened the greatcoat and was fumbling in the breast-pocket of his coat. He produced a letter which he handed to Harold, who took it with trembling hand. By this time the reins had fallen slack and the horse was walking quietly. There was moonlight, but not enough to read by. Harold bent over and lifted the driving-lamp next to him and turned it so that he could read the envelope. He could hardly keep either lamp or paper still, his hand trembled so when he saw that the direction was in Stephen's handwriting. He was handing it back when Leonard said again:

'Open it! Read it! You must do so; I tell you, you must! You called me a liar, and now must read the proof that I am not. If you don't I shall have to ask Stephen to make you!' Before Harold's mind flashed a rapid thought of what the girl might suffer in being asked to take part in such a quarrel. He could not himself even act to the best advantage unless he knew the truth . . . he took the letter from the envelope and held it before the lamp, the paper fluttering as though in a breeze from the trembling of his hand. Leonard looked on, the dull glare of his eyes brightening with malignant pleasure as he beheld the other's concern. He owed him a grudge, and by God he would pay it. Had he not been struck—throttled—called a liar! . . .

As he read the words Harold's face cleared. 'Why, you infernal young scoundrel!' he said angrily, 'that letter is nothing but a simple note from a young girl to an old friend—playmate asking him to come to see her about some trivial thing. And you construe it into a proposal of marriage. You hound!' He held the letter whilst he spoke, heedless of the outstretched hand of the other waiting to take it back. There was a dangerous glitter in Leonard's eyes. He knew his man and he knew the truth of what he had himself said, and he felt, with all the strength of his base soul, how best he could torture him. In the very strength of Harold's anger, in the poignancy of his concern, in the relief to his soul expressed in his eyes and his voice, his antagonist realised the jealousy of one who honours—and loves. Second by second Leonard grew more sober, and more and better able to carry his own idea into act.

'Give me my letter!' he began.

'Wait!' said Harold as he put the lamp back into its socket. 'That will do presently. Take back what you said just now!'

'What? Take back what?'

'That base lie; that Miss Norman asked you to marry her.'

Leonard felt that in a physical struggle for the possession of the letter he would be outmatched; but his passion grew colder and more malignant, and in a voice that cut like the hiss of a snake he spoke slowly and deliberately. He was all sober now; the drunkenness of brain and blood was lost, for the time, in the strength of his cold passion.

'It is true. By God it is true; every word of it! That letter, which you want to steal, is only a proof that I went to meet her on Caester Hill by her own appointment. When I got there, she was waiting for me. She began to talk about a châlet there, and at first I didn't know what she meant—'

There was such conviction, such a triumphant truth in his voice, that Harold was convinced.

'Stop!' he thundered; 'stop, don't tell me anything. I don't want to hear. I don't want to know.' He covered his face with his hands and groaned. It was not as though the speaker were a stranger, in which case he would have been by now well on in his death by strangulation; he had known Leonard all his life, and he was a friend of Stephen's. And he was speaking truth.

The baleful glitter of Leonard's eyes grew brighter still. He was as a serpent when he goes to strike. In this wise he struck.

'I shall not stop. I shall go on and tell you all I choose. You have called me liar—twice. You have also called me other names. Now you shall hear the truth, the whole truth, and nothing but the truth. And if you won't listen to me some one else will.' Harold groaned again; Leonard's eyes brightened still more, and the evil smile on his face grew broader as he began more and more to feel his power. He went on to speak with a cold deliberate malignancy, but instinctively so sticking to absolute truth that he could trust himself to hurt most. The other listened, cold at heart and physically; his veins and arteries seemed stagnant.

'I won't tell you anything of her pretty embarrassments; how her voice fell as she pleaded; how she blushed and stammered. Why, even I, who am used to women and their pretty ways and their passions and their flushings and their stormy upbraidings, didn't quite know for a while what she was driving at. So at last she spoke out pretty plainly, and told me what a fond wife she'd make me if I would only take her!' Harold said nothing; he only rocked a little as one in pain, and his hands fell. The other went on:

'That is what happened this morning on Caester Hill under the trees where I met Stephen Norman by her own appointment; honestly what happened. If you don't believe me now you can ask Stephen. My Stephen!' he added in a final burst of venom as in a gleam of moonlight through a rift in the shadowy wood he saw the ghastly pallor of Harold's face. Then he added abruptly as he held out his hand:

'Now give me my letter!'

In the last few seconds Harold had been thinking. And as he had been thinking for the good, the safety, of Stephen, his thoughts flew swift and true. This man's very tone, the openness of his malignity, the underlying scorn when he spoke of her whom others worshipped, showed him the danger—the terrible immediate danger in which she stood from such a man. With the instinct of a mind working as truly for the woman he loved as the needle does to the Pole he spoke quietly, throwing a sneer into the tone so as to exasperate his companion—it was brain against brain now, and for Stephen's sake:

'And of course you accepted. You naturally would!' The other fell into the trap. He could not help giving an extra dig to his opponent by proving him once more in the wrong.

'Oh no, I didn't! Stephen is a fine girl; but she wants taking down a bit. She's too high and mighty just at present, and wants to boss a chap too much. I mean to be master in my own house; and she's got to begin as she will have to go on. I'll let her wait a bit: and then I'll yield by degrees to her lovemaking. She's a fine girl, for all her red head; and she won't be so bad after all!'

Harold listened, chilled into still and silent amazement. To hear Stephen spoken of in such a way appalled him. She of all women! . . . Leonard never knew how near sudden death he was, as he lay back in his seat, his eyes getting dull again and his chin sinking. The drunkenness which had been arrested by his passion was reasserting itself. Harold saw his state in time and arrested his own movement to take him by the throat and dash him to the ground. Even as he looked at him in scornful hate, the cart gave a lurch and Leonard fell forward. Instinctively Harold swept an arm round him and held him up. As he did so the unconsciousness of arrested sleep came; Leonard's chin sank on his breast and he breathed stertorously.

As he drove on, Harold's thoughts circled in a tumult. Vague ideas of extreme measures which he ought to take flashed up and paled away. Intention revolved upon itself till its weak side was exposed, and, it was abandoned. He could not doubt the essential truth of Leonard's statement regarding the proposal of marriage. He did not understand this nor did he try to. His own love for the girl and the bitter awaking to its futility made him so hopeless that in his own desolation all the mystery of her doing and the cause of it was merged and lost.

His only aim and purpose now was her safety. One thing at least he could do: by fair means or foul stop Leonard's mouth, so that others need not know her shame! He groaned aloud as the thought came to him. Beyond this first step he could do nothing, think of nothing as yet. And he could not take this first step till Leonard had so far sobered that he could understand.

And so waiting for that time to come, he drove on through the silent night.

CHAPTER-13
Harold's Resolve

As they went on their way Harold noticed that Leonard's breathing became more regular, as in honest sleep. He therefore drove slowly so that the other might be sane again before they should arrive at the gate of his father's place; he had something of importance to say before they should part.

Seeing him sleeping so peacefully, Harold passed a strap round him to prevent him falling from his seat. Then he could let his thoughts run more freely. Her safety was his immediate concern; again and again he thought over what he should say to Leonard to ensure his silence.

Whilst he was pondering with set brows, he was startled by Leonard's voice at his side:

'Is that you, Harold? I must have been asleep!' Harold remained silent, amazed at the change. Leonard went on, quite awake and coherent:

'By George! I must have been pretty well cut. I don't remember a thing after coming down the stairs of the club and you and the hall-porter helping me up here. I say, old chap, you have strapped me up all safe and tight. It was good of you to take charge of me. I hope I haven't been a beastly nuisance!' Harold answered grimly:

'It wasn't exactly what I should have called it!' Then, after looking keenly at his companion, he said: 'Are you quite awake and sober now?'

'Quite.' The answer came defiantly; there was something in his questioner's tone which was militant and aggressive. Before speaking further Harold pulled up the horse. They were now crossing bare moorland, where anything within a mile could have easily been seen. They were quite alone, and would be undisturbed. Then he turned to his companion.

'You talked a good deal in your drunken sleep—if sleep it was. You appeared to be awake!' Leonard answered:

'I don't remember anything of it. What did I say?'

'I am going to tell you. You said something so strange and so wrong that you must answer for it. But first I must know its truth.'

'Must! You are pretty dictatorial,' said Leonard angrily. 'Must answer for it! What do you mean?'

'Were you on Caester Hill to-day?'

'What's that to you?' There was no mistaking the defiant, quarrelsome intent.

'Answer me! were you?' Harold's voice was strong and calm.

'What if I was? It is none of your affair. Did I say anything in what you have politely called my drunken sleep?'

'You did.'

'What did I say?'

'I shall tell you in time. But I must know the truth as I proceed. There is some one else concerned in this, and I must know as I go on. You can easily judge by what I say if I am right.'

'Then ask away and be damned to you!' Harold's calm voice seemed to quell the other's turbulence as he went on:

'Were you on Caester Hill this morning?'

'I was.'

'Did you meet Miss --- a lady there?'

'What . . . I did!'

'Was it by appointment?' Some sort of idea or half-recollection seemed to come to Leonard; he fumbled half consciously in his breast-pocket. Then he broke out angrily:

'You have taken my letter!'

'I know the answer to that question,' said Harold slowly. 'You showed me the letter yourself, and insisted on my reading it.' Leonard's heart began to quail. He seemed to have an instinctive dread of what was coming. Harold went on calmly and remorselessly:

'Did a proposal of marriage pass between you?'

'Yes!' The answer was defiantly given; Leonard began to feel that his back was against the wall.

'Who made it?' The answer was a sudden attempt at a blow, but Harold struck down his hand in time and held it. Leonard, though a fairly strong man, was powerless in that iron grasp.

'You must answer! It is necessary that I know the truth.'

'Why must you? What have you to do with it? You are not my keeper! Nor Stephen's; though I dare say you would like to be!' The insult cooled Harold's rising passion, even whilst it wrung his heart.

'I have to do with it because I choose. You may find the answer if you wish in your last insult! Now, clearly understand me, Leonard Everard. You know me of old; and you know that what I say I shall do. One way or another, your life or mine may hang on your answers to me—if necessary!' Leonard felt himself pulled up. He knew well the strength and purpose of the man. With a light laugh, which he felt to be, as it was, hollow, he answered:

'Well, schoolmaster, as you are asking questions, I suppose I may as well answer them. Go on! Next!' Harold went on in the same calm, cold voice:

'Who made the proposal of marriage?'

'She did.'

'Did . . . Was it made at once and directly, or after some preliminary suggestion?'

'After a bit. I didn't quite understand at first what she was driving at.' There was a long pause. With an effort Harold went on:

'Did you accept?' Leonard hesitated. With a really wicked scowl he eyed his big, powerfully-built companion, who still had his hand as in a vice. Then seeing no resource, he answered:

'I did not! That does not mean that I won't, though!' he added defiantly. To his surprise Harold suddenly released his hand. There was a grimness in his tone as he said:

'That will do! I know now that you have spoken the truth, sober as well as drunk. You need say no more. I know the rest. Most men—even brutes like you, if there are any—would have been ashamed even to think the things you said, said openly to me, you hound. You vile, traitorous, mean-souled hound!'

'What did I say?'

'I know what you said; and I shall not forget it.' He went on, his voice deepening into a stern judicial utterance, as though he were pronouncing a sentence of death:

'Leonard Everard, you have treated vilely a lady whom I love and honour more than I love my own soul. You have insulted her to her face and behind her back. You have made such disloyal reference to her and to her mad act in so trusting you, and have so shown your intention of causing, intentionally or unintentionally, woe to her, that I tell you here and now that you hold henceforth your life in your hand. If you ever mention to a living soul what you have told me twice to-night, even though you should be then her husband; if you should cause her harm though she should then be your wife; if you should cause her dishonour in public or in private, I shall kill you. So help me God!'

Not a word more did he say; but, taking up the reins, drove on in silence till they arrived at the gate of Brindehow, where he signed to him to alight.

He drove off in silence.

When he arrived at his own house he sent the servant to bed, and then went to his study, where he locked himself in. Then, and then only, did he permit his thoughts to have full range. For the first time since the blow had fallen he looked straight in the face the change in his own life. He had loved Stephen so long and so honestly that it seemed to him now as if that love had been the very foundation of his life. He could not remember a time when he had not loved her; away back to the time when he, a big boy, took her, a little girl, under his care, and devoted himself to her. He had grown into the belief that so strong and so consistent an affection, though he had never spoken it or even hinted at it or inferred it, had become a part of her life as well as of his own. And this was the end of that dreaming! Not only did she not care for him, but found herself with a heart so empty that she needs must propose marriage to another man! There was surely something, more than at present he knew of or could understand, behind such an act done by her. Why should she ask Everard to marry her? Why should she ask any man? Women didn't do such things! . . . Here he paused. 'Women didn't do such things.' All at once there came back to him fragments of discussions—in which Stephen had had a part, in which matters of convention had been dealt with. Out of these dim and shattered memories came a comfort to his heart, though his brain could not as yet grasp the reason of it. He knew that Stephen had held an unconventional idea as to the equality of the sexes. Was it possible that she was indeed testing one of her theories?

The idea stirred him so that he could not remain quiet. He stood up, and walked the room. Somehow he felt light beginning to dawn, though he could not tell its source, or guess at the final measure of its fulness. The fact of Stephen having done such a thing was hard to bear; but it was harder to think that she should have done such a thing without a motive; or worse: with love of Leonard as a motive! He shuddered as he paused. She could not love such a man. It was monstrous! And yet she had done this thing...

'Oh, if she had had any one to advise her, to restrain her! But she had no mother! No mother! Poor Stephen!'

The pity of it, not for himself but for the woman he loved, overcame him. Sitting down heavily before his desk, he put his face on his hands, and his great shoulders shook.

Long, long after the violence of his emotion had passed, he sat there motionless, thinking with all the power and sincerity he knew; thinking for Stephen's good.

When a strong man thinks unselfishly some good may come out of it. He may blunder; but the conclusion of his reasoning must be in the main right. So it was with Harold. He knew that he was ignorant of women, and of woman's nature, as distinguished from man's. The only woman he had ever known well was Stephen; and she in her youth and in her ignorance of the world and herself was hardly sufficient to supply to him data for his present needs. To a clean-minded man of his age a woman is something divine. It is only when in later life disappointment and experience have hammered bitter truth into his brain, that he begins to realise that woman is not angelic but human. When he knows more, and finds that she is like himself, human and limited but with qualities of purity and sincerity and endurance which put his own to shame, he realises how much better a helpmate she is for man than could be the vague, unreal creations of his dreams. And then he can thank God for His goodness that when He might have given us Angels He did give us women!

Of one thing, despite the seeming of facts, he was sure: Stephen did not love Leonard. Every fibre of his being revolted at the thought. She of so high a nature; he of so low. She so noble; he so mean. Bah! the belief was impossible.

Impossible! Herein was the manifestation of his ignorance; anything is possible where love is concerned! It was characteristic of the man that in his mind he had abandoned, for the present at all events, his own pain. He still loved Stephen with all the strength of his nature, but for him the selfish side ceased to exist. He was trying to serve Stephen; and every other thought had to give way. He had been satisfied that in a manner she loved him in some way and in some degree; and he had hoped that in the fulness of time the childish love would ripen, so that in the end would come a mutual affection which was of the very essence of Heaven. He believed still that she loved him in some way; but the future that was based on hope had now been wiped out with a sudden and unsparing hand. She had actually proposed marriage to another man. If the idea of a marriage with him had ever crossed her mind she could have had no doubt of her feeling toward another. . . . And yet? And yet he could not believe that she loved Leonard; not even if all trains of reasoning should end by leading to that point. One thing he had at present to accept, that whatever might be the measure of affection Stephen might have for him, it was not love as he understood it. He resolutely turned his back on the thought of his own side of the matter, and tried to find some justification of Stephen's act.

'Seek and ye shall find; knock and it shall be opened to ye' has perhaps a general as well as a special significance. It is by patient tireless seeking that many a precious thing has been found. It was after many a long cycle of thought that the seeking and the knocking had effectual result. Harold came to believe, vaguely at first but more definitely as the evidence nucleated, that Stephen's act was due to some mad girlish wish to test her own theory; to prove to herself the correctness of her own reasoning, the fixity of her own purpose. He did not go on analysing further; for as he walked the room with a portion of the weight taken from his heart he noticed that the sky was beginning to quicken. The day would soon be upon him, and there was work to be done. Instinctively he knew that there was trouble in store for Stephen, and he felt that in such an hour he should be near her. All her life she had been accustomed to him. In her sorrows to confide in him, to tell him her troubles so that they might dwindle and pass away; to enhance her pleasures by making him a sharer in them.

Harold was inspirited by the coming of the new day. There was work to be done, and the work must be based on thought. His thoughts must take a practical turn; what was he to do that would help Stephen? Here there dawned on him for the first time the understanding of a certain humiliation which she had suffered; she had been refused! She who had stepped so far out of the path of maidenly reserve in which she had always walked as to propose marriage to a man, had been refused! He did not, could not, know to the full the measure of such humiliation to a woman; but he could guess at any rate a part. And that guessing made him grind his teeth in impotent rage.

But out of that rage came an inspiration. If Stephen had been humiliated by the refusal of one man, might not this be minimised if she in turn might refuse another? Harold knew so well the sincerity of his own love and the depth of his own devotion that he was satisfied that he could not err in giving the girl the opportunity of refusing him. It would be some sort of balm to her wounded spirit to know that Leonard's views were not shared by all men. That there were others who would deem it a joy to serve as her slaves. When she had refused him she would perhaps feel easier in her mind. Of course if she did not refuse him . . . Ah! well, then would the gates of Heaven open . . . But that would never be. The past could not be blotted out! All he could do would be to serve her. He would go early. Such a man as Leonard Everard might make some new complication, and the present was quite bad enough.

It was a poor enough thing for him, he thought at length. She might trample on him; but it was for her sake. And to him what did it matter? The worst had come. All was over now!

CHAPTER-14

The Beech Grove

On the morning following the proposal Stephen strolled out into a beech grove, some little distance from the house, which from childhood had been a favourite haunt of hers. It was not in the immediate road to anywhere, and so there was no occasion for any of the household or the garden to go through it or near it. She did not put on a hat, but took only a sunshade, which she used in passing over the lawn. The grove was on the side of the house away from her own room and the breakfast-room. When she had reached its shade she felt that at last she was alone.

The grove was a privileged place. Long ago a great number of young beeches had been planted so thickly that as they grew they shot up straight and branchless in their struggle for the light. Not till they had reached a considerable altitude had they been thinned; and then the thinning had been so effected that, as the high branches began to shoot out in the freer space, they met in time and interlaced so closely that they made in many places a perfect screen of leafy shade. Here and there were rifts or openings through which the light passed; under such places the grass was fine and green, or the wild hyacinths in due season tinged the earth with blue. Through the grove some wide alleys had been left: great broad walks where the soft grass grew short and fine, and to whose edges came a drooping of branches and an upspringing of undergrowth of laurel and rhododendron. At the far ends of these walks were little pavilions of marble built in the classic style which ruled for garden use two hundred years ago. At the near ends some of them were close to the broad stretch of water from whose edges ran back the great sloping banks of emerald sward dotted here and there with great forest trees. The grove was protected by a ha-ha, so that it was never invaded from without, and the servants of the house, both the domestics and the gardeners and grooms, had been always forbidden to enter it. Thus by long usage it had become a place of quiet and solitude for the members of the family.

To this soothing spot had come Stephen in her pain. The long spell of self-restraint during that morning had almost driven her to frenzy, and she sought solitude as an anodyne to her tortured soul. The long anguish of a third sleepless night, following on a day of humiliation and terror, had destroyed for a time the natural resilience of a healthy nature. She had been for so long in the prison of her own purpose with Fear as warder; the fetters of conventional life had so galled her that here in the accustomed solitude of this place, in which from childhood she had been used to move and think freely, she felt as does a captive who has escaped from an irksome durance. As Stephen had all along been free of movement and speech, no such opportunities of freedom called to her. The pent-up passion in her, however, found its own relief. Her voice was silent, and she moved with slow steps, halting often between the green tree-trunks in the cool shade; but her thoughts ran free, and passion found a vent. No stranger seeing the tall, queenly girl moving slowly through the trees could have imagined the fierce passion which blazed within her, unless he had been close enough to see her eyes. The habit of physical restraint to which all her life she had been accustomed, and which was intensified by the experience of the past thirty-six hours, still ruled her, even here. Gradually the habit of security began to prevail, and the shackles to melt away. Here had she come in all her childish troubles. Here had she fought with herself, and conquered herself. Here the spirits of the place were with her and not against her. Here memory in its second degree, habit, gave her the full sense of spiritual freedom.

As she walked to and fro the raging of her spirit changed its objective: from restraint to its final causes; and chief amongst them the pride which had been so grievously hurt. How she loathed the day that had passed, and how more than all she hated herself for her part in it; her mad, foolish, idiotic, self-importance which gave her the idea of such an act and urged her to the bitter end of its carrying out; her mulish obstinacy in persisting when every fibre of her being had revolted at the doing, and when deep in her inmost soul was a deterring sense of its futility. How could she have stooped to have done such a thing: to ask a man . . . oh! the shame of it, the shame of it all! How could she have been so blind as to think that such a man was worthy! . . .

In the midst of her whirlwind of passion came a solitary gleam of relief: she knew with certainty that she did not love Leonard; that she had never loved him. The coldness of disdain to him, the fear of his future acts which was based on disbelief of the existence of that finer nature with which she had credited him, all proved to her convincingly that he could never really have been within the charmed circle of her inner life. Did she but know it, there was an even stronger evidence of her indifference to him in the ready manner in which her thoughts flew past him in their circling sweep. For a moment she saw him as the centre of a host of besetting fears; but her own sense of superior power nullified the force of the vision. She was able to cope with him and his doings, were there such need. And so her mind flew back to the personal side of her trouble: her blindness, her folly, her shame.

In truth she was doing good work for herself. Her mind was working truly and to a beneficent end. One by one she was overcoming the false issues of her passion and drifting to an end in which she would see herself face to face and would place so truly the blame for what had been as to make it a warning and ennobling lesson of her life. She moved more quickly, passing to and fro as does a panther in its cage when the desire of forest freedom is heavy upon it.

That which makes the irony of life will perhaps never be understood in its casual aspect by the finite mind of man. The 'why' and 'wherefore' and the 'how' of it is only to be understood by that All-wise intelligence which can scan the future as well as the present, and see the far far-reaching ramifications of those schemes of final development to which the manifestation of completed character tend.

To any mortal it would seem a pity that to Stephen in her solitude, when her passion was working itself out to an end which might be good, should come an interruption which would throw it back upon itself in such a way as to multiply its malignant force. But again it is a part of the Great Plan that instruments whose use man's finite mind could never predicate should be employed: the seeming good to evil, the seeming evil to good.

As she swept to and fro, her raging spirit compelling to violent movement, Stephen's eyes were arrested by the figure of a man coming through the aisles of the grove. At such a time any interruption of her passion was a cause for heightening anger; but the presence of a person was as a draught to a full-fed furnace. Most of all, in her present condition of mind, the presence of a man—for the thought of a man lay behind all her trouble, was as a tornado striking a burning forest. The blood of her tortured heart seemed to leap to her brain and to suffuse her eyes. She 'saw blood'!

It mattered not that the man whom she saw she knew and trusted. Indeed, this but added fuel to the flame. In the presence of a stranger some of her habitual self-restraint would doubtless have come back to her. But now the necessity for such was foregone; Harold was her alter ego, and in his presence was safety. He was, in this aspect, but a higher and more intelligent rendering of the trees around her. In another aspect he was an opportune victim, something to strike at. When the anger of a poison snake opens its gland, and the fang is charged with venom, it must strike at something. It does not pause or consider what it may be; it strikes, though it may be at stone or iron. So Stephen waited till her victim was within distance to strike. Her black eyes, fierce with passion and blood-rimmed as a cobra's, glittered as he passed among the tree-trunks towards her, eager with his errand of devotion.

Harold was a man of strong purpose. Had he not been, he would never have come on his present errand. Never, perhaps, had any suitor set forth on his quest with a heavier heart. All his life, since his very boyhood, had been centred round the girl whom to-day he had come to serve. All his thought had been for her: and to-day all he could expect was a gentle denial of all his hopes, so that his future life would be at best a blank.

But he would be serving Stephen! His pain might be to her good; ought to be, to a certain extent, to her mental ease. Her wounded pride would find some solace . . . As he came closer the feeling that he had to play a part, veritably to act one, came stronger and stronger upon him, and filled him with bitter doubt as to his power. Still he went on boldly. It had been a part of his plan to seem to come eagerly, as a lover should come; and so he came. When he got close to Stephen, all the witchery of her presence came upon him as of old. After all, he loved her with his whole soul; and the chance had come to tell her so. Even under the distressing conditions of his suit, the effort had its charm.

Stephen schooled herself to her usual attitude with him; and that, too, since the effort was based on truth came with a certain ease to her. At the present time, in her present frame of mind, nothing in the wide world could give her pleasure; the ease which came, if it did not change her purpose, increased her power. Their usual salutation, begun when she was a little baby, was 'Good morning, Stephen!' 'Good morning, Harold!' It had become so much a custom that now it came mechanically on her part. The tender reference to childhood's days, though it touched her companion to the quick, did not appeal to her since she had no special thought of it. Had such a thought come to her it might have softened her even to tears, for Harold had been always deep in her heart. As might have been expected from her character and condition of mind, she was the first to begin:

'I suppose you want to see me about something special, Harold, you have come so early.'

'Yes, Stephen. Very special!'

'Were you at the house?' she asked in a voice whose quietness might have conveyed a warning. She was so suspicious now that she suspected even Harold of—of what she did not know. He answered in all simplicity:

'No. I came straight here.'

'How did you know I should be here?' Her voice was now not only quiet but sweet. Without thinking, Harold blundered on. His intention was so single-minded, and his ignorance of woman so complete, that he did not recognise even elementary truths:

'I knew you always came here long ago when you were a child when you were in—' Here it suddenly flashed upon him that if he seemed to expect that she was in trouble as he had purposed saying, he would give away his knowledge of what had happened and so destroy the work to which he had set himself. So he finished the sentence in a lame and impotent manner, which, however, saved complete annihilation as it was verbally accurate: 'in short frocks.' Stephen needed to know little more. Her quick intelligence grasped the fact that there was some purpose afoot which she did not know or understand. She surmised, of course, that it was some way in connection with her mad act, and she grew cooler in her brain as well as colder in her heart as she prepared to learn more. Stephen had changed from girl to woman in the last twenty-four hours; and all the woman in her was now awake. After a moment's pause she said with a winning smile:

'Why, Harold, I've been in long frocks for years. Why should I come here on this special day on that account?' Even as she was speaking she felt that it would be well to abandon this ground of inquiry. It had clearly told her all it could. She would learn more by some other means. So she went on in a playful way, as a cat—not a kitten—does when it has got a mouse:

'That reason won't work, Harold. It's quite rusty in the joints. But never mind it! Tell me why you have come so early?' This seemed to Harold to be a heaven-sent opening; he rushed in at once:

'Because, Stephen, I wanted to ask you to be my wife! Oh! Stephen, don't you know that I love you? Ever since you were a little girl! When you were a little girl and I a big boy I loved you. I have loved you ever since with all my heart, and soul, and strength. Without you the world is a blank to me! For you and your happiness I would do anything—anything!'

This was no acting. When once the barrier of beginning had been broken, his soul seemed to pour itself out. The man was vibrant through all his nature; and the woman's very soul realised its truth. For an instant a flame of gladness swept through her; and for the time it lasted put all other thought aside.

But suspicion is a hard metal which does not easily yield to fire. It can come to white heat easily enough, but its melting-point is high indeed. When the flame had leaped it had spent its force; the reaction came quick. Stephen's heart seemed to turn to ice, all the heat and life rushing to her brain. Her thoughts flashed with convincing quickness; there was no time for doubting amid their rush. Her life was for good or ill at the crossing of the ways. She had trusted Harold thoroughly. The habit of her whole life from her babyhood up had been to so look to him as comrade and protector and sympathetic friend. She was so absolutely sure of his earnest devotion that this new experience of a riper feeling would have been a joy to her, if it should be that his act was all spontaneous and done in ignorance of her shame. 'Shame' was the generic word which now summarised to herself her thought of her conduct in proposing to Leonard. But of this she must be certain. She could not, dare not, go farther till this was settled. With the same craving for certainty with which she convinced herself that Leonard understood her overtures, and with the same dogged courage with which she pressed the matter on him, she now went on to satisfy her mind.

'What did you do yesterday?'

'I was at Norcester all day. I went early. By the way, here is the ribbon you wanted; I think it's exactly the same as the pattern.' As he spoke he took a tissue-piper parcel from his pocket and handed it to her.

'Thanks!' she said. 'Did you meet any friends there?'

'Not many.' He answered guardedly; he had a secret to keep.

'Where did you dine?'

'At the club!' He began to be uneasy at this questioning; but he did not see any way to avoid answering without creating some suspicion.

'Did you see any one you knew at the club?' Her voice as she spoke was a little harder, a little more strained. Harold noticed the change, rather by instinct than reason. He felt that there was danger in it, and paused. The pause seemed to suddenly create a new fury in the breast of Stephen. She felt that Harold was playing with her. Harold! If she could not trust him, where then was she to look for trust in the world? If he was not frank with her, what then meant his early coming; his seeking her in the grove; his proposal of marriage, which seemed so sudden and so inopportune? He must have seen Leonard, and by some means have become acquainted with her secret of shame . . . His motive?

Here her mind halted. She knew as well as if it had been trumpeted from the skies that Harold knew all. But she must be certain . . . Certain!

She was standing erect, her hands held down by her sides and clenched together till the knuckles were white; all her body strung high—like an over-pitched violin. Now she raised her right hand and flung it downward with a passionate jerk.

'Answer me!' she cried imperiously. 'Answer me! Why are you playing with me? Did you see Leonard Everard last night? Answer me, I say. Harold An Wolf, you do not lie! Answer me!'

As she spoke Harold grew cold. From the question he now knew that Stephen had guessed his secret. The fat was in the fire with a vengeance. He did not know what to do, and still remained silent. She did not give him time to think, but spoke again, this time more coldly. The white terror had replaced the red:

'Are you not going to answer me a simple question, Harold? To be silent now is to wrong me! I have a right to know!'

In his trouble, for he felt that say what he would he could only give her new pain, he said humbly:

'Don't ask me, Stephen! Won't you understand that I want to do what is best for you? Won't you trust me?' Her answer came harshly. A more experienced man than Harold, one who knew women better, would have seen how overwrought she was, and would have made pity the pivot of his future bearing and acts and words while the interview lasted; pity, and pity only. But to Harold the high ideal was ever the same. The Stephen whom he loved was no subject for pity, but for devotion only. He knew the nobility of her nature and must trust it to the end. When her silence and her blazing eyes denied his request, he answered her query in a low voice:

'I did!' Even whilst he spoke he was thankful for one thing, he had not been pledged in any way to confidence. Leonard had forced the knowledge on him; and though he would have preferred a million times over to be silent, he was still free to speak. Stephen's next question came more coldly still:

'Did he tell you of his meeting with me?'

'He did.'

'Did he tell you all?' It was torture to him to answer; but he was at the stake and must bear it.

'I think so! If it was true.'

'What did he tell you? Stay! I shall ask you the facts myself; the broad facts. We need not go into details . . . '

'Oh, Stephen!' She silenced his pleading with an imperious hand.

'If I can go into this matter, surely you can. If I can bear the shame of telling, you can at least bear that of listening. Remember that knowing—knowing what you know, or at least what you have heard—you could come here and propose marriage to me!' This she said with a cold, cutting sarcasm which sounded like the rasping of a roughly-sharpened knife through raw flesh. Harold groaned in spirit; he felt a weakness which began at his heart to steal through him. It took all his manhood to bear himself erect. He dreaded what was coming, as of old the once-tortured victim dreaded the coming torment of the rack.

CHAPTER-15

The End of The Meeting

Stephen went on in her calm, cold voice:

'Did he tell you that I had asked him to marry me?' Despite herself, as she spoke the words a red tide dyed her face. It was not a flush; it was not a blush; it was a sort of flood which swept through her, leaving her in a few seconds whiter than before. Harold saw and understood. He could not speak; he lowered his head silently. Her eyes glittered more coldly. The madness that every human being may have once was upon her. Such a madness is destructive, and here was something more vulnerable than herself.

'Did he tell you how I pressed him?' There was no red tide this time, nor ever again whilst the interview lasted. To bow in affirmation was insufficient; with an effort he answered:

'I understood so.' She answered with an icy sarcasm:

'You understood so! Oh, I don't doubt he embellished the record with some of his own pleasantries. But you understood it; and that is sufficient.' After a pause she went on:

'Did he tell you that he had refused me?'

'Yes!' Harold knew now that he was under the torture, and that there was no refusing. She went on, with a light laugh, which wrung his heart even more than her pain had done . . . Stephen to laugh like that!

'And I have no doubt that he embellished that too, with some of his fine masculine witticisms. I understood myself that he was offended at my asking him. I understood it quite well; he told me so!' Then with feminine intuition she went on:

'I dare say that before he was done he said something kindly of the poor little thing that loved him; that loved him so much, and that she had to break down all the bounds of modesty and decorum that had made the women of her house honoured for a thousand years! And you listened to him whilst he spoke! Oh-h-h!' she quivered with her white-hot anger, as the fierce heat in the heart of a furnace quivers. But her voice was cold again as she went on:

'But who could help loving him? Girls always did. It was such a beastly nuisance! You "understood" all that, I dare say; though perhaps he did not put it in such plain words!' Then the scorn, which up to now had been imprisoned, turned on him; and he felt as though some hose of deathly chill was being played upon him.

'And yet you, knowing that only yesterday, he had refused me—refused my pressing request that he should marry me, come to me hot-foot in the early morning and ask me to be your wife. I thought such things did not take place; that men were more honourable, or more considerate, or more merciful! Or at least I used to think so; till yesterday. No! till to-day. Yesterday's doings were my own doings, and I had to bear the penalty of them myself. I had come here to fight out by myself the battle of my shame . . .'

Here Harold interrupted her. He could not bear to hear Stephen use such a word in connection with herself.

'No! You must not say "shame." There is no shame to you, Stephen. There can be none, and no one must say it in my presence!' In her secret heart of hearts she admired him for his words; she felt them at the moment sink into her memory, and knew that she would never forget the mastery of his face and bearing. But the blindness of rage was upon her, and it is of the essence of this white-hot anger that it preys not on what is basest in us, but on what is best. That Harold felt deeply was her opportunity to wound him more deeply than before.

'Even here in the solitude which I had chosen as the battleground of my shame you had need to come unasked, unthought of, when even a lesser mind than yours, for you are no fool, would have thought to leave me alone. My shame was my own, I tell you; and I was learning to take my punishment. My punishment! Poor creatures that we are, we think our punishment will be what we would like best: to suffer in silence, and not to have spread abroad our shame!' How she harped on that word, though she knew that every time she uttered it, it cut to the heart of the man who loved her. 'And yet you come right on top of my torture to torture me still more and illimitably. You come, you who alone had the power to intrude yourself on my grief and sorrow; power given you by my father's kindness. You come to me without warning, considerately telling me that you knew I would be here because I had always come here when I had been in trouble.

No—I do you an injustice. “In trouble” was not what you said, but that I had come when I had been in short frocks. Short frocks! And you came to tell me that you loved me. You thought, I suppose, that as I had refused one man, I would jump at the next that came along. I wanted a man. God! God! what have I done that such an affront should come upon me? And come, too, from a hand that should have protected me if only in gratitude for my father’s kindness!’ She was eyeing him keenly, with eyes that in her unflinching anger took in everything with the accuracy of sun-painting. She wanted to wound; and she succeeded.

But Harold had nerves and muscles of steel; and when the call came to them they answered. Though the pain of death was upon him he did not flinch. He stood before her like a rock, in all his great manhood; but a rock on whose summit the waves had cast the wealth of their foam, for his face was as white as snow. She saw and understood; but in the madness upon her she went on trying new places and new ways to wound:

‘You thought, I suppose, that this poor, neglected, despised, rejected woman, who wanted so much to marry that she couldn’t wait for a man to ask her, would hand herself over to the first chance comer who threw his handkerchief to her; would hand over herself—and her fortune!’

‘Oh, Stephen! How can you say such things, think such things?’ The protest broke from him with a groan. His pain seemed to inflame her still further; to gratify her hate, and to stimulate her mad passion:

‘Why did I ever see you at all? Why did my father treat you as a son; that when you had grown and got strong on his kindness you could thus insult his daughter in the darkest hour of her pain and her shame!’ She almost choked with passion. There was now nothing in the whole world that she could trust. In the pause he spoke:

‘Stephen, I never meant you harm. Oh, don’t speak such wild words. They will come back to you with sorrow afterwards! I only meant to do you good. I wanted . . . ’ Her anger broke out afresh:

‘There; you speak it yourself! You only wanted to do me good. I was so bad that any kind of a husband . . . Oh, get out of my sight! I wish to God I had never seen you! I hope to God I may never see you again! Go! Go! Go!’

This was the end! To Harold’s honest mind such words would have been impossible had not thoughts of truth lain behind them. That Stephen—his Stephen, whose image in his mind shut out every other woman in the world, past, present, and future—should say such things to any one, that she should think such things, was to him a deadly blow. But that she should say them to him! . . . Utterance, even the utterance which speaks in the inmost soul, failed him. He had in some way that he knew not hurt—wounded—killed Stephen; for the finer part was gone from the Stephen that he had known and worshipped so long. She wished him gone; she wished she had never seen him; she hoped to God never to see him again. Life for him was over and done! There could be no more happiness in the world; no more wish to work, to live! . . .

He bowed gravely; and without a word turned and walked away.

Stephen saw him go, his tall form moving amongst the tree trunks till finally it was lost in their massing. She was so filled with the tumult of her passion that she looked, unmoved. Even the sense of his going did not change her mood. She raged to and fro amongst the trees, her movements getting quicker and quicker as her excitement began to change from mental to physical; till the fury began to exhaust itself. All at once she stopped, as though arrested by a physical barrier; and with a moan sank down in a helpless heap on the cool moss.

* * * * *

Harold went from the grove as one seems to move in a dream. Little things and big were mixed up in his mind. He took note, as he went towards the town by the byroads, of everything around him in his usual way, for he had always been one of those who notice unconsciously, or rather unintentionally. Long afterwards he could shut his eyes and recall every step of the way from the spot where he had turned from Stephen to the railway station outside Norcester. And on many and many such a time when he opened them again the eyelids were wet. He wanted to get away quickly, silently, unobserved. With the instinct of habitual thought his mind turned London-ward. He met but few persons, and those only cottiers. He saluted them in his usual cheery way, but did not stop to speak with any. He was about to take a single ticket to London when it struck him that this might look odd, so he asked for a return. Then, his mind being once more directed towards concealment of purpose, he sent a telegram to his housekeeper telling her that he was called away to London on business. It was only when he was far on his journey that he gave thought to ways and means, and took stock of his possessions. Before he took out his purse and pocket-book he made up his mind that he would be content with what it was, no matter how little. He had left Normanstand and all belonging to it for ever, and was off to hide himself in whatever part of the world would afford him the best opportunity. Life was over! There was nothing to look forward to; nothing to look back at! The present was a living pain whose lightest element was despair. As, however, he got further and further away, his practical mind began to work; he thought over matters so as to arrange in his mind how best he could dispose of his affairs, so to cause as little comment as might be, and to save the possibility of worry or distress of any kind to Stephen.

Even then, in his agony of mind, his heart was with her; it was not the least among his troubles that he would have to be away from her when perhaps she would need him most. And yet whenever he would come to this point in his endless chain of thought, he would have to stop for a while, overcome with such pain that his power of thinking was paralysed. He would never, could never, be of service to her again. He had gone out of her life, as she had gone out of his life; though she never had, nor never could out of his thoughts. It was all over! All the years of sweetness, of hope, and trust, and satisfied and justified faith in each other, had been wiped out by that last terrible, cruel meeting. Oh! how could she have said such things to him! How could she have thought them! And there she was now in all the agony of her unrestrained passion. Well he knew, from his long experience of her nature, how she must have suffered to be in such a state of mind, to have so forgotten all the restraint of her teaching and her life! Poor, poor Stephen! Fatherless now as well as motherless; and friendless as well as fatherless! No one to calm her in the height of her wild abnormal passion! No one to comfort her when the fit had passed! No one to sympathise with her for all that she had suffered! No one to help her to build new and better hopes out of the wreck of her mad ideas! He would cheerfully have given his life for her. Only last night he was prepared to kill, which was worse than to die, for her sake. And now to be far away, unable to help, unable even to know how she fared. And behind her eternally the shadow of that worthless man who had spurned her love and flouted her to a chance comer in his drunken delirium. It was too bitter to bear. How could God lightly lay such a burden on his shoulders who had all his life tried to walk in sobriety and chastity and in all worthy and manly ways! It was unfair! It was unfair! If he could do anything for her? Anything! Anything! . . . And so the unending whirl of thoughts went on!

The smoke of London was dim on the horizon when he began to get back to practical matters. When the train drew up at Euston he stepped from it as one to whom death would be a joyous relief!

He went to a quiet hotel, and from there transacted by letter such business matters as were necessary to save pain and trouble to others. As for himself, he made up his mind that he would go to Alaska, which he took to be one of the best places in the as yet uncivilised world for a man to lose his identity. As a security at the start he changed his name; and as John Robinson, which was not a name to attract public attention, he shipped as a passenger on the *Scoriac* from London to New York.

The *Scoriac* was one of the great cargo boats which take a certain number of passengers. The few necessaries which he took with him were chosen with an eye to utility in that frozen land which he sought. For the rest, he knew nothing, nor did he care how or whither he went. His vague purpose was to cross the American Continent to San Francisco, and there to take passage for the high latitudes north of the Yukon River.

*****

When Stephen began to regain consciousness her first sensation was one of numbness. She was cold in the back, and her feet did not seem to exist; but her head was hot and pulsating as though her brain were a living thing. Then her half-open eyes began to take in her surroundings. For another long spell she began to wonder why all around her was green. Then came the inevitable process of reason. Trees! It is a wood! How did I come here? why am I lying on the ground?

All at once wakened memory opened on her its flood-gates, and overwhelmed her with pain. With her hands pressed to her throbbing temples and her burning face close to the ground, she began to recall what she could of the immediate past. It all seemed like a terrible dream. By degrees her intelligence came back to its normal strength, and all at once, as does one suddenly wakened from sleep to the knowledge of danger, she sat up.

Somehow the sense of time elapsed made Stephen look at her watch. It was half-past twelve. As she had come into the grove immediately after breakfast, and as Harold had almost immediately joined her, and as the interview between them had been but short, she must have lain on the ground for more than three hours. She rose at once, trembling in every limb. A new fear began to assail her; that she had been missed at home, and that some one might have come to look for her. Up to now she had not been able to feel the full measure of pain regarding what had passed, but which would, she knew, come to her in the end. It was too vague as yet; she could not realise that it had really been. But the fear of discovery was immediate, and must be guarded against without delay. As well as she could, she tidied herself and began to walk slowly back to the house, hoping to gain her own room unnoticed. That her general intelligence was awake was shown by the fact that before she left the grove she remembered that she had forgotten her sunshade. She went back and searched till she had found it.

Gaining her room without meeting any one, she at once change her dress, fearing that some soil or wrinkle might betray her. Resolutely she put back from her mind all consideration of the past; there would be time for that later on. Her nerves were already much quieter than they had been. That long faint, or lapse into insensibility, had for the time taken the place of sleep. There would be a price to be paid for it later; but for the present it had served its purpose. Now and again she was disturbed by one thought; she could not quite remember what had occurred after Harold had left, and just before she became unconscious. She dared not dwell upon it, however. It would doubtless all come back to her when she had leisure to think the whole matter over as a connected narrative.

When the gong sounded for lunch she went down, with a calm exterior, to face the dreaded ordeal of another meal.

Luncheon passed off without a hitch. She and her aunt talked as usual over all the small affairs of the house and the neighbourhood, and the calm restraint was in itself soothing. Even then she could not help feeling how much convention is to a woman's life. Had it not been for these recurring trials of set hours and duties she could never have passed the last day and night without discovery of her condition of mind. That one terrible, hysterical outburst was perhaps the safety valve. Had it been spread over the time occupied in conventional duties its force even then might have betrayed her; but without the necessity of nerving herself to conventional needs, she would have infallibly betrayed herself by her negative condition.

After lunch she went to her own boudoir where, when she had shut the inner door, no one was allowed to disturb her without some special need in the house or on the arrival of visitors. This 'sporting oak' was the sign of 'not at home' which she had learned in her glimpse of college life. Here in the solitude of safety, she began to go over the past, resolutely and systematically.

She had already been so often over the memory of the previous humiliating and unhappy day that she need not revert to it at present. Since then had she not quarrelled with Harold, whom she had all her life so trusted that her quarrel with him seemed to shake the very foundations of her existence? As yet she had not remembered perfectly all that had gone on under the shadow of the beech grove. She dared not face it all at once, even as yet. Time must elapse before she should dare to cry; to think of her loss of Harold was to risk breaking down altogether. Already she felt weak. The strain of the last forty-eight hours was too much for her physical strength. She began to feel, as she lay back in her cushioned chair, that a swoon is no worthy substitute for sleep. Indeed it had seemed to make the need for sleep even more imperative.

It was all too humiliating! She wanted to think over what had been; to recall it as far as possible so as to fix it in her mind, whilst it was still fresh. Later on, some action might have to be based on her recollection. And yet . . . How could she think when she was so tired . . . tired . . .

Nature came to the poor girl's relief at last, and she fell into a heavy sleep . . .

It was like coming out of the grave to be dragged back to waking life out of such a sleep, and so soon after it had begun. But the voice seemed to reach to her inner consciousness in some compelling way. For a second she could not understand; but as she rose from the cushions the maid's message repeated, brought her wide awake and alert in an instant:

'Mr. Everard, young Mr. Everard, to see you, miss!'

CHAPTER-16

A Private Conversation

The name braced Stephen at once. Here was danger, an enemy to be encountered; all the fighting blood of generations leaped to the occasion. The short spell of sleep had helped to restore her. There remained still quite enough of mental and nervous excitement to make her think quickly; the words were hardly out of the maid's mouth before her resolution was taken. It would never do to let Leonard Everard see she was diffident about meeting him; she would go down at once. But she would take the precaution of having her aunt present; at any rate, till she should have seen how the land lay. Her being just waked from sleep would be an excuse for asking her aunt to see the visitor till she came down. So she said to the maid:

'I have been asleep. I must have got tired walking in the wood in the heat. Ask Auntie to kindly see Mr. Everard in the blue drawing-room till I come down. I must tidy my hair; but I will be down in a few minutes.'

'Shall I send Marjorie to you, miss?'

'No! Don't mind; I can do what I want myself. Hurry down to Miss Rowly!'

How she regarded Leonard Everard now was shown in her instinctive classing him amongst her enemies.

When she entered the room she seemed all aglow. She wanted not only to overcome but to punish; and all the woman in her had risen to the effort. Never in her life had Stephen Norman looked more radiantly beautiful, more adorable, more desirable. Even Leonard Everard felt his pulses quicken as he saw that glowing mass of beauty standing out against the cold background of old French tapestry. All the physical side of him leaped in answer to the call of her beauty; and even his cold heart and his self-engrossed brain followed with slower gait. He had been sitting opposite Miss Rowly in one of the windows, twirling his hat in nervous suspense.

He jumped up, and, as she came towards him, went forward rapidly to greet her. No one could mistake the admiration in his eyes. Ever since he had made up his mind to marry her she had assumed a new aspect in his thoughts. But now her presence swept away all false imaginings; from the moment that her loveliness dawned upon him something like love began to grow within his breast. Stephen saw the look and it strengthened her. He had so grievously wounded her pride the previous day that her victory on this was a compensation which set her more at her old poise.

Her greeting was all sweetness: she was charmed to see him. How was his father, and what was the news? Miss Rowly looked on with smiling visage. She too had seen the look of admiration in his eyes, and it pleased her. Old ladies, especially when they are maiden ladies, always like to see admiration in the eyes of young men when they are turned in the direction of any girl dear to them.

They talked for some time, keeping all the while, by Stephen's clever generalship, to the small-talk of the neighbourhood and the minor events of social importance. As the time wore on she could see that Leonard was growing impatient, and evidently wanted to see her alone. She ignored, however, all his little private signalling, and presently ordered tea to be brought. This took some little time; when it had been brought and served and drunk, Leonard was in a smothered fume of impatience. She was glad to see that as yet her aunt had noticed nothing, and she still hoped that she would be able to so prolong matters, that she would escape without a private interview. She did not know the cause of Leonard's impatience: that he must see her before the day passed. She too was an egoist, in her own way; in the flush of belief of his subjugation she did not think of attributing to him any other motive than his desire for herself. As she had made up her mind on the final issue she did not want to be troubled by a new 'scene.'

But, after all, Leonard was a man; and man's ways are more direct than woman's. Seeing that he could not achieve his object in any other way, he said out suddenly, thinking, and rightly, that she would not wish to force an issue in the presence of her aunt:

'By the way, Miss Norman,' he had always called her 'Miss Norman' in her aunt's presence: 'I want to have two minutes with you before I go. On a matter of business,' he added, noticing Miss Rowly's surprised look. The old lady was old-fashioned even for her age; in her time no young man would have asked to see a young lady alone on business. Except on one kind of business; and with regard to that kind of business gentlemen had to obtain first the confidence and permission of guardians. Leonard saw the difficulty and said quickly:

'It is on the matter you wrote to me about!'

Stephen was prepared for a nasty shock, but hardly for so nasty a one as this. There was an indelicacy about it which went far beyond the bounds of thoughtless conventionality. That such an appeal should be made to her, and in such a way, savoured of danger. Her woman's intuition gave her the guard, and at once she spoke, smilingly and gently as one recalling a matter in which the concern is not her own:

'Of course! It was selfish of me not to have thought of it, and to have kept you so long waiting. The fact is, Auntie, that Leonard—I like to call him Leonard, since we were children together, and he is so young; though perhaps it would be more decorous nowadays to say "Mr. Everard"—has consulted me about his debts. You know, Auntie dear, that young men will be young men in such matters; or perhaps you do not, since the only person who ever worried you has been myself. But I stayed at Oxford and I know something of young men's ways; and as I am necessarily more or less of a man of business, he values my help. Don't you, Leonard?' The challenge was so direct, and the position he was in so daringly put, that he had to acquiesce. Miss Rowly, who had looked on with a frown of displeasure, said coldly:

'I know you are your own mistress, my dear. But surely it would be better if Mr. Everard would consult with his solicitor or his father's agent, or some of his gentlemen friends, rather than with a young lady whose relations with him, after all, are only those of a neighbour on visiting terms. For my own part, I should have thought that Mr. Everard's best course would have been to consult his own father! But the things that gentlemen, as well as ladies do, have been sadly changed since my time!' Then, rising in formal dignity, she bowed gravely to the visitor before leaving the room.

But the position of being left alone in the room with Leonard did not at all suit Stephen's plans. Rising quickly she said to her aunt:

'Don't stir, Auntie. I dare say you are right in what you say; but I promised Mr. Everard to go into the matter. And as I have brought the awkwardness on myself, I suppose I must bear it. If Mr. Everard wants to see me alone, and I suppose he is diffident in speaking on such a matter before you—he didn't play with you, you know!—we can go out on the lawn. We shan't be long!' Before Leonard could recover his wits she had headed him out on the lawn.

Her strategy was again thoroughly good. The spot she chose, though beyond earshot, was quite in the open and commanded by all the windows in that side of the house. A person speaking there might say what he liked, but his actions must be discreet.

On the lawn Stephen tripped ahead; Leonard followed inwardly raging. By her clever use of the opening she had put him in a difficulty from which there was no immediate means of extrication. He could not quarrel overtly with Stephen; if he did so, how could he enter on the pressing matter of his debts? He dared not openly proclaim his object in wishing to marry her, for had he done so her aunt might have interfered, with what success he could not be sure. In any case it would cause delay, and delay was what he could not afford. He felt that in mentioning his debts at just such a movement he had given Stephen the chance she had so aptly taken. He had to be on his good behaviour, however; and with an apprehension that was new to him he followed her.

An old Roman marble seat was placed at an angle from the house so that the one of the two occupants within its curve must almost face the house, whilst the other gave to it at least a quarter-face. Stephen seated herself on the near side, leaving to Leonard the exposed position. As soon as he was seated, she began:

'Now, Leonard, tell me all about the debts?' She spoke in tones of gay friendliness, but behind the mask of her cheerfulness was the real face of fear. Down deep in her mind was a conviction that her letter was a pivotal point of future sorrow. It was in the meantime quite apparent to her that Leonard kept it as his last resource; so her instinct was to keep it to the front and thus minimise its power.

Leonard, though inwardly weakened by qualms of growing doubt, had the animal instinct that, as he was in opposition, his safety was in attacking where his opponent most feared. He felt that there was some subtle change in his companion; this was never the same Stephen Norman whom only yesterday he had met upon the hill! He plunged at once into his purpose.

'But it wasn't about my debts you asked me to meet you, Stephen.'

'You surprise me, Leonard! I thought I simply asked you to come to meet me. I know the first subject I mentioned when we began to talk, after your grumbling about coming in the heat, was your money matters.' Leonard winced, but went on:

'It was very good of you, Stephen; but really that is not what I came to speak of to-day. At first, at all events!' he added with a sublime naïvetté, as the subject of his debts and his imperative want of money rose before him. Stephen's eyes flashed; she saw more clearly than ever through his purpose. Such as admission at the very outset of the proffer of marriage, which she felt was coming, was little short of monstrous. Her companion did not see the look of mastery on her face; he was looking down at the moment. A true lover would have been looking up.

'I wanted to tell you, Stephen, that I have been thinking over what you said to me in your letter, and what you said in words; and I want to accept!' As he was speaking he was looking her straight in the face.

Stephen answered slowly with a puzzled smile which wrinkled up her forehead:

'Accept what I said in my letter! why, Leonard, what do you mean? That letter must have had a lot more in it than I thought. I seem to remember that it was simply a line asking you to meet me. Just let me look at it; I should like to be sure of what actually is!' As she spoke she held out her hand. Leonard was nonplussed; he did not know what to say. Stephen made up her mind to have the letter back. Leonard was chafing under the position forced upon him, and tried to divert his companion from her purpose. He knew well why she had chosen that exposed position for their interview. Now, as her outstretched hand embarrassed him, he made reprisal; he tried to take it in his in a tender manner.

She instantly drew back her hand and put it behind her in a decided manner. She was determined that whatever might happen she would not let any watcher at the windows, by chance or otherwise, see any sign of tenderness on her part. Leonard, thinking that his purpose had been effected, went on, breathing more freely:

'Your letter wasn't much. Except of course that it gave me the opportunity of listening to what you said; to all your sweet words. To your more than sweet proposal!'

'Yes! It must have been sweet to have any one, who was in a position to do so, offer to help you when you knew that you were overwhelmed with debts!' The words were brutal. Stephen felt so; but she had no alternative. Leonard had some of the hard side of human nature; but he had also some of the weak side. He went on blindly:

'I have been thinking ever since of what you said, and I want to tell you that I would like to do as you wish!' As he spoke, his words seemed even to him to be out of place. He felt it would be necessary to throw more fervour into the proceedings. The sudden outburst which followed actually amused Stephen, even in her state of fear:

'Oh, Stephen, don't you know that I love you! You are so beautiful! I love you! I love you! Won't you be my wife?'

This was getting too much to close quarters. Stephen said in a calm, business-like way:

'My dear Leonard, one thing at a time! I came out here, you know, to speak of your debts; and until that is done, I really won't go into any other matter. Of course if you'd rather not . . . ' Leonard really could not afford this; matters were too pressing with him. So he tried to affect a cheery manner; but in his heart was a black resolve that she should yet pay for this.

'All right! Stephen. Whatever you wish I will do; you are the queen of my heart, you know!'

'How much is the total amount?' said Stephen.

This was a change to the prosaic which made sentiment impossible. He gave over, for the time.

'Go on!' said Stephen, following up her advantage. 'Don't you even know how much you owe?'

'The fact is, I don't. Not exactly. I shall make up the amount as well as I can and let you know. But that's not what I came about to-day.' Stephen was going to make an angry gesture of dissent. She was not going to have that matter opened up. She waited, however, for Leonard was going on after his momentary pause. She breathed more freely after his first sentence. He was unable evidently to carry on a double train of thought.

'It was about that infernal money-lenders' letter that the Governor got!' Stephen got still less anxious. This open acknowledgment of his true purpose seemed to clear the air.

'What is the amount?' Leonard looked quickly at her; the relief of her mind made her tone seem joyful.

'A monkey! Five hundred pounds, you know. But then there's three hundred for interest that has to be paid also. It's an awful lot of money, isn't it?' The last phrase was added on seeing Stephen's surprised look.

'Yes!' she answered quietly. 'A great deal of money—to waste!' They were both silent for a while. Then she said:

'What does your father say to it?'

'He was in an awful wax. One of these beastly duns had written to him about another account and he was in a regular fury. When I told him I would pay it within a week, he said very little, which was suspicious; and then, just when I was going out, he sprung this on me. Mean of him! wasn't it? I need expect no help from him.' As he was speaking he took a mass of letters from his pocket and began to look among them for the money-lenders' letter.

'Why, what a correspondence you have there. Do you keep all your letters in your pockets?' said Stephen quietly.

'All I don't tear up or burn. It wouldn't do to let the Governor into my secrets. He might know too much!'

'And are all those letters from duns?'

'Mostly, but I only keep those letters I have to attend to and those I care for.'

'Show me the bundle!' she said. Then seeing him hesitate, added:

'You know if I am to help you to get clear you must take me into your confidence. I dare say I shall have to see a lot more letters than these before you are quite clear!' Her tone was too quiet. Knowing already the silent antagonism between them he began to suspect her; knowing also that her own letter was not amongst them, he used his wits and handed them over without a word. She, too, suspected him. After his tacit refusal to give her the letter, she almost took it for granted that it was not amongst them. She gave no evidence of her feeling, however, but opened and read the letters in due sequence; all save two, which, being in a female hand, she gave back without a word. There was a calmness and an utter absence of concern, much less of jealousy, about this which disconcerted him. Throughout her reading Stephen's face showed surprise now and again; but when she came to the last, which was that of the usurers, it showed alarm. Being a woman, a legal threat had certain fears of its own.

'There must be no delay about this!' she said.

'What am I to do?' he answered, a weight off his mind that the fiscal matter had been practically entered on.

'I shall see that you get the money!' she said quietly. 'It will be really a gift, but I prefer it to be as a loan for many reasons.' Leonard made no comment. He found so many reasons in his own mind that he thought it wise to forbear from asking any of hers. Then she took the practical matter in hand:

'You must wire to these people at once to say that you will pay the amount on the day after to-morrow. If you will come here to-morrow at four o'clock the money will be ready for you. You can go up to town by the evening train and pay off the debt first thing in the morning. When you bring the receipt

I shall speak to you about the other debts; but you must make out a full list of them. We can't have any half-measure. I will not go into the matter till I have all the details before me!' Then she stood up to go.

As they walked across the lawn, she said:

'By the way, don't forget to bring that letter with you. I want to see what I really did say in it!' Her tone was quiet enough, and the wording was a request; but Leonard knew as well as if it had been spoken outright as a threat that if he did not have the letter with him when he came things were likely to be unpleasant.

The farther he got from Normanstand on his way home the more discontented Leonard grew. Whilst he had been in Stephen's presence she had so dominated him, not only by her personality but by her use of her knowledge of his own circumstances, that he had not dared to make protest or opposition; but now he began to feel how much less he was to receive than he had expected. He had come prepared to allow Stephen to fall into his arms, fortune and all. But now, although he had practical assurance that the weight of his debts would be taken from him, he was going away with his tail between his legs. He had not even been accepted as a suitor, he who had himself been wooed only a day before. His proposal of marriage had not been accepted, had not even been considered by the woman who had so lately broken ironclad convention to propose marriage to him. He had been treated merely as a scapegrace debtor who had come to ask favours from an old friend. He had even been treated like a bad boy; had been told that he had wasted money; had been ordered, in no doubtful way, to bring the full schedule of his debts. And all the time he dared not say anything lest the thing shouldn't come off at all. Stephen had such an infernally masterly way with her! It didn't matter whether she was proposing to him, or he was proposing to her, he was made to feel small all the same. He would have to put up with it till he had got rid of the debts!

And then as to the letter. Why was she so persistent about seeing it? Did she want to get it into her hands and then keep it, as Harold An Wolf had done? Was it possible that she suspected he would use it to coerce her; she would call it 'blackmail,' he supposed. This being the very thing he had intended to do, and had done, he grew very indignant at the very thought of being accused of it. It was, he felt, a very awkward thing that he had lost possession of the letter. He might need it if Stephen got nasty. Then Harold might give it to her, as he had threatened to do. He thought he would call round that evening by Harold's house, and see if he couldn't get back the letter. It belonged to him; Harold had no right to keep it. He would see him before he and Stephen got putting their heads together. So, on his way home, he turned his steps at once to Harold's house.

He did not find him in. The maid who opened the door could give him no information; all she could say was that Mrs. Dingle the housekeeper had got a telegram from Master saying that he had been called suddenly away on business.

This was a new source of concern to Leonard. He suspected a motive of some sort; though what that motive could be he could not hazard the wildest guess. On his way home he called at the post-office and sent a telegram to Cavendish and Cecil, the name of the usurers' firm, in accordance with Stephen's direction. He signed it: 'Jasper Everard.'

CHAPTER-17
A Business Transaction

When Stephen had sent off her letter to the bank she went out for a stroll; she knew it would be no use trying to get rest before dinner. That ordeal, too, had to be gone through. She found herself unconsciously going in the direction of the grove; but when she became aware of it a great revulsion overcame her, and she shuddered.

Slowly she took her way across the hard stretch of finely-kept grass which lay on the side of the house away from the wood. The green sward lay like a sea, dotted with huge trees, singly, or in clumps as islands. In its far-stretching stateliness there was something soothing. She came back to the sound of the dressing-gong with a better strength to resist the trial before her. Well she knew her aunt would have something to say on the subject of her interference in Leonard Everard's affairs.

Her fears were justified, for when they had come into the drawing-room after dinner Miss Rowly began:

'Stephen dear, is it not unwise of you to interfere in Mr. Everard's affairs?'

'Why unwise, Auntie?'

'Well, my dear, the world is censorious. And when a young lady, of your position and your wealth, takes a part in a young man's affairs tongues are apt to wag. And also, dear, debts, young men's debts, are hardly the subjects for a girl's investigation. Remember, that we ladies live very different lives from men; from some men, I should say, for your dear father was the best of men, and I should think that in all his life there was nothing which he would have wished concealed. But, my dear, young men are less restrained in their ways than we are, than we have to be for our own safety and protection.' The poor lady was greatly perturbed at having to speak in such a way. Stephen saw her distress; coming over to her, she sat down and took her hand. Stephen had a very tender side to her nature, and she loved very truly the dear old lady who had taken her mother's place and had shown her all a mother's love. Now, in her loneliness and woe and fear, she clung to her in spirit. She would have liked to have clung to her physically; to have laid her head on her bosom, and have cried her heart out. The time for tears had not come. Hourly she felt more and more the weight that a shameful secret is to carry. She knew, however, that she could set her aunt's mind at rest on the present subject; so she said:

'I think you are right, Auntie dear. It would have been better if I had asked you first; but I saw that Leonard was in distress, and wormed the cause of it from him. When I heard that it was only debt I offered to help him. He is an old friend, you know, Auntie. We were children together; and as I have much more money than I can ever want or spend, I thought I might help him. I am afraid I have let myself in for a bigger thing than I intended; but as I have promised I must go on with it. I dare say, Auntie, that you are afraid that I may end by getting in love with him, and marrying him. Don't you, dear?' This was said with a hug and a kiss which gave the old lady delight. Her instinct told her what was coming. She nodded her head in acquiescence. Stephen went on gravely:

'Put any such fear out of your mind. I shall never marry him. I can never love him.' She was going to say 'could never love him,' when she remembered.

'Are you sure, my dear? The heart is not always under one's own control.'

'Quite sure, Auntie. I know Leonard Everard; and though I have always liked him, I do not respect him. Why, the very fact of his coming to me for money would make me reconsider any view I had formed, had nothing else ever done so. You may take it, Auntie dear, that in the way you mean Leonard is nothing to me; can never be anything to me!' Here a sudden inspiration took her. In its light a serious difficulty passed, and the doing of a thing which had a fear of its own became easy. With a conviction in her tone, which in itself aided her immediate purpose, she said:

'I shall prove it to you. That is, if you will not mind doing something which will save me an embarrassment.'

'You know I will do anything, my dearest, which an old woman can do for a young one!' Stephen squeezed the mittened hand which she held as she went on:

'As I said, I have promised to lend him some money. The first instalment is to be given him to-morrow; he is to call for it in the afternoon. Will you give it to him for me?'

'Gladly, my dear,' said the old lady, much relieved. Stephen continued:

'One other thing, Auntie, I want you to do for me: not to think of the amount, or to say a word to me about it. It is a large sum, and I dare say it will frighten you a little. But I have made up my mind to it. I am learning a great deal out of this, Auntie dear; and I am quite willing to pay for my knowledge. After all, money is the easiest and cheapest way of paying for knowledge! Don't you agree with me?'

Miss Rowly gulped down her disappointment. She felt that she ought not to say too much, now that Stephen had set aside her graver fears. She consoled herself with the thought that even a large amount of money would cause no inconvenience to so wealthy a woman as Stephen. Beyond this, as she would have the handing over of the money to Leonard, she would know the amount. If advisable, she could remonstrate. She could if necessary consult, in confidence, with Harold. Her relief from her greater fear, and her gladness at this new proof of her niece's confidence, were manifested in the extra affection with which she bade her good-night.

Stephen did not dare to breathe freely till she was quite alone; and as she lay quiet in her bed in the dark she thought before sleep came.

Her first feeling was one of thankfulness that immediate danger was swerving from her. Things were so shaping themselves that she need not have any fear concerning Leonard. For his own sake he would have to keep silent. If he intended to blackmail her she would have the protection of her aunt's knowledge of the loan, and of her participation in it. The only weapon that remained to him was her letter; and that she would get from him before furnishing the money for the payment of his other debts.

These things out of the way, her thoughts turned to the matter of the greater dread; that of which all along she had feared to think for a moment: Harold!

Harold! and her treatment of him!

The first reception of the idea was positive anguish. From the moment he had left her till now there had been no time when a consideration of the matter was possible. Time pressed, or circumstances had interfered, or her own personal condition had forbidden. Now, when she was alone, the whole awful truth burst on her like an avalanche. Stephen felt the issue of her thinking before the thinking itself was accomplished; and it was with a smothered groan that she, in the darkness, held up her arms with fingers linked in desperate concentration of appeal.

Oh, if she could only take back one hour of her life, well she knew what that hour would be! Even that shameful time with Leonard on the hill-top seemed innocuous beside the degrading remembrance of her conduct to the noble friend of her whole life.

Sadly she turned over in her bed, and with shut eyes put her burning face on the pillow, to hide, as it were, from herself her abject depth of shame.

Leonard lounged through the next morning with what patience he could. At four o'clock he was at the door of Normanstand in his dogcart. This time he had a groom with him and a suitcase packed for a night's use, as he was to go on to London after his interview with Stephen. He had lost sight altogether of the matter of Stephen's letter, or else he would have been more nervous.

He was taken into the blue drawing-room, where shortly Miss Rowly joined him. He had not expected this. His mental uneasiness manifested itself in his manner, and his fidgeting was not unobserved by the astute old lady. He was disconcerted; 'overwhelmed' would better have described his feelings when she said:

'Miss Norman is sorry she can't see you to-day as she is making a visit; but she has given me a message for you, or rather a commission to discharge. Perhaps you had better sit down at the table; there are writing materials there, and I shall want a receipt of some sort.'

'Stephen did not say anything about a receipt!' The other smiled sweetly as she said in a calm way:

'But unfortunately Miss Norman is not here; and so I have to do the best I can. I really must have some proof that I have fulfilled my trust. You see, Mr. Everard, though it is what lawyers call a "friendly" transaction, it is more or less a business act; and I must protect myself.'

Leonard saw that he must comply, for time pressed. He sat down at the table. Taking up a pen and drawing a sheet of paper towards him, he said with what command of his voice he could:

'What am I to write?' The old lady took from her basket a folded sheet of notepaper, and, putting on her reading-glasses, said as she smoothed it out:

'I think it would be well to say something like this—"I, Leonard Everard, of Brindehow, in the Parish of Normanstand, in the County of Norcester, hereby acknowledge the receipt from Miss Laetitia Rowly of nine hundred pounds sterling lent to me in accordance with my request, the same being to clear me of a pressing debt due by me.'

When he had finished writing the receipt Miss Rowly looked it over, and handing it back to him, said:

'Now sign; and date!' He did so with suppressed anger.

She folded the document carefully and put it in her pocket. Then taking from the little pouch which she wore at her belt a roll of notes, she counted out on the table nine notes of one hundred pounds each. As she put down the last she said:

'Miss Norman asked me to say that a hundred pounds is added to the sum you specified to her, as doubtless the usurers would, since you are actually behind the time promised for repayment, require something extra as a solatium or to avoid legal proceedings already undertaken. In fact that they would "put more salt on your tail." The expression, I regret to say, is not mine.'

Leonard folded up the notes, put them into his pocket-book, and walked away. He did not feel like adding verbal thanks to the document already signed. As he got near the door the thought struck him; turning back he said:

'May I ask if Stephen said anything about getting the document?'

'I beg your pardon,' she said icily, 'did you speak of any one?'

'Miss Norman, I meant!' Miss Rowly's answer to this came so smartly that it left an added sting. Her arrow was fledged with two feathers so that it must shoot true: her distrust of him and his own impotence.

'Oh no! Miss Norman knows nothing of this. She simply asked me to give you the money. This is my own doing entirely. You see, I must exercise my judgment on my dear niece's behalf. Of course it may not be necessary to show her the receipt; but if it should ever be advisable it is always there.'

He looked at her with anger, not unmixed with admiration, as, bowing rather lower than necessary, he went out of the door, saying sotto voce, between his teeth:

'When my turn comes out you go! Neck and crop! Quick! Normanstand isn't big enough to hold us both!'

CHAPTER-18

More Business

When Leonard tendered the eight hundred pounds in payment of his debt of five hundred, Mr. Cavendish at first refused to take it. But when Leonard calmly but firmly refused to pay a single penny beyond the obligations already incurred, including interest on the full sum for one day, he acquiesced. He knew the type of man fully; and knew also that in all probability it would not be long before he would come to the Firm again on a borrowing errand. When such time should come, he would put an extra clause into his Memorandum of Agreement which would allow the Firm full power to make whatever extra charge they might choose in case of the slightest default in making payment.

Leonard's visits to town had not of late been many, and such as he had had were not accompanied with a plethora of cash. He now felt that he had earned a holiday; and it was not till the third morning that he returned to Brindehow. His father made no comment on his absence; his only allusion to the subject was:

'Back all right! Any news in town?' There was, however, an unwonted suavity in his manner which made Leonard a little anxious. He busied himself for the balance of the morning in getting together all his unpaid accounts and making a schedule of them. The total at first amazed almost as much as it frightened him. He feared what Stephen would say. She had already commented unfavourably on the one amount she had seen. When she was face to face with this she might refuse to pay altogether. It would therefore be wise to propitiate her. What could he do in this direction? His thoughts naturally turned to the missing letter. If he could get possession of it, it would either serve as a sop or a threat. In the one case she would be so glad to have it back that she would not stick at a few pounds; in the other it would 'bring her to her senses' as he put in his own mind his intention of blackmail.

He was getting so tightened up in situation that as yet he could only do as he was told, and keep his temper as well as he could.

Altogether it was in a chastened mood that he made his appearance at Normanstand later in the afternoon. He was evidently expected, for he was shown into the study without a word. Here Miss Rowly and Stephen joined him. Both were very kind in manner. After the usual greetings and commonplaces Stephen said in a brisk, businesslike way:

'Have you the papers with you?' He took the bundle of accounts from his pocket and handed them to her. After his previous experience he would have suggested, had he dared, that he should see Stephen alone; but he feared the old lady. He therefore merely said:

'I am afraid you will find the amount very large. But I have put down everything!'

So he had; and more than everything. At the last an idea struck him that as he was getting so much he might as well have a little more. He therefore added several good-sized amounts which he called 'debts of honour.' This would, he thought, appeal to the feminine mind. Stephen did not look at the papers at once. She stood up, holding them, and said to Miss Rowly:

'Now, if you will talk to Mr. Everard I will go over these documents quietly by myself. When I have been through them and understand them all I shall come back; and we will see what can be done.' She moved gracefully out of the room, closing the door behind her. As is usual with women, she had more than one motive for her action in going away. In the first place, she wished to be alone whilst she went over the schedule of the debts. She feared she might get angry; and in the present state of her mind towards Leonard the expression of any feeling, even contempt, would not be wise. Her best protection from him would be a manifest kindly negation of any special interest. In the second place, she believed that he would have her letter with the other papers, and she did not wish her aunt to see it, lest she should recognise the writing. In her boudoir, with a beating heart, she untied the string and looked through the papers.

Her letter was not among them.

For a few seconds she stood stock still, thinking. Then, with a sigh, she sat down and began to read the list of debts, turning to the originals now and again for details. As she went on, her wonder and disgust grew; and even a sense of fear came into her thoughts. A man who could be so wildly reckless and so selfishly unscrupulous was to be feared. She knew his father was a comparatively poor man, who could not possibly meet such a burden. If he were thus to his father, what might he be to her if he got a chance.

The thought of what he might have been to her, had he taken the chance she had given him, never occurred to her. This possibility had already reached the historical stage in her mind.

She made a few pencil notes on the list; and went back to the study. Her mind was made up.

She was quite businesslike and calm, did not manifest the slightest disapproval, but seemed to simply accept everything as facts. She asked Leonard a few questions on subjects regarding which she had made notes, such as discounts. Then she held the paper out to him and without any preliminary remark said:

'Will you please put the names to these?'

'How do you mean?' he asked, flushing.

'The names of the persons to whom these sums marked "debt of honour" are due.' His reply came quickly, and was a little aggressive; he thought this might be a good time to make a bluff:

'I do not see that that is necessary. I can settle them when I have the money.' Slowly and without either pause or flurry Stephen replied, looking him straight in the eyes as she handed him the papers:

'Of course it is not necessary! Few things in the world really are! I only wanted to help you out of your troubles; but if you do not wish me to . . . !' Leonard interrupted in alarm:

'No! no! I only spoke of these items. You see, being "debts of honour" I ought not to give the names.' Looking with a keen glance at her set face he saw she was obdurate; and, recognising his defeat, said as calmly as he could, for he felt raging:

'All right! Give me the paper!' Bending over the table he wrote. When she took the paper, a look half surprised, half indignant, passed over her face. Her watchful aunt saw it, and bending over looked also at the paper. Then she too smiled bitterly.

Leonard had printed in the names! The feminine keenness of both women had made his intention manifest. He did not wish for the possibility of his handwriting being recognised. His punishment came quickly. With a dazzling smile Stephen said to him:

'But, Leonard, you have forgotten to put the addresses!'

'Is that necessary?'

'Of course it is! Why, you silly, how is the money to be paid if there are no addresses?'

Leonard felt like a rat in a trap; but he had no alternative. So irritated was he, and so anxious to hide his irritation that, forgetting his own caution, he wrote, not in printing characters but in his own handwriting, addresses evolved from his own imagination. Stephen's eyes twinkled as he handed her the paper: he had given himself away all round.

Leonard having done all that as yet had been required of him, felt that he might now ask a further favour, so he said:

'There is one of those bills which I have promised to pay by Monday.'

'Promised?' said Stephen with wide-opened eyes. She had no idea of sparing him, she remembered the printed names. 'Why, Leonard, I thought you said you were unable to pay any of those debts?'

Again he had put himself in a false position. He could not say that it was to his father he had made the promise; for he had already told Stephen that he had been afraid to tell him of his debts. In his desperation, for Miss Rowly's remorseless glasses were full on him, he said:

'I thought I was justified in making the promise after what you said about the pleasure it would be to help me. You remember, that day on the hilltop?'

If he had wished to disconcert her he was mistaken; she had already thought over and over again of every form of embarrassment her unhappy action might bring on her at his hands. She now said sweetly and calmly, so sweetly and so calmly that he, with knowledge of her secret, was alarmed:

'But that was not a promise to pay. If you will remember it was only an offer, which is a very different thing. You did not accept it then!' She was herself somewhat desperate, or she would not have sailed so close to the wind.

'Ah, but I accepted later!' he said quickly, feeling in his satisfaction in an epigrammatic answer a certain measure of victory. He felt his mistake when she went on calmly:

'Offers like that are not repeated. They are but phantoms, after all. They come at their own choice, when they do come; and they stay but the measure of a breath or two. You cannot summon them!' Leonard fell into the current of the metaphor and answered:

'I don't know that even that is impossible. There are spells which call, and recall, even phantoms!'

'Indeed!' Stephen was anxious to find his purpose.

Leonard felt that he was getting on, that he was again acquiring the upper hand; so he pushed on the metaphor, more and more satisfied with himself:

'And it is wonderful how simple some spells, and these the most powerful, can be. A remembered phrase, the recollection of a pleasant meeting, the smell of a forgotten flower, or the sight of a forgotten letter; any or all of these can, through memory, bring back the past. And it is often in the past that the secret of the future lies!'

Miss Rowly felt that something was going on before her which she could not understand. Anything of this man's saying which she could not fathom must be at least dangerous; so she determined to spoil his purpose, whatever it might be.

'Dear me! That is charmingly poetic! Past and future; memory and the smell of flowers; meetings and letters! It is quite philosophy. Do explain it all, Mr. Everard!' Leonard was not prepared to go on under the circumstances. His own mention of 'letter,' although he had deliberately used it with the intention of frightening Stephen, had frightened himself. It reminded him that he had not brought, had not got, the letter; and that as yet he was not certain of getting the money. Stephen also had noted the word, and determined not to pass the matter by. She said gaily:

'If a letter is a spell, I think you have a spell of mine, which is a spell of my own weaving. You were to show me the letter in which I asked you to come to see me. It was in that, I think you said, that I mentioned your debts; but I don't remember doing so. Show it to me!'

'I have not got it with me!' This was said with mulish sullenness.

'Why not?'

'I forgot.'

'That is a pity! It is always a pity to forget things in a business transaction; as this is. I think, Auntie, we must wait till we have all the documents, before we can complete this transaction!'

Leonard was seriously alarmed. If the matter of the loan were not gone on with at once the jeweller's bill could not be paid by Monday, and the result would be another scene with his father. He turned to Stephen and said as charmingly as he could, and he was all in earnest now:

'I'm awfully sorry! But these debts have been so worrying me that they put lots of things out of my head. That bill to be paid on Monday, when I haven't a feather to fly with, is enough to drive a fellow off his chump. The moment I lay my hands on the letter I shall keep it with me so that I can't forget it again. Won't you forgive me for this time?'

'Forgive!' she answered, with a laugh. 'Why it's not worth forgiveness! It is not worth a second thought! All right! Leonard, make your mind easy; the bill will be paid on Monday!' Miss Rowly said quietly:

'I have to be in London on Monday afternoon; I can pay it for you.' This was a shock to Leonard; he said impulsively:

'Oh, I say! Can't I . . . ' His words faded away as the old lady again raised her lorgnon and gazed at him calmly. She went on:

'You know, my dear, it won't be even out of my way, as I have to call at Mr. Malpas's office, and I can go there from the hotel in Regent Street.' This was all news to Stephen. She did not know that her aunt had intended going to London; and indeed she did not know of any business with Mr. Malpas, whose firm had been London solicitor to the Rowlys for several generations. She had no doubt, however, as to the old lady's intention. It was plain to her that she wanted to help. So she thanked her sweetly. Leonard could say nothing. He seemed to be left completely out of it. When Stephen rose, as a hint to him that it was time for him to go, he said humbly, as he left:

'Would it be possible that I should have the receipt before Monday evening? I want to show it to my father.'

'Certainly!' said the old lady, answering him. 'I shall be back by the two o'clock train; and if you happen to be at the railway station at Norcester when I arrive I can give it to you!'

He went away relieved, but vindictive; determined in his own mind that when he had received the money for the rest of the debts he would see Stephen, when the old lady was not present, and have it out with her.

CHAPTER-19

A Letter

On Monday evening after dinner Mr. Everard and his son sat for a while in silence. They had not met since morning; and in the presence of the servants conversation had been scrupulously polite. Now, though they were both waiting to talk, neither liked to begin. The older man was outwardly placid, when Leonard, a little flushed and a little nervous of voice, began:

'Have you had any more bills?' He had expected none, and thus hoped to begin by scoring against his father. It was something of a set-down when the latter, taking some papers from his breast-pocket, handed them to him, saying:

'Only these!' Leonard took them in silence and looked at them. All were requests for payment of debts due by his son.

In each case the full bill was enclosed. He was silent a while; but his father spoke:

'It would almost seem as if all these people had made up their minds that you were of no further use to them.' Then without pausing he said, but in a sharper voice:

'Have you paid the jewellers? This is Monday!' Without speaking Leonard took leisurely from his pocket folded paper. This he opened, and, after deliberately smoothing out the folds, handed it to his father. Doubtless something in his manner had already convinced the latter that the debt was paid. He took the paper in as leisurely a way as it had been given, adjusted his spectacles, and read it. Seeing that his son had scored this time, he covered his chagrin with an appearance of paternal satisfaction.

'Good!' For many reasons he was glad the debt was paid He was himself too poor a man to allow the constant drain his son's debts, and too careful of his position to be willing have such exposure as would come with a County Court action against his son. All the same, his exasperation continued. Neither was his quiver yet empty. He shot his next arrow:

'I am glad you paid off those usurers!' Leonard did not like the definite way he spoke. Still in silence, he took from his pocket a second paper, which he handed over unfolded. Mr. Everard read it, and returned it politely, with again one word:

'Good!' For a few minutes there was silence. The father spoke again:

'Those other debts, have you paid them?' With a calm deliberation so full of tacit rudeness that it made his father flush Leonard answered:

'Not yet, sir! But I shall think of them presently. I don't care to be bustled by them; and I don't mean to!' It was apparent that though he spoke verbally of his creditors, his meaning was with regard to others also.

'When will they be paid?' As his son hesitated, he went on:

'I am alluding to those who have written to me. I take it that as my estate is not entailed, and as you have no income except from me, the credit which has been extended to you has been rather on my account than your own. Therefore, as the matter touches my own name, I am entitled to know something of what is going on.' His manner as well as his words was so threatening that Leonard was a little afraid. He might imperil his inheritance. He answered quickly:

'Of course, sir, you shall know everything. After all, you know, my affairs are your affairs!'

'I know nothing of the sort. I may of course be annoyed by your affairs, even dishonoured, in a way, by them. But I accept no responsibility whatever. As you have made your bed, so must you lie on it!'

'It's all right, sir, I assure you. All my debts, both those you know of and some you don't, I shall settle very shortly.'

'How soon?' The question was sternly put.

'In a few days. I dare say a week at furthest will see everything straightened out.'

The elder man stood, saying gravely as he went to the door:

'You will do well to tell me when the last of them is paid. There is something which I shall then want to tell you!' Without waiting for reply he went to his study.

Leonard went to his room and made a systematic, though unavailing, search for Stephen's letter; thinking that by some chance he might have recovered it from Harold and had overlooked it.

The next few days he passed in considerable suspense. He did not dare go near Normanstand until he was summoned, as he knew he would be when he was required.

* * * * *

When Miss Rowly returned from her visit to London she told Stephen that she had paid the bill at the jeweller's, and had taken the precaution of getting a receipt, together with a duplicate for Mr. Everard. The original was by her own request made out as received from Miss Laetitia Rowly in settlement of the account of Leonard Everard, Esq.; the duplicate merely was 'recd. in settlement of the account of—,' etc. Stephen's brows bent hit thought as she said:

'Why did you have it done that way, Auntie dear?' The other answered quietly:

'I had a reason, my dear; good reason! Perhaps I shall tell you all about it some day; in the meantime I want you not to ask me anything about it. I have a reason for that too. Stephen, won't you trust me in this, blindfold?' There was something so sweet and loving in the way she made the request that Stephen was filled with emotion. She put her arms round her aunt's neck and hugged her tight. Then laying her head on her bosom she said with a sigh:

'Oh, my dear, you can't know how I trust you; or how much your trust is to me. You never can know!'

The next day the two women held a long consultation over the schedule of Leonard's debts. Neither said a word of disfavour, or even commented on the magnitude. The only remark touching on the subject was made by Miss Rowly:

'We must ask for proper discounts. Oh, the villainy of those tradesmen! I do believe they charge double in the hope of getting half. As to jewellers . . . !' Then she announced her intention of going up to town again on Thursday, at which visit she would arrange for the payment of the various debts. Stephen tried to remonstrate, but she was obdurate. She held Stephen's hand in hers and stroked it lovingly as she kept on repeating:

'Leave it all to me, dear! Leave it all to me! Everything shall be paid as you wish; but leave it to me!'

Stephen acquiesced. This gentle yielding was new in her; it touched the elder lady to the quick, even whilst it pained her. Well she knew that some trouble must have gone to the smoothing of that imperious nature.

Stephen's inner life in these last few days was so bitterly sad that she kept it apart from all the routine of social existence. Into it never came now, except as the exciting cause of all the evil, a thought of Leonard. The saddening memory was of Harold. And of him the sadness was increased and multiplied by a haunting fear. Since he had walked out of the grove she had not seen him nor heard from him. This was in itself strange; for in all her life, when she was at home and he too, never a day passed without her seeing him. She had heard her aunt say that word had come of his having made a sudden journey to London, from which he had not yet returned. She was afraid to make inquiries. Partly lest she might hear bad news—this was her secret fear; partly lest she might bring some attention to herself in connection with his going. Of some things in connection with her conduct to him she was afraid to think at all. Thought, she felt, would come in time, and with it new pains and new shames, of which as yet she dared not think.

One morning came an envelope directed in Harold's hand. The sight made her almost faint. She rejoiced that she had been first down, and had opened the postbag with her own key. She took the letter to her room and shut herself in before opening it. Within were a few lines of writing and her own letter to Leonard in its envelope. Her head beat so hard that she could scarcely see; but gradually the writing seemed to grow out of the mist:

'The enclosed should be in your hands. It is possible that it may comfort you to know that it is safe. Whatever may come, God love and guard you.'

For a moment joy, hot and strong, blazed through her. The last words were ringing through her brain. Then came the cold shock, and the gloom of fear. Harold would never have written thus unless he was going away! It was a farewell!

For a long time she stood, motionless, holding the letter in her hand. Then she said, half aloud:

'Comfort! Comfort! There is no more comfort in the world for me! Never, never again! Oh, Harold! Harold!'

She sank on her knees beside her bed, and buried her face in her cold hands, sobbing in all that saddest and bitterest phase of sorrow which can be to a woman's heart: the sorrow that is dry-eyed and without hope.

Presently the habit of caution which had governed her last days woke her to action. She bathed her eyes, smoothed her hair, locked the letter and its enclosure in the little jewel-safe let into the wall, and came down to breakfast.

The sense of loss was so strong on her that she forgot herself. Habit carried her on without will or voluntary effort, and, so faithfully worked to her good that even the loving eyes of her aunt—and the eyes of love are keen—had no suspicion that any new event had come into her life.

Not till she was alone in her room that night did Stephen dare to let her thoughts run freely. In the darkness her mind began to work truly, so truly that she began at the first step of logical process: to study facts. And to study them she must question till she found motive.

Why had Harold sent her the letter? His own words said that it should be in her hands. Then, again, he said it might comfort her to know the letter was safe. How could it comfort her? How did he get possession of the letter?

There she began to understand; her quick intuition and her old knowledge of Harold's character and her new knowledge of Leonard's, helped her to reconstruct causes. In his interview with her he had admitted that Leonard had told him much, all. He would no doubt have refused to believe him, and Leonard would have shown him, as proof, her letter asking him to meet her. He would have seen then, as she did now, how much the possession of that letter might mean to any one.

Good God! to 'any one.' Could it have been so to Harold himself . . . that he thought to use it as an engine, to force her to meet his wishes—as Leonard had already tried to do! The mistrust, founded on her fear, was not dead yet . . . No! no! no! Her whole being resented such a monstrous proposition! Besides, there was proof. Thank God! there was proof. A blackmailer would have stayed close to her, and would have kept the letter; Harold did neither. Her recognition of the truth was shown in her act, when, stretching out her arms in the darkness, she whispered pleadingly:

'Forgive me, Harold!'

And Harold, far away where the setting sun was lying red on the rim of the western sea, could not hear her. But perhaps God did.

As, then, Harold's motive was not of the basest, it must have been of the noblest. What would be a man's noblest motive under such circumstances? Surely self-sacrifice!

And yet there could be no doubt as to Harold's earnestness when he had told her that he loved her . . .

Here Stephen covered her face in one moment of rapture. But the gloom that followed was darker than the night. She did not pursue the thought. That would come later when she should understand.

And yet, so little do we poor mortals know the verities of things, so blind are we to things thrust before our eyes, that she understood more in that moment of ecstasy than in all the reasoning that preceded and followed it. But the reasoning went on:

If he really loved, and told her so, wherein was the self-sacrifice? She had reproached him with coming to her with his suit hotfoot upon his knowledge of her shameful proffer of herself to another man; of her refusal by him. Could he have been so blind as not to have seen, as she did, the shameful aspect of his impulsive act? Surely, if he had thought, he must have seen! . . . And he must have thought; there had been time for it. It was at dinner that he had seen Leonard; it was after breakfast when he had seen her . . . And if he had seen then . . .

In an instant it all burst upon her; the whole splendid truth. He had held back the expression of his long love for her, waiting for the time when her maturity might enable her to understand truly and judge wisely; waiting till her grief for the loss of her father had become a story of the past; waiting for God knows what a man's mind sees of obstacles when he loves. But he had spoken it out when it was to her benefit. What, then, had been his idea of her benefit? Was it that he wished to meet the desire that she had manifested to have some man to—to love? . . . The way she covered her face with her hands whilst she groaned aloud made her answer to her own query a perfect negative.

Was it, then, to save her from the evil of marrying Leonard in case he should repent of his harshness, and later on yield himself to her wooing? The fierce movement of her whole body, which almost threw the clothes from her bed, as the shameful recollection rolled over her, marked the measure of her self-disdain.

One other alternative there was; but it seemed so remote, so far-fetched, so noble, so unlike what a woman would do, that she could only regard it in a shamefaced way. She put the matter to herself questioningly, and with a meekness which had its roots deeper than she knew. And here out of the depths of her humility came a noble thought. A noble thought, which was a noble truth. Through the darkness of the night, through the inky gloom of her own soul came with that thought a ray of truth which, whilst it showed her her own shrivelled unworthiness, made the man whom she had dishonoured with insults worse than death stand out in noble relief. In that instant she guessed at, and realised, Harold's unselfish nobility of purpose, the supreme effort of his constant love. Knowing the humiliation she must have suffered at Leonard's hands, he had so placed himself that even her rejection of him might be some solace to her wounded spirit, her pride.

Here at last was truth! She knew it in the very marrow of her bones.

This time she did not move. She thought and thought of that noble gentleman who had used for her sake even that pent-up passion which, for her sake also, he had suppressed so long.

In that light, which restored in her eyes and justified so fully the man whom she had always trusted, her own shame and wrongdoing, and the perils which surrounded her, were for the time forgotten.

And its glory seemed to rest upon her whilst she slept.

CHAPTER-20

Confidences

Miss Rowly had received a bulky letter by the morning's post. She had not opened it, but had allowed it to rest beside her plate all breakfast-time. Then she had taken it away with her to her own sitting-room. Stephen did not appear to take any notice of it. She knew quite well that it was from some one in London whom her aunt had asked to pay Leonard's bills. She also knew that the old lady had some purpose in her reticence, so she waited. She was learning to be patient in these days. Miss Rowly did say anything about it that day, or the next, or the next. The third-morning, she received another letter which she had read in an enlightening manner. She began its perusal with set brow frowning, then she nodded her head and smiled. She put the letter back in its envelope and placed it in the little bag always carried. But she said nothing. Stephen wondered, but waited.

That night, when Stephen's maid had left her, there came a gentle tap at her door, and an instant after the door opened. The tap had been a warning, not a request; it had in a measure prepared Stephen, who was not surprised to see her Aunt in dressing-gown, though it was many a long day since she had visited her niece's room at night. She closed the door behind her, saying:

'There is something I want to talk to you about, dearest, and I thought it would be better to do so when there could not be any possible interruption. And besides,' here there was a little break in her voice, 'I could hardly summon up my courage in the daylight.' She stopped, and the stopping told its own story. In an instant Stephen's arm's were round her, all the protective instinct in her awake, at the distress of the woman she loved. The old lady took comfort from the warmth of the embrace, and held her tight whilst she went on:

'It is about these bills, my dear. Come and sit down and put a candle near me. I want you to read something.'

'Go on, Auntie dear,' she said gravely. The old lady, after a pause, spoke with a certain timidity:

'They are all paid; at least all that can be. Perhaps I had better read you the letter I have had from my solicitors:

'"Dear Madam,—In accordance with your instructions we have paid all the accounts mentioned in Schedule A (enclosed). We have placed for your convenience three columns: (1) the original amount of each account, (2) the amount of discount we were able to arrange, and (3) the amount paid. We regret that we have been unable to carry out your wishes with regard to the items enumerated in Schedule B (enclosed). We have, we assure you, done all in our power to find the gentlemen whose names and addresses are therein given. These were marked 'Debt of honour' in the list you handed to us. Not having been able to obtain any reply to our letters, we sent one of our clerks first to the addresses in London, and afterwards to Oxford. That clerk, who is well used to such inquiries, could not find trace of any of the gentlemen, or indeed of their existence. We have, therefore, come to the conclusion that, either there must be some error with regard to (a) names, (b) addresses, or (c) both; or that no such persons exist. As it would be very unlikely that such errors could occur in all the cases, we can only conclude that there have not been any such persons. If we may hazard an opinion: it is possible that, these debts being what young men call 'debts of honour,' the debtor, or possibly the creditors, may not have wished the names mentioned. In such case fictitious names and addresses may have been substituted for the real ones. If you should like any further inquiry instituted we would suggest that you ascertain the exact names and addresses from the debtor. Or should you prefer it we would see the gentleman on your behalf, on learning from you his name and address. We can keep, in the person of either one of the Firm or a Confidential Clerk as you might prefer, any appointment in such behalf you may care to make.

'"We have already sent to you the receipted account from each of the creditors as you directed, viz. 'Received from Miss Laetitia Rowly in full settlement to date of the account due by Mr. Leonard Everard the sum of,' etc. etc. And also, as you further directed, a duplicate receipt of the sum-total due in each case made out as 'Received in full settlement to date of account due by,' etc. etc. The duplicate receipt was pinned at the back of each account so as to be easily detachable.

'"With regard to finance we have carried out your orders, etc."' She hurried on the reading. "These sums, together with the amounts of nine hundred pounds sterling, and seven hundred pounds sterling lodged to the account of Miss Stephen Norman in the Norcester branch of the Bank as repayment of moneys advanced to you as by your written instructions, have exhausted the sum, etc."' She folded up the letter with the schedules, laying the bundle of accounts on the table. Stephen paused; she felt it necessary to collect herself before speaking.

'Auntie dear, will you let me see that letter? Oh, my dear, dear Auntie, don't think I mistrust you that I ask it. I do because I love you, and because I want to love you more if it is possible to do so.' Miss Rowly handed her the letter. She rose from the arm of the chair and stood beside the table as though to get better light from the candle than she could get from where she had sat.

She read slowly and carefully to the end; then folded up the letter and handed it to her aunt. She came back to her seat on the edge of the chair, and putting her arms round her companion's neck looked her straight in the eyes. The elder woman grew embarrassed under the scrutiny; she coloured up and smiled in a deprecatory way as she said:

'Don't look at me like that, darling; and don't shake your head so. It is all right! I told you I had my reasons, and you said you would trust me. I have only done what I thought best!'

'But, Auntie, you have paid away more than half your little fortune. I know all the figures. Father and uncle told me everything. Why did you do it? Why did you do it?' The old woman held out her arms as she said:

'Come here, dear one, and sit on my knee as you used to when you were a child, and I will whisper you.' Stephen sprang from her seat and almost threw herself into the loving arms. For a few seconds the two, clasped tight to each other's heart, rocked gently to and fro. The elder kissed the younger and was kissed impulsively in return. Then she stroked the beautiful bright hair with her wrinkled hand, and said admiringly:

'What lovely hair you have, my dear one!' Stephen held her closer and waited.

'Well, my dear, I did it because I love you!'

'I know that, Auntie; you have never done anything else my life!'

'That is true, dear one. But it is right that I should do this. Now you must listen to me, and not speak till I have done. Keep your thoughts on my words, so that you may follow my thoughts. You can do your own thinking about them afterwards. And your own talking too; I shall listen as long as you like!'

'Go on, I'll be good!'

'My dear, it is not right that you should appear to have paid the debts of a young man who is no relation to you and who will, I know well, never be any closer to you than he is now.' She hurried on, as though fearing an interruption, but Stephen felt that her clasp tightened. 'We never can tell what will happen as life goes on. And, as the world is full of scandal, one cannot be too careful not to give the scandalmongers anything to exercise their wicked spite upon. I don't trust that young man! he is a bad one all round, or I am very much mistaken. And, my dear, come close to me! I cannot but see that you and he have some secret which he is using to distress you!' She paused, and her clasp grew closer still as Stephen's head sank on her breast. 'I know you have done something or said something foolish of which he has a knowledge. And I know my dear one, that whatever it was, and no matter how foolish it may have been, it was not a wrong thing. God knows, we are all apt to do wrong things as well as foolish ones; the best of us. But such is not for you! Your race, your father and mother, your upbringing, yourself and the truth and purity which are yours would save you from anything which was in itself wrong. That I know, my dear, as well as I know myself! Ah! better, far better! for the gods did not think it well to dower me as they have dowered you. The God of all the gods has given you the ten talents to guard; and He knows, as I do, that you will be faithful to your trust.'

There was a solemn ring in her voce as the words were spoken which went through the young girl's heart. Love and confidence demanded in return that she should have at least the relief of certain acquiescence; there is a possible note of pain in the tensity of every string! Stephen lifted her head proudly and honestly, though her cheeks were scarlet, saying with a consciousness of integrity which spoke directly soul to soul:

'You are right, dear! I have done something very foolish; very, very foolish! But it was nothing which any one could call wrong. Do not ask me what it was. I need only tell you this: that it was an outrage on convention. It was so foolish, and based on such foolish misconception; it sprang from such over-weening, arrogant self-opinion that it deserves the bitter punishment which will come; which is coming; which is with me now! It was the cause of something whose blackness I can't yet realise; but of which I will tell you when I can speak of it. But it was not wrong in itself, or in the eyes of God or man!' The old woman said not a word. No word was needed, for had she not already expressed her belief? But Stephen felt her relief in the glad pressure of her finger-tips. In a voice less strained and tense Miss Rowly went on:

'What need have I for money, dear? Here I have all that any woman, especially at my age, can need. There is no room even for charity; you are so good to all your people that my help is hardly required. And, my dear one, I know—I know,' she emphasised the word as she stroked the beautiful hair, 'that when I am gone my own poor, the few that I have looked after all my life, will, not suffer when my darling thinks of me!' Stephen fairly climbed upon her as she said, looking in the brave old eyes:

'So help me God, my darling, they shall never want!'

Silence for a time; and then Miss Rowly's voice again:

'Though it would not do for the world to know that a young maiden lady had paid the debts of a vicious young man, it makes no matter if they be paid by an old woman, be the same maid, wife, or widow! And really, my dear, I do not see how any money I might have could be better spent than in keeping harm away from you.'

'There need not be any harm at all, Auntie.'

'Perhaps not, dear! I hope not with all my heart. But I fear that young man. Just fancy him threatening you, and in your own house; in my very presence! Oh! yes, my dear. He meant to threaten, anyhow! Though I could not exactly understand what he was driving at, I could see that he was driving at something. And after all that you were doing for him, and had done for him! I mean, of course, after all that I had done for him, and was doing for him. It is mean enough, surely, for a man to beg, and from a woman; but to threaten afterwards. Ach! But I think, my dear, it is checkmate to him this time. All along the line the only proof that is of there being any friendliness towards him from this house points to me. And moreover, my dear, I have a little plan in my head that will tend to show him up even better, in case he may ever try to annoy us. Look at me when next he is here. I mean to do a little play-acting which will astonish him, I can tell you, if it doesn't frighten him out of the house altogether. But we won't talk of that yet. You will understand when you see it!' Her eyes twinkled and her mouth shut with a loud snap as she spoke.

After a few minutes of repose, which was like a glimpse of heaven to Stephen's aching heart, she spoke again:

'There was something else that troubled you more than even this. You said you would tell me when you were able to speak of it . . . Why not speak now? Oh! my dear, our hearts are close together to-night; and in all your life, you will never have any one who will listen with greater sympathy than I will, or deal more tenderly with your fault, whatever it may have been.

Tell me, dear! Dear!' she whispered after a pause, during which she realised the depth of the girl's emotion by her convulsive struggling to keep herself in check.

All at once the tortured girl seemed to yield herself, and slipped inertly from her grasp till kneeling down she laid her head in the motherly lap and sobbed. Miss Rowly kept stroking her hair in silence. Presently the girl looked up, and with a pang the aunt saw that her eyes were dry. In her pain she said:

'You sob like that, my child, and yet you are not crying; what is it, oh! my dear one? What is it that hurts you so that you cannot cry?'

And then the bitter sobbing broke out again, but still alas! without tears. Crouching low, and still enclosing her aunt's waist with her outstretched arms and hiding her head in her breast; she said:

'Oh! Auntie, I have sent Harold away!'

'What, my dear? What?' said the old lady astonished. 'Why, I thought there was no one in the world that you trusted so much as Harold!'

'It is true. There was—there is no one except you whom I trust so much. But I mistook something he said. I was in a blind fury at the time, and I said things that I thought my father's daughter never could have said. And she never thought them, even then! Oh, Auntie, I drove him away with all the horrible things I could say that would wound him. And all because he acted in a way that I see now was the most noble and knightly in which any man could act. He that my dear father had loved, and honoured, and trusted as another son. He that was a real son to him, and not a mock sop like me. I sent him away with such fierce and bitter pain that his poor face was ashen grey, and there was woe in his eyes that shall make woe in mine whenever I shall see them in my mind, waking or sleeping. He, the truest friend . . . the most faithful, the most tender, the most strong, the most unselfish! Oh! Auntie, Auntie, he just turned and bowed and went away. And he couldn't do anything else with the way I spoke to him; and now I shall never see him again!'

The young girl's eyes ware still dry, but the old woman's were wet. For a few minutes she kept softly stroking the bowed heat till the sobbing grew less and less, and then died away; and the girl lay still, collapsed in the abandonment of dry-eyed grief.

Then she rose, and taking off her dressing-gown, said tenderly:

'Let me stay with you to-night, dear one? Go to sleep in my arms, as you did long ago when there was any grief that you could not bear.'

So Stephen lay in those loving arms till her own young breast ceased heaving, and she breathed softly. Till dawn she slept on the bosom of her who loved her so well.

CHAPTER-21

The Duty of Courtesy

Leonard was getting tired of waiting when he received his summons to Normanstand. But despite his impatience he was ill pleased with the summons, which came in the shape of a polite note from Miss Rowly asking him to come that afternoon at tea-time. He had expected to hear from Stephen.

'Damn that old woman! You'd think she was working the whole show!' However, he turned up at a little before five o'clock, spruce and dapper and well dressed and groomed as usual. He was shown, as before, into the blue drawing-room. Miss Rowly, who sat there, rose as he entered, and coming across the room, greeted him, as he thought, effusively. He actually winced when she called him 'my dear boy' before the butler.

She ordered tea to be served at once, and when it had been brought she said to the butler:

'Tell Mannerly to bring me a large thick envelope which is on the table in my room. It is marked L.E. on the outside.' Presently an elderly maid handed her the envelope and withdrew. When tea was over she opened the envelope, and taking from it a number of folios, looked over them carefully; holding them in her lap, she said quietly:

'You will find writing materials on the table. I am all ready now to hand you over the receipts.' His eyes glistened. This was good news at all events; the debts were paid. In a rapid flash of thought he came to the conclusion that if the debts were actually paid he need not be civil to the old lady. He felt that he could have been rude to her if he had actual possession of the receipts. As it was, however, he could not yet afford to have any unpleasantness. There was still to come that lowering interview with his father; and he could not look towards it satisfactorily until he had the assurance of the actual documents that he was safe. Miss Rowly was, in her own way, reading his mind in his face. Her lorgnon seemed to follow his every expression like a searchlight. He remembered his former interview with her, and how he had been bested in it; so he made up his mind to acquiesce in time. He went over to the table and sat down. Taking a pen he turned to Miss Rowly and said:

'What shall I write?' She answered calmly:

'Date it, and then say, "Received from Miss Laetitia Rowly the receipts for the following amounts from the various firms hereunder enumerated."' She then proceeded to read them, he writing and repeating as he wrote. Then she added:

'"The same being the total amount of my debts which she has kindly paid for me."' He paused here; she asked.

'Why don't you go on?'

'I thought it was Stephen—Miss Norman,' he corrected, catching sight of her lorgnon, 'who was paying them.'

'Good Lord, man,' she answered, 'what does it matter who has paid them, so long as they are paid?'

'But I didn't ask you to pay them,' he went on obstinately. There was a pause, and then the old lady, with a distinctly sarcastic smile, said:

'It seems to me, young man, that you are rather particular as to how things are done for you. If you had begun to be just a little bit as particular in making the debts as you are in the way of having them paid, there would be a little less trouble and expense all round. However, the debts have been paid, and we can't unpay them. But of course you can repay me the money if you like. It amounts in all to four thousand three hundred and seventeen pounds, twelve shillings and sixpence, and I have paid every penny of it out of my own pocket. If you can't pay it yourself, perhaps your father would like to do so.'

The last shot told; he went on writing: '"Kindly paid for me,"' she continued in the same even voice:

'"In remembrance of my mother, of whom she was an acquaintance." Now sign it!' He did so and handed it to her. She read it over carefully, folded it, and put it in her pocket. She then stood. He rose also; and as he moved to the door—he had not offered to shake hands with her—he said:

'I should like to see, Miss Norman.'

'I am afraid you will have to wait.'

'Why?'

'She is over at Heply Regis. She went there for Lady Heply's ball, and will remain for a few days. Good afternoon!' The tone in which the last two words were spoken seemed in his ears like the crow of the victor after a cock-fight.

As he was going out of the room a thought struck her. She felt he deserved some punishment for his personal rudeness to her. After all, she had paid half her fortune for him, though not on his account; and not only had he given no thanks, but had not even offered the usual courtesy of saying good-bye. She had intended to have been silent on the subject, and to have allowed him to discover it later. Now she said, as if it was an after-thought:

'By the way, I did not pay those items you put down as "debts of honour"; you remember you gave the actual names and addresses.'

'Why not?' the question came from him involuntarily. The persecuting lorgnon rose again:

'Because they were all bogus! Addresses, names, debts, honour! Good afternoon!'

He went out flaming; free from debt, money debts; all but one. And some other debts—not financial—whose magnitude was exemplified in the grinding of his teeth.

After breakfast next morning he said to his father:

'By the way, you said you wished to speak to me, sir.' There was something in the tone of his voice which called up antagonism.

'Then you have paid your debts?'

'All!'

'Good! Now there is something which it is necessary I should call your attention to. Do you remember the day on which I handed you that pleasing epistle from Messrs. Cavendish and Cecil?'

'Certainly, sir.'

'Didn't you send a telegram to them?'

'I did.'

'You wrote it yourself?'

'Certainly.'

'I had a courteous letter from the money-lenders, thanking me for my exertions in securing the settlement of their claim, and saying that in accordance with the request in my telegram they had held over proceedings until the day named. I did not quite remember having sent any telegram to them, or any letter either. So, being at a loss, I went to our excellent postmaster and requested that he would verify the sending of a telegram to London from me. He courteously looked up the file; which was ready for transference to the G.P.O., and showed me the form. It was in your handwriting.' He paused so long that Leonard presently said:

'Well!'

'It was signed Jasper Everard. Jasper Everard! my name; and yet it was sent by my son, who was christened, if I remember rightly, Leonard!' Then he went on, only in a cold acrid manner which made his son feel as though a February wind was blowing on his back:

'I think there need not have been much trouble in learning to avoid confusing our names. They are really dissimilar. Have you any explanation to offer of the—the error, let us call it?' A bright thought struck Leonard.

'Why, sir,' he said, 'I put it in your name as they had written to you. I thought it only courteous.' The elder man winced; he had not expected the excuse. We went on speaking in the same calm way, but his tone was more acrid than before:

'Good! of course! It was only courteous of you! Quite so! But I think it will be well in the future to let me look after my own courtesy; as regards my signature at any rate. You see, my dear boy, a signature is queer sort of thing, and judges and juries are apt to take a poor view of courtesy as over against the conventions regarding a man, writing his own name. What I want to tell you is this, that on seeing that signature I made a new will. You see, my estate is not entailed, and therefore I think it only right to see that in such a final matter justice is done all round. I therefore made a certain provision of which I am sure you will approve. Indeed, since I am assured of the payment of your debts, I feel justified in my action. I may say, inter alia, that I congratulate you on either the extent of your resources or the excellence of your friendships, or both. I confess that the amounts brought to my notice were rather large; more especially in proportion to the value of the estate which you are some day to inherit. For you are of course to inherit some day, my dear boy. You are my only son, and it would be hardly—hardly courteous of me not to leave it to you. But I have put a clause in my will to the effect that the trustee's are to pay all debts of your accruing which can be proved against you, before handing over to you either the estate itself or the remainder after its sale and the settlement of all claims. That's all. Now run away, my boy; I have some important work to do.'

* * * * *

The day after her return from Heply Regis, Stephen was walking in the wood when she thought she heard a slight rustling of leaves some way behind her. She looked round, expecting to see some one; but the leafy path was quite clear. Her suspicion was confirmed; some one was secretly following her. A short process of exclusions pointed to the personality of the some one. Tramps and poachers were unknown in Normanstand, and there was no one else whom she could think of who had any motive in following her in such a way; it must be Leonard Everard. She turned and walked rapidly in the opposite direction. As this would bring her to the house Leonard had to declare his presence at once or else lose the opportunity of a private interview which he sought. When she saw him she said at once and without any salutation:

'What are you doing there; why are you following me?'

'I wanted to see you alone. I could not get near you on account of that infernal old woman.' Stephen's face grew hard.

'On account of whom?' she asked with dangerous politeness.

'Miss Rowly; your aunt.'

'Don't you think, Mr. Everard,' she said icily, 'that it is at least an unpardonable rudeness to speak that way, and to me, of the woman I love best in all the world?'

'Sorry!' he said in the offhand way of younger days, 'I apologise. Fact is, I was angry that she wouldn't let me see you.'

'Not let you see me!' she said as if amazed. 'What do mean?'

'Why, I haven't been able to see you alone ever since I went to meet you on Caester Hill.'

'But why should you see me alone?' she asked as if still in amazement. 'Surely you can say anything you have to say before my aunt.' With an unwisdom for which an instant later he blamed himself he blurted out:

'Why, old girl, you yourself did not think her presence necessary when you asked me to meet you on the hill.'

'When was that?' She saw that he was angry and wanted to test him; to try how far he would venture. He was getting dangerous; she must know the measure of what she had to fear.

He fell into the trap at once. His debts being paid, fear was removed, and all the hectoring side of the man was aroused. His antagonist was a woman; and he had already had in his life so many unpleasant scenes with women that this was no new experience. This woman had, by her own indiscretion, put a whip into his hand; and, if necessary to secure his own way, by God! he meant to use it! These last days had made her a more desirable possession in his eyes. The vastness of her estate had taken hold on him, and his father's remorseless intention with regard to his will would either keep him with very limited funds, or leave him eventually a pauper if he forestalled his inheritance. The desire of her wealth had grown daily, and it was now the main force in bringing him here to-day. And to this was now added the personal desire which her presence evoked. Stephen, at all times beautiful, had never looked more lovely. In the days since she had met him on the hilltop, a time that to her seemed so long ago, she had grown to be a woman, and there is some subtle inconceivable charm in completed womanhood. The reaction from her terrible fear and depression had come, and her strong brilliant youth was manifesting itself. Her step was springy and her eyes were bright; and the glow of fine health, accentuated by the militant humour of the present moment, seemed to light up her beautiful skin. In herself she was desirable, very desirable; Leonard felt his pulses quicken and his blood leap as he looked at her. Even his prejudice against her red hair had changed to something like hungry admiration. Leonard felt for the first moment since he had known her that she was a woman; and that, with relation to her, he was a man.

And at the moment all the man in him asserted itself. It was with half love, as he saw it, and half self-assertion that he answered her question:

'The day you asked me to marry you! Oh! what a fool I was not to leap at such a chance! I should have taken you in my arms then and kissed you till I showed you how much I loved you. But that will all come yet; the kissing is still to come! Oh! Stephen, don't you see that I love you? Won't you tell me that you love me still? Darling!' He almost sprang at her, his arms extended to clasp her.

'Stop!' Her voice rang like a trumpet. She did not mean to submit to physical violence, and in the present state of her feeling, an embrace from him would be a desecration. He was now odious to her; she positively loathed him.

Before her uplifted hand and those flashing eyes, he stopped as one stricken into stone. In that instant she knew she was safe; and with a woman's quickness of apprehension and resolve, made up her mind what course to pursue. In a calm voice she said quietly:

'Mr. Everard, you have followed me in secret, and without my permission. I cannot talk here with you, alone. I absolutely refuse to do so; now or at any other time. If you have anything especial to say to me you will find me at home at noon to-morrow. Remember, I do not ask you to come. I simply yield to the pressure of your importunity. And remember also that I do not authorise you in any way to resume this conversation. In fact, I forbid it. If you come to my house you must control yourself to my wish!'

Then with a stately bow, whose imperious distance inflamed him more than ever, and without once looking back she took her way home, all agitated inwardly and with fast beating heart.

CHAPTER-22

Fixing The Bounds

Leonard came towards Normanstand next forenoon in considerable mental disturbance. In the first place he was seriously in love with Stephen, and love is in itself a disturbing influence.

Leonard's love was all of the flesh; and as such had power at present to disturb him, as it would later have power to torture him. Again, he was disturbed by the fear of losing Stephen, or rather of not being able to gain her. At first, ever since she had left him on the path from the hilltop till his interview the next day, he had looked on her possession as an 'option,' to the acceptance of which circumstances seemed to be compelling him. But ever since, that asset seemed to have been dwindling; and now he was almost beginning to despair. He was altogether cold at heart, and yet highly strung with apprehension, as he was shown into the blue drawing-room.

Stephen came in alone, closing the door behind her. She shook hands with him, and sat down by a writing-table near the window, pointing to him to sit on an ottoman a little distance away. The moment he sat down he realised that he was at a disadvantage; he was not close to her, and he could not get closer without manifesting his intention of so doing. He wanted to be closer, both for the purpose of his suit and for his own pleasure; the proximity of Stephen began to multiply his love for her. He thought that to-day she looked better than ever, of a warm radiant beauty which touched his senses with unattainable desire. She could not but notice the passion in his eyes, and instinctively her eyes wandered to a silver gong placed on the table well within reach. The more he glowed, the more icily calm she sat, till the silence between them began to grow oppressive. She waited, determined that he should be the first to speak. Recognising the helplessness of silence, he began huskily:

'I came here to-day in the hope that you would listen to me.' Her answer, given with a conventional smile, was not helpful:

'I am listening.'

'I cannot tell you how sorry I am that I did not accept your offer. If I had know when I was coming that day that you loved me . . . ' She interrupted him, calm of voice, and with uplifted hand:

'I never said so, did I? Surely I could not have said such a thing! I certainly don't remember it?' Leonard was puzzled.

'You certainly made me think so. You asked me to marry you, didn't you?' Her answer came calmly, though in a low voice:

'I did.'

'Then if you didn't love me, why did you ask me to marry you?' It was his nature to be more or less satisfied when he had put any one opposed to him proportionally in the wrong; and now his exultation at having put a poser manifested itself in his tone. This, however, braced up Stephen to cope with a difficult and painful situation. It was with a calm, seemingly genial frankness, that she answered, smilingly:

'Do you know, that is what has been puzzling me from that moment to this!' Her words appeared to almost stupefy Leonard. This view of the matter had not occurred to him, and now the puzzle of it made him angry.

'Do you mean to say,' he asked hotly, 'that you asked a man to marry you when you didn't even love him?'

'That is exactly what I do mean! Why I did it is, I assure you, as much a puzzle to me as it is to you. I have come to the conclusion that it must have been from my vanity. I suppose I wanted to dominate somebody; and you were the weakest within range!'

'Thank you!' He was genuinely angry by this time, and, but for a wholesome fear of the consequences, would have used strong language.

'I don't see that I was the weakest about.' Somehow this set her on her guard. She wanted to know more, so she asked:

'Who else?'

'Harold An Wolf! You had him on a string already!' The name came like a sword through her heart, but the bitter comment braced her to further caution. Her voice seemed to her to sound as though far away:

'Indeed! And may I ask you how you came to know that?' Her voice seemed so cold and sneering to him that he lost his temper still further.

'Simply because he told me so himself.' It pleased him to do in ill turn to Harold. He did not forget that savage clutch at his throat; and he never would. Stephen's senses were all alert. She saw an opportunity of learning something, and went on with the same cold voice:

'And I suppose it was that pleasing confidence which was the cause of your refusal of my offer of marriage; of which circumstance you have so thoughtfully and so courteously reminded me.' This, somehow, seemed of good import to Leonard. If he could show her that his intention to marry her was antecedent to Harold's confidence, she might still go back to her old affection for him. He could not believe that it did not still exist; his experience of other women showed him that their love outlived their anger, whether the same had been hot or cold.

'It had nothing in the world to do with it. He never said a word about it till he threatened to kill me—the great brute!' This was learning something indeed! She went on in the same voice:

'And may I ask you what was the cause of such sanguinary intention?'

'Because he knew that I was going to marry you!' As he spoke he felt that he had betrayed himself; he went on hastily, hoping that it might escape notice:

'Because he knew that I loved you. Oh! Stephen, don't you know it now! Can't you see that I love you; and that I want you for my wife!'

'But did he threaten to kill you out of mere jealousy? Do you still go in fear of your life? Will it be necessary to arrest him?' Leonard was chagrined at her ignoring of his love-suit, and in his self-engrossment answered sulkily:

'I'm not afraid of him! And, besides, I believe he has bolted. I called at his house yesterday, and his servant said they hadn't heard a word from him.' Stephen's heart sank lower and lower. This was what she had dreaded. She said in as steady a voice as she could muster:

'Bolted! Has he gone altogether?'

'Oh, he'll come back all right, in time. He's not going to give up the jolly good living he has here!'

'But why has he bolted? When he threatened to kill you did he give any reason?' There was too much talk about Harold. It made him angry; so he answered in an offhand way:

'Oh, I don't know. And, moreover, I don't care!'

'And now,' said Stephen, having ascertained what she wanted to know, 'what is it that you want to speak to me about?'

Her words fell on Leonard like a cold douche. Here had he been talking about his love for her, and yet she ignored the whole thing, and asked him what he wanted to talk about.

'What a queer girl you are. You don't seem to attend to what a fellow is saying. Here have I been telling you that I love you, and asking you to marry me; and yet you don't seem to have even heard me!' She answered at once, quite sweetly, and with a smile of superiority which maddened him:

'But that subject is barred!'

'How do you mean? Barred!'

'Yes. I told you yesterday!'

'But, Stephen,' he cried out quickly, all the alarm in him and all the earnestness of which he was capable uniting to his strengthening, 'can't you understand that I love you, with all my heart? You are so beautiful; so beautiful!' He felt now in reality what he was saying.

The torrent of his words left no opening for her objection; it swept all merely verbal obstacles before it. She listened, content in a measure. So long as he sat at the distance which she had arranged before his coming she did not fear any personal violence. Moreover, it was a satisfaction to her now to hear him, who had refused her, pleading in vain. The more sincere his eloquence, the larger her satisfaction; she had no pity for him now.

'I know I was a fool, Stephen! I had my chance that day on the hilltop; and if I had felt then as I feel now, as I have felt every moment since, I would not have been so cold. I would have taken you in my arms and held you close and kissed you, again, and again, and again. Oh, darling! I love you! I love you! I love you!' He held out his arms imploringly. 'Won't you love me? Won't—'

He stopped, paralysed with angry amazement. She was laughing.

He grew purple in the face; his hands were still outstretched. The few seconds seemed like hours.

'Forgive me!' she said in a polite tone, suddenly growing grave. 'But really you looked so funny, sitting there so quietly, and speaking in such a way, that I couldn't help it. You really must forgive me! But remember, I told you the subject was barred; and as, knowing that, you went on, you really have no one but yourself to blame!' Leonard was furious, but managed to say as he dropped his arms:

'But I love you!'

'That may be, now,' she went on icily. 'But it is too late. I do not love you; and I have never loved you! Of course, had you accepted my offer of marriage you should never have known that. No matter how great had been my shame and humiliation when I had come to a sense of what I had done, I should have honourably kept my part of the tacit compact entered into when I made that terrible mistake. I cannot tell you how rejoiced and thankful I am that you took my mistake in such a way. Of course, I do not give you any credit for it; you thought only of yourself, and did that which you liked best!'

'That is a nice sort of thing to tell a man!' he interrupted with cynical frankness.

'Oh, I do not want to hurt you unnecessarily; but I wish there to be no possible misconception in the matter. Now that I have discovered my error I am not likely to fall into it again; and that you may not have any error at all, I tell you now again, that I have not loved you, do not love you, and never will and never can love you.' Here an idea struck Leonard and he blurted out:

'But do you not think that something is due to me?'

'How do you mean?' Her brows were puckered with real wonder this time.

'For false hopes raised in my mind. If I did not love you before, the very act of proposing to me has made me love you; and now I love you so well that I cannot live without you!' In his genuine agitation he was starting up, when the sight of her hand laid upon the gong arrested him. She laughed as she said:

'I thought that the privilege of changing one's mind was a female prerogative! Besides, I have done already something to make reparation to you for the wrong of . . . of—I may put it fairly, as the suggestion is your own—of not having treated you as a woman!'

'Damn!'

'As you observe so gracefully, it is annoying to have one's own silly words come back at one, boomerang fashion. I made up my mind to do something for you; to pay off your debts.' This so exasperated him that he said out brutally:

'No thanks to you for that! As I had to put up with the patronage and the lecturings, and the eyeglass of that infernal old woman, I don't intend . . . '

Stephen stood up, her hand upon the gong:

'Mr. Everard, if you do not remember that you are in my drawing-room, and speaking of my dear and respected aunt, I shall not detain you longer!'

He sat down at once, saying surlily:

'I beg your pardon. I forgot. You make me so wild that—that . . . ' He chewed the ends of his moustache angrily. She resumed her seat, taking her hand from the gong. Without further pause she continued:

'Quite right! It has been Miss Rowly who paid your debts. At first I had promised myself the pleasure; but from something in your speech and manner she thought it better that such an act should not be done by a woman in my position to a man in yours. It might, if made public, have created quite a wrong impression in the minds of many of our friends.'

There was something like a snort from Leonard. She ignored it:

'So she paid the money herself out of her own fortune. And, indeed, I must say that you do not seem to have treated her with much gratitude.'

'What did I say or do that put you off doing the thing yourself?'

'I shall answer it frankly: It was because you manifested, several times, in a manner there was no mistaking, both by words and deeds, an intention of levying blackmail on me by using your knowledge of my ridiculous, unmaidenly act. No one can despise, or deplore, or condemn that act more than I do; so that rather than yield a single point to you, I am, if necessary, ready to face the odium which the public knowledge of it might produce. What I had intended to do for you in the way of compensation for false hopes raised to you by that act has now been done. That it was done by my aunt on my behalf, and not by me, matters to you no more than it did to your creditors, who, when they received the money, made no complaint of injury to their feelings on that account.

'Now, when you think the whole matter over in quietness, you will, knowing that I am ready at any time to face if necessary the unpleasant publicity, be able to estimate what damage you would do to yourself by any exposé. It seems to me that you would come out of it pretty badly all round. That, however, is not my affair; it entirely rests with yourself. I think I know how women would regard it. I dare say you best know how men would look at it; and at you!'

Leonard knew already how the only man who knew of it had taken it, and the knowledge did not reassure him!

'You jade! You infernal, devilish, cruel, smooth-tongued jade!' He stood as bespoke. She stood too, and stood watching him with her hand on the gong. After a pause of a couple of seconds she said gravely:

'One other thing I should wish to say, and I mean it. Understand me clearly, that I mean it! You must not come again into my grounds without my special permission. I shall not allow my liberty to be taken away, or restricted, by you. If there be need at any time to come to the house, come in ceremonious fashion, by the avenues which are used by others. You can always speak to me in public, or socially, in the most friendly manner;

as I shall hope to be able to speak to you. But you must never transgress the ordinary rules of decorum. If you do, I shall have to take, for my own protection, another course. I know you now! I am willing to blot out the past; but it must be the whole past that is wiped out!'

She stood facing him; and as he looked at her clear-cut aquiline face, her steady eyes, her resolute mouth, her carriage, masterly in its self-possessed poise, he saw that there was no further hope for him. There was no love and no fear.

'You devil!' he hissed.

She struck the gong; her aunt entered the room.

'Oh, is that you, Auntie? Mr. Everard has finished his business with me!' Then to the servant, who had entered after Miss Rowly:

'Mr. Everard would like his carriage. By the way,' she added, turning to him in a friendly way as an afterthought, 'will you not stay, Mr. Everard, and take lunch with us? My aunt has been rather moping lately; I am sure your presence would cheer her up.'

'Yes, do stay, Mr. Everard!' added Miss Rowly placidly. 'It would make a pleasant hour for us all.'

Leonard, with a great effort, said with conventional politeness:

'Thanks, awfully! But I promised my father to be home for lunch!' and he withdrew to the door which the servant held open.

He went out filled with anger and despair, and, sad for him, with a fierce, overmastering desire—love he called it—for the clever, proud, imperious beauty who had so outmatched and crushed him.

That beautiful red head, which he had at first so despised, was henceforth to blaze in his dreams.

CHAPTER-23

The Man

On the *Scoriac* Harold An Wolf, now John Robinson, kept aloof from every one. He did not make any acquaintances, did not try to. Some of those at table with him, being ladies and gentlemen, now and again made a polite remark; to which he answered with equal politeness. Being what he was he could not willingly offend any one; and there was nothing in his manner to repel any kindly overture to acquaintance. But this was the full length his acquaintanceship went; so he gradually felt himself practically alone. This was just what he wished; he sat all day silent and alone, or else walked up and down the great deck that ran from stem to stern, still always alone. As there were no second-class or steerage passengers on the *Scoriac*, there were no deck restraints, and so there was ample room for individual solitude. The travellers, however, were a sociable lot, and a general feeling of friendliness was abroad. The first four days of the journey were ideally fine, and life was a joy. The great ship, with bilge keels, was as steady as a rock.

Among the other passengers was an American family consisting of Andrew Stonehouse, the great ironmaster and contractor, with his wife and little daughter.

Stonehouse was a remarkable man in his way, a typical product of the Anglo-Saxon under American conditions. He had started in young manhood with nothing but a good education, due in chief to his own industry and his having taken advantage to the full of such opportunities as life had afforded to him. By unremitting work he had at thirty achieved a great fortune, which had, however; been up to then entirely invested and involved in his businesses. With, however, the colossal plant at his disposal, and by aid of the fine character he had won for honesty and good work, he was able within the next ten years to pile up a fortune vast even in a nation where multi-millionaires are scattered freely. Then he had married, wisely and happily. But no child had come to crown the happiness of the pair who so loved each other till a good many years had come and gone. Then, when the hope of issue had almost passed away, a little daughter came. Naturally the child was idolised by her parents, and thereafter every step taken by either was with an eye to her good. When the rigour of winter and the heat of summer told on the child in a way which the more hardy parents had never felt, she was whirled away to some place with more promising conditions of health and happiness. When the doctors hinted that an ocean voyage and a winter in Italy would be good, those too were duly undertaken. And now, the child being in perfect health, the family was returning before the weather should get too hot to spend the summer at their châlet amongst the great pines on the slopes of Mount Ranier. Like the others on board, Mr. and Mrs. Stonehouse had proffered travellers' civilities to the sad, lonely young man. As to the others, he had shown thanks for their gracious courtesy; but friendship, as in other cases, did not advance. The Stonehouses were not in any way chagrined; their lives were too happy and too full for them to take needless offence. They respected the young man's manifest desire for privacy; and there, so far as they were concerned, the matter rested.

But this did not suit the child. Pearl was a sweet little thing, a real blue-eyed, golden-haired little fairy, full of loving-kindness. All the mother-instinct in her, and even at six a woman-child can be a mother—theoretically, went out towards the huge, lonely, sad, silent young man. She insisted on friendship with him; insisted shamelessly, with the natural inclination of innocence which rises high above shame. Even the half-hearted protests of the mother, who loved to see the child happy, did not deter her; after the second occasion of Pearl's seeking him, as she persisted, Harold could but remonstrate with the mother in turn; the ease of the gentle lady and the happiness of her child were more or less at stake. When Mrs. Stonehouse would say:

'There, darling! You must be careful not to annoy the gentleman,' Pearl would turn a rosy all-commanding face to her and answer:

'But, mother, I want him to play with me. You must play with me!' Then, as the mother would look at him, he would say quickly, and with genuine heartiness too:

'Oh please, madam, do let her play with me! Come, Pearl, shall you ride a cock-horse or go to market the way the gentleman rides?' Then the child would spring on his knee with a cry of delight, and their games began.

The presence of the child and her loving ways were unutterably sweet to Harold; but his pleasure was always followed by a pain that rent him as he thought of that other little one, now so far away, and of those times that seemed so long since gone.

But the child never relaxed in her efforts to please; and in the long hours of the sea voyage the friendship between her and the man grew, and grew. He was the biggest and strongest and therefore most lovely thing on board the ship, and that sufficed her. As for him, the child manifestly loved and trusted him, and that was all-in-all to his weary, desolate heart.

The fifth day out the weather began to change; the waves grew more and more mountainous as the day wore on and the ship advanced west. Not even the great bulk and weight of the ship, which ordinarily drove through the seas without pitch or roll, were proof against waves so gigantic. Then the wind grew fiercer and fiercer, coming in roaring squalls from the south-west. Most of those on board were alarmed, for the great waves were dreadful to see; and the sound of the wind was a trumpet-call to fear.

The sick stayed in their cabins; the rest found an interest if not a pleasure on deck. Among the latter were the Stonehouses, who were old travellers. Even Pearl had already had more sea-voyages than fall to most people in their lives. As for Harold, the storm seemed to come quite naturally to him and he paced the deck like a ship-master.

It was fortunate for the passengers that most of them had at this period of the voyage got their sea legs; otherwise walking on the slippery deck, that seemed to heave as the rolling of the vessel threw its slopes up or down, would have been impossible. Pearl was, like most children, pretty sure-footed; holding fast to Harold's hand she managed to move about ceaselessly. She absolutely refused to go with any one else. When her mother said that she had better sit still she answered:

'But, mother, I am quite safe with The Man!' 'The Man' was the name she had given Harold, and by which she always now spoke of him. They had had a good many turns together, and Harold had, with the captain's permission, taken her up on the bridge and showed her how to look out over the 'dodger' without the wind hurting her eyes. Then came the welcome beef-tea hour, and all who had come on deck were cheered and warmed with the hot soup. Pearl went below, and Harold, in the shelter of the charthouse, together with a good many others, looked out over the wild sea.

Harold, despite the wild turmoil of winds and seas around him, which usually lifted his spirits, was sad, feeling lonely and wretched; he was suffering from the recoil of his little friend's charming presence. Pearl came on deck again looking for him. He did not see her, and the child, seeing an opening for a new game, avoided both her father and mother, who also stood in the shelter of the charthouse, and ran round behind it on the weather side, calling a loud 'Boo!' to attract Harold's attention as she ran.

A few seconds later the *Scoriac* put her nose into a coming wave at just the angle which makes for the full exercise of the opposing forces. The great wave seemed to strike the ship on the port quarter like a giant hammer; and for an instant she stood still, trembling. Then the top of the wave seemed to leap up and deluge her. The wind took the flying water and threw it high in volumes of broken spray, which swept not only the deck but the rigging as high as the top of the funnels. The child saw the mass of water coming, and shrieking flew round the port side of the charthouse. But just as she turned down the open space between it and the funnel the vessel rolled to starboard. At the same moment came a puff of wind of greater violence than ever. The child, calling out, half in simulated half in real fear, flew down the slope. As she did so the gale took her, and in an instant whirled her, almost touching her mother, over the rail into the sea.

Mrs. Stonehouse shrieked and sprang forward as though to follow her child. She was held back by the strong arm of her husband. They both slipped on the sloping deck and fell together into the scuppers. There was a chorus of screams from all the women present. Harold, with an instinctive understanding of the dangers yet to be encountered, seized a red tam-o'-shanter from the head of a young girl who stood near.

Her exclamation of surprise was drowned in the fearful cry 'Man overboard!' and all rushed down to the rail and saw Harold, as he emerged from the water, pull the red cap over his head and then swim desperately towards the child, whose golden hair was spread on the rising wave.

The instant after Pearl's being swept overboard might be seen the splendid discipline of a well-ordered ship. Every man to his post, and every man with a knowledge of his duty. The First Officer called to the Quartermaster at the wheel in a voice which cut through the gale like a trumpet:

'Hard a port! Hard!'

The stern of the great ship swung away to port in time to clear the floating child from the whirling screw, which would have cut her to pieces in an instant. Then the Officer after tearing the engine-room signal to 'Starboard engine full speed astern,' ran for the lifebuoy hanging at the starboard end of the bridge. This he hurled far into the sea. As it fell the attached rope dragged with it the signal, which so soon as it reaches water bursts into smoke and flame—signal by day and night. This done, and it had all been done in a couple of seconds, he worked the electric switch of the syren, which screamed out quickly once, twice, thrice. This is the dread sound which means 'man overboard,' and draws to his post every man on the ship, waking or sleeping.

The Captain was now on the bridge and in command, and the First Officer, freed from his duty there, ran to the emergency boat, swung out on its davits on the port side.

All this time, though only numbered by seconds, the *Scoriac* was turning hard to starboard, making a great figure of eight; for it is quicker to turn one of these great sea monsters round than to stop her in mid career. The aim of her Captain in such cases is to bring her back to the weather side of the floating buoy before launching the boat.

On deck the anguish of the child's parents was pitiable. Close to the rail, with her husband's arms holding her tight to it, the distressed mother leaned out; but always moving so that she was at the nearest point of the ship to her child. As the ship passed on it became more difficult to see the heads. In the greater distance they seemed to be quite close together. All at once, just as a great wave which had hidden them in the farther trough passed on, the mother screamed out:

'She's sinking! she's sinking! Oh, God! Oh, God!' and she fell on her knees, her horrified eyes, set in a face of ashen grey, looking out between the rails.

But at the instant all eyes saw the man's figure rise in the water as he began to dive. There was a hush which seemed deadly; the onlookers feared to draw breath. And then the mother's heart leaped and her cry rang out again as two heads rose together in the waste of sea:

'He has her! He has her! He has her! Oh, thank God! Thank God!' and for a single instant she hid her face in her hands.

Then when the fierce 'hurrah' of all on board had been hushed in expectation, the comments broke forth. Most of the passengers had by this time got glasses of one kind or another.

'See! He's putting the cap on the child's head. He's a cool one that. Fancy him thinking of a red cap at such a time!'

'Ay! we could see that cap, when it might be we couldn't see anything else.'

'Look!' this from an old sailor standing by his boat, 'how he's raisin' in the water. He's keeping his body between her an' the spindrift till the squall has passed. That would choke them both in a wind like this if he didn't know how to guard against it. He's all right; he is! The little maid is safe wi' him.'

'Oh, bless you! Bless you for those words,' said the mother, turning towards him. 'At this moment the Second Officer, who had run down from the bridge, touched Mr. Stonehouse on the shoulder.

'The captain asked me to tell you, sir, that you and Mrs. Stonehouse had better come to him on the bridge. You'll see better from there.'

They both hurried up, and the mother again peered out with fixed eyes. The Captain tried to comfort her; laying his strong hand on her shoulder, he said:

'There, there! Take comfort, ma'am. She is in the hands of God! All that mortal man can do is being done. And she is safer with that gallant young giant than she could be with any other man on the ship. Look, how he is protecting her! Why he knows that all that can be done is being done. He is waiting for us to get to him, and is saving himself for it. Any other man who didn't know so much about swimming as he does would try to reach the lifebuoy; and would choke the two of them with the spindrift in the trying. Mind how he took the red cap to help us see them. He's a fine lad that; a gallant lad!'

CHAPTER-24

From The Deeps

Presently the Captain handed Mrs. Stonehouse a pair of binoculars. For an instant she looked through them, then handed them back and continued gazing out to where the two heads appeared—when they did appear on the crest of the waves like pin-heads. The Captain said half to himself and half to the father:

'Mother's eyes! Mother's eyes!' and the father understood.

As the ship swept back to the rescue, her funnels sending out huge volumes of smoke which the gale beat down on the sea to leeward, the excitement grew tenser and tenser. Men dared hardly breathe; women wept and clasped their hands convulsively as they prayed. In the emergency boat the men sat like statues, their oars upright, ready for instant use. The officer stood with the falls in his hand ready to lower away.

When opposite the lifebuoy, and about a furlong from Harold and Pearl, the Captain gave the signal 'Stop,' and then a second later: 'Full speed astern.'

'Ready, men! Steady!' As the coming wave slipping under the ship began to rise up her side, the officer freed the falls and the boat sank softly into the lifting sea.

Instantly the oars struck the water, and as the men bent to them a cheer rang out.

* * * * *

Harold and Pearl heard, and the man turning his head for a moment saw that the ship was close at hand, gradually drifting down to the weather side of them. He raised the child in his arms, saying:

'Now, Pearl, wave your hand to mother and say, hurrah!' The child, fired into fresh hope, waved her tiny hand and cried 'Hurrah! Hurrah!' The sound could not reach the mother's ears; but she saw, and her heart leaped. She too waved her hand, but she uttered no sound. The sweet high voice of the child crept over the water to the ears of the men in the boat, and seemed to fire their arms with renewed strength.

A few more strokes brought them close, Harold with a last effort raised the child in his arms as the boat drove down on them. The boatswain leaning over the bow grabbed the child, and with one sweep of his strong arm took her into the boat. The bow oarsman caught Harold by the wrist. The way of the boat took him for a moment under water; but the next man; pulling his oar across the boat, stooped over and caught him by the collar, and clung fast. A few seconds more and he was hauled abroad. A wild cheer from all on the *Scoriac* came, sweeping down on the wind.

When once the boat's head had been turned towards the ship, and the oars had bent again to their work, they came soon within shelter. When they had got close enough ropes were thrown out, caught and made fast; and then came down one of the bowlines which the seamen held ready along the rail of the lower deck. This was seized by the boatswain, who placed it round him under his armpits. Then, standing with the child in his arms he made ready to be pulled up. Pearl held out her arms to Harold, crying in fear:

'No, no, let The Man take me! I want to go with The Man!' He said quietly so as not to frighten her:

'No, no, dear! Go with him! He can do this better than I can!' So she clung quietly to the seaman, holding her face pressed close against his shoulder. As the men above pulled at the rope, keeping it as far as possible from the side of the vessel, the boatswain fended himself off with his feet. In a few seconds he was seized by eager hands and pulled over the rail, tenderly holding and guarding the child all the while. In an instant she was in the arms of her mother, who had thrown herself upon her knees and pressed her close to her loving heart. The child put her little arms around her neck and clung to her. Then looking up and seeing the grey pallor of her face, which even her great joy could not in a moment efface, she stroked it and said:

'Poor mother! Poor mother! And now I have made you all wet!' Then, feeling her father's hand on her head she turned and leaped into his arms, where he held her close.

Harold was the next to ascend. He came amid a regular tempest of cheers, the seamen joining with the passengers. The officers, led by the Captain waving his cap from the bridge, joined in the paean.

The boat was cast loose. An instant after the engine bells tinkled: 'Full speed ahead.'

Mrs. Stonehouse had no eyes but for her child, except for one other. When Harold leaped down from the rail she rushed at him, all those around instinctively making way for her. She flung her arms around him and kissed him, and then before he could stop her sank to her knees at his feet, and taking his hand kissed it. Harold was embarrassed beyond all thinking. He tried to take away his hand, but she clung tight to it.

'No, no!' she cried. 'You saved my child!'

Harold was a gentleman and a kindly one. He said no word till she had risen, still holding his hand, when he said quietly:

'There! there! Don't cry. I was only too happy to be of service. Any other man on board would have done the same. I was the nearest, and therefore had to be first. That was all!'

Mr. Stonehouse came to him and said as he grasped Harold's hand so hard that his fingers ached:

'I cannot thank you as I would. But you are a man and will understand. God be good to you as you have been good to my child; and to her mother and myself!' As he turned away Pearl, who had now been holding close to her mother's hand, sprang to him holding up her arms. He raised her up and kissed her. Then he placed her back in her mother's arms.

All at once she broke down as the recollection of danger swept back upon her. 'Oh, Mother! Mother!' she cried, with a long, low wail, which touched every one of her hearers to the heart's core.

'The hot blankets are all ready. Come, there is not a moment to be lost. I'll be with you when I have seen the men attended to!'

So the mother, holding her in her arms and steadied by two seamen lest she should slip on the wet and slippery deck, took the child below.

Harold was taken by another set of men, who rubbed him down till he glowed, and poured hot brandy and water into him till he had to almost use force against the superabundance of their friendly ministrations.

For the remainder of that day a sort of solemn gladness ruled on the *Scoriac*. The Stonehouse family remained in their suite, content in glad thankfulness to be with Pearl, who lay well covered up on the sofa sleeping off the effects of the excitement and the immersion, and the result of the potation which the Doctor had forced upon her. Harold was simply shy, and objecting to the publicity which he felt to be his fate, remained in his cabin till the trumpet had blown the dinner call.

CHAPTER-25

A Little Child Shall Lead

After dinner Harold went back to his cabin; locking himself in, he lay down on the sofa. The gloom of his great sorrow was heavy on him; the reaction from the excitement of the morning had come.

He was recalled to himself by a gentle tapping. Unlocking and opening the door he saw Mr. Stonehouse, who said with trouble in his voice:

'I came to you on account of my little child.' There he stopped with a break in his voice. Harold, with intent to set his mind at ease and to stave off further expressions of gratitude, replied:

'Oh, pray don't say anything. I am only too glad that I was privileged to be of service. I only trust that the dear little girl is no worse for her—her adventure!'

'That is why I am here,' said the father quickly. 'My wife and I are loth to trouble you. But the poor little thing has worked herself into a paroxysm of fright and is calling for you. We have tried in vain to comfort or reassure her. She will not be satisfied without you. She keeps calling on "The Man" to come and help her. I am loth to put you to further strain after all you have gone through to-day; but if you would come—' Harold was already in the passage as he spoke:

'Of course I'm coming. If I can in any way help it is both a pleasure and a duty to be with her.' Turning to the father he added:

'She is indeed a very sweet and good child. I shall never forget how she bore herself whilst we waited for aid to come.'

'You must tell her mother and me all about it,' said the father; much moved.

When they came close to the Stonehouses' suite of rooms they heard Pearl's voice rising with a pitiful note of fear:

'Where is The Man? Oh! where is The Man? Why doesn't he come to me? He can save me! I want to be with The Man!' When the door opened and she saw him she gave shriek of delight, and springing from the arms of her mother fairly leaped into Harold's arms which were outstretched to receive her. She clung to him and kissed him again and again, rubbing her little hands all over his face as though to prove to herself that he was real and not a dream. Then with a sigh she laid her head on his breast, the reaction of sleep coming all at once to her. With a gesture of silence Harold sat down, holding the child in his arms. Her mother laid a thick shawl over and sat down close to Harold. Mr. Stonehouse stood quiet in the doorway with the child's nurse peering anxiously over his shoulder.

After a little while, when he thought she was asleep, Harold rose and began to place her gently in the bunk. But the moment he did so she waked with a scream. The fright in her eyes was terrible. She clung to him, moaning and crying out between her sobs:

'Don't leave me! Don't leave me! Don't leave me!' Harold was much moved and held the little thing tight in his strong arms, saying to her:

'No darling! I shan't leave you! Look in my eyes, dear, and I will promise you, and then you will be happy. Won't you?'

She looked quickly up in his face. Then she kissed him lovingly, and rested her head, but not sleepily this time, on his breast said:

'Yes! I'm not afraid now! I'm going to stay with The Man!' Presently Mrs. Stonehouse, who had been thinking of ways and means, and of the comfort of the strange man who had been so good to her child, said:

'You will sleep with mother to-night, darling. Mr. . . . The Man,' she said this with an appealing look of apology to Harold, 'The Man will stay by you till you are asleep . . . ' But she interrupted, not fretfully or argumentatively, but with a settled air of content:

'No! I'm going to sleep with The Man!'

'But, dear one,' the mother expostulated, 'The Man will want sleep too.'

'All right, mother. He can sleep too. I'll be very good and lie quite quiet; but oh! mother, I can't sleep unless his arms are round me. I'm afraid if they're not the sea will get me!' and she clung closer to Harold, tightening her arms round his neck.

'You will not mind?' asked Mrs. Stonehouse timidly to Harold; and, seeing acquiescence in his face, added in a burst of tearful gratitude:

'Oh! you are good to her to us all!'

'Hush!' Harold said quietly. Then he said to Pearl, in a cheerful matter-of-fact way which carried conviction to the child's mind:

'Now, darling, it is time for all good little girls to be asleep, especially when they have had an—an interesting day. You wait here till I put my pyjamas on, and then I'll come back for you. And mother and father shall come and see you nicely tucked in!'

'Don't be long!' the child anxiously called after him as he hurried away. Even trust can have its doubts.

In a few minutes Harold was back, in pyjamas and slipper and a dressing-gown. Pearl, already wrapped in a warm shawl by her mother, held out her arms to Harold, who lifted her.

The Stonehouses' suite of rooms was close to the top of the companion-way, and as Harold's stateroom was on the saloon deck, the little procession had, much to the man's concern, run the gauntlet of the thong of passengers whom the bad weather had kept indoors. When he came out of the day cabin carrying the child there was a rush of all the women to make much of the little girl. They were all very kind and no troublesome; their interest was natural enough, and Harold stopped whilst they petted the little thing.

The little procession followed. Mr. and Mrs. Stonehouse coming next, and last the nurse, who manifested a phase of the anxiety of a hen who sees her foster ducklings waddling toward a pond.

When Harold was in his bunk the little maid was brought in.

When they had all gone and the cabin was dark, save for the gleam from the nightlight which the careful mother had placed out of sight in the basin at the foot of the bunk, Harold lay a long time in a negative state, if such be possible, in so far as thought was concerned.

Presently he became conscious of a movement of the child his arms; a shuddering movement, and a sort of smothered groan. The little thing was living over again in sleep the perils and fears of the day. Instinctively she put up her hands and felt the a round her. Then with a sigh clasped her arms round his neck, and with a peaceful look laid her head upon his breast. Even through the gates of sleep her instinct had recognised and realised protection.

And then this trust of a little child brought back the man to his nobler self. Once again came back to him that love which he had had, and which he knew now that he had never lost, for the little child that he had seen grow into full womanhood; whose image must dwell in his heart of hearts for evermore.

The long night's sleep quite restored Pearl. She woke fairly early and without any recurrence of fear. At first she lay still, fearing she would wake The Man, but finding that he was awake—he had not slept a wink all night—she kissed him and then scrambled out of bed.

It was still early morning, but early hours rule on shipland. Harold rang for the steward, and when the man came he told him to tell Mr. Stonehouse that the child was awake. His delight when he found the child unfrightened looking out of the port was unbounded.

CHAPTER-26

A Noble Offer

That day Harold passed in unutterable gloom. The reaction was strong on him; and all his woe, his bitter remembrance of the past and his desolation for the future, were with him unceasingly.

In the dusk of the evening he wandered out to his favourite spot, the cable-tank on top of the aft wheelhouse. Here he had been all alone, and his loneliness had the added advantage that from the isolated elevation he could see if anyone approached. He had been out there during the day, and the Captain, who had noticed his habit had had rigged up a canvas dodger on the rail on the weather side. When he sat down on the coiled hawsers in the tank he was both secluded and sheltered. In this peaceful corner his thoughts ran freely and in sympathy with the turmoil of wind and wave.

How unfair it all was! Why had he been singled out for such misery? What gleam of hope or comfort was left to his miserable life since he had heard the words of Stephen; those dreadful words which had shattered in an instant all the cherished hopes of his life. Too well he remembered the tone and look of scorn with which the horrible truths had been conveyed to him. In his inmost soul he accepted them as truths; Stephen's soul had framed them and Stephen's lips had sent them forth.

From his position behind the screen he did not see the approaching figure of Mr. Stonehouse, and was astonished when he saw his head rise above the edge of the tank as he climbed the straight Jacob's ladder behind the wheelhouse. The elder man paused as he saw him and said in an apologetic way:

'Will you forgive my intruding on your privacy? I wanted to speak to you alone; and as I saw you come here a while ago I thought it would be a good opportunity.' Harold was rising as he spoke.

'By all means. This place is common property. But all the same I am honoured in your seeking me.' The poor fellow wished to be genial; but despite his efforts there was a strange formality in the expression of his words. The elder man understood, and said as he hurried forward and sank beside him:

'Pray don't stir! Why, what a cosy corner this is. I don't believe at this moment there is such peace in the ship!'

Once again the bitterness of Harold's heart broke out in sudden words:

'I hope not! There is no soul on board to whom I could wish such evil!' The old man said as he laid his hand softly on the other's shoulder:

'God help you, my poor boy, if such pain is in your heart!' Mr. Stonehouse looked out at the sea, at last turning his face to him again he spoke:

'If you feel that I intrude on you I earnestly ask you to forgive me; but I think that the years between your age and mine as well as my feeling towards the great obligation which I owe you will plead for excuse. There is something I would like to say to you, sir; but I suppose I must not without your permission. May I have it?'

'If you wish, sir. I can at least hear it.'

The old man bowed and went on:

'I could not but notice that you have some great grief bearing upon you; and from one thing or another—I can tell you the data if you wish me to do so—I have come to the conclusion that you are leaving your native land because of it.' Here Harold, wakened to amazement by the readiness with which his secret had been divined, said quickly, rather as an exclamation than interrogation:

'How on earth did you know that!' His companion, taking it as a query, answered:

'Sir, at your age and with your strength life should be a joy; and yet you are sad: Companionship should be a pleasure; yet you prefer solitude. That you are brave and unselfish I know; I have reason, thank God! to know it. That you are kindly and tolerant is apparent from your bearing to my little child this morning; as well as your goodness of last night, the remembrance of which her mother and I will bear to our graves; and to me now. I have not lived all these years without having had trouble in my own heart; and although the happiness of late years has made it dim, my gratitude to you who are so sad brings it all back to me.' He bowed, and Harold, wishing to avoid speaking of his sorrow, said:

'You are quite right so far as I have a sorrow; and it is because of it I have turned my back on home. Let it rest at that!' His companion bowed gravely and went on.

‘I take it that you are going to begin life afresh in the new country. In such case I have a proposition to make. I have a large business; a business so large that I am unable to manage it all myself. I was intending that when I arrived at home I would set about finding a partner. The man I want is not an ordinary man. He must have brains and strength and daring.’ He paused. Harold felt what was coming, but realised, as he jumped at the conclusion, that it would not do for him to take for granted that he was the man sought. He waited; Mr. Stonehouse went on:

‘As to brains, I am prepared to take the existence of such on my own judgment. I have been reading men, and in this aspect specially, all my life. The man I have thought of has brains. I am satisfied of that, without proof. I have proof of the other qualities.’ He paused again; as Harold said nothing he continued in a manner ill at ease:

‘My difficulty is to make the proposal to the man I want. It is so difficult to talk business to a man to whom you under great obligation; to whom you owe everything. He might take a friendly overture ill.’ There was but one thing to be said and Harold said it. His heart warmed to the kindly old man and he wished to spare him pain; even if he could not accept him proposition:

‘He couldn’t take it ill; unless he was an awful bounder.’

‘It was you I thought of!’

‘I thought so much, sir;’ said Harold after a pause, ‘and I thank you earnestly and honestly. But it is impossible.’

‘Oh, my dear sir!’ said the other, chagrined as well as surprised. ‘Think again! It is really worth your while to think of it, no matter what your ultimate decision may be!’

Harold shook his head. There was a long silence. The old man wished to give his companion time to think; and indeed he thought that Harold was weighing the proposition in his mind. As for Harold, he was thinking how best he could make his absolute refusal inoffensive. He must, he felt, give some reason; and his thoughts were bent on how much of the truth he could safely give without endangering his secret. Therefore he spoke at last in general terms:

‘I can only ask you, sir, to bear with me and to believe that I am very truly and sincerely grateful to you for your trust. But the fact is, I cannot go anywhere amongst people. Of course you understand that I am speaking in confidence; to you alone and to none other?’

‘Absolutely!’ said Mr. Stonehouse gravely. Harold went on:

'I must be alone. I can only bear to see people on this ship because it is a necessary way to solitude.'

'You "cannot go anywhere amongst people"! Pardon me. I don't wish to be unduly inquisitive; but on my word I fail to understand!' Harold was in a great difficulty. Common courtesy alone forbade that he should leave the matter where it was; and in addition both the magnificently generous offer which had been made to him, and the way in which accident had thrown him to such close intimacy with Pearl's family, required that he should be at least fairly frank. At last in a sort of cold desperation he said:

'I cannot meet anyone . . . There it something that happened . . . Something I did . . . Nothing can make it right . . . All I can do is to lose myself in the wildest, grimmest, wilderness in the world; and fight my pain . . . my shame . . . !'

A long silence. Then the old man's voice came clear and sweet, something like music, in the shelter from the storm:

'But perhaps time may mend things. God is very good . . . !' Harold answered out of the bitterness of his heart. He felt that his words were laden with an anger which he did not feel, but he did not see his way to alter them:

'Nothing can mend this thing! It is at the farthest point of evil; and there is no going on or coming back. Nothing can wipe out what is done; what is past!'

Again silence, and again the strong, gentle voice:

'God can do much! Oh my dear young friend, you who have been such a friend to me and mine, think of this.'

'God Himself can do nothing here! It is done! And that is the end!' He turned his head; it was all he could do to keep from groaning. The old man's voice vibrated with earnest conviction as he spoke:

'You are young and strong and brave! Your heart is noble! You can think quickly in moments of peril; therefore your brain is sound and alert. Now, may I ask you a favour? it is not much. Only that you will listen, without interruption, to what, if I have your permission, I am going to say. Do not ask me anything; do not deny; do not interrupt! Only listen! May I ask this?'

'By all means! It is not much!' he almost felt like smiling as he spoke. Mr. Stonehouse, after a short pause, as if arranging his thoughts, spoke:

'Let me tell you what I am. I began life with nothing but a fair education such as all our American boys get. But from a good mother I got an idea that to be honest was the best of all things; from a strenuous father, who, however, could not do well for himself, I learned application to work and how best to use and exercise such powers as were in me. From the start things prospered with me. Men who knew me trusted me; some came with offers to share in my enterprise. Thus I had command of what capital I could use; I was able to undertake great works and to carry them through. Fortune kept growing and growing; for as I got wealthier I found newer and larger and more productive uses for my money. And in all my work I can say before God I never willingly wronged any man. I am proud to be able to say that my name stands good wherever it has been used. It may seem egotistical that I say such things of myself. It may seem bad taste; but I speak because I have a motive in so doing. I want you to understand at the outset that in my own country, wherever I am known and in my own work, my name is a strength.'

He paused a while. Harold sat still; he knew that such man would not, could not, speak in such a way without a strong motive; and to learn that motive he waited.

'When you were in the water making what headway you could in that awful sea—when my little child's life hung in the balance, and the anguish of my wife's heart nearly tore my heart in two, I said to myself, "If we had a son I should wish him to be like that." I meant it then, and I mean it now! Come to me as you are! Faults, and past, and all. Forget the past! Whatever it was we will together try to wipe it out. Much may be done in restoring where there has been any wrong-doing. Take my name as your own. It will protect you from the result of what ever has been, and give you an opportunity to find your place again. You are not bad in heart I know. Whatever you have done has not been from base motives. Few of us are spotless as to facts. You and I will show ourselves—for unless God wills to the opposite we shall confide in none other—that a strong, brave man may win back all that was lost. Let me call you by my name and hold you as the son of my heart; and it will be a joy and pleasure to my declining years.'

As he had spoken, Harold's thought's had at first followed in some wonderment. But gradually, as his noble purpose unfolded, based as it was on a misconception as to the misdoing of which he himself had spoken, he had been almost stricken dumb. At the first realisation of what was intended he could not have spoken had he tried; but at the end he had regained his thoughts and his voice. There was still wonderment in it, as realising from the long pause that the old man had completed his suggestion, he spoke:

'If I understand aright you are offering me your name! Offering to share your honour with me. With me, whom, if again I understand, you take as having committed some crime?'

'I inferred from what you said and from your sadness, your desire to shun your kind, that there was, if not a crime, some fault which needed expiation.'

'But your honour, sir; your honour!' There was a proud look in the old man's eyes as he said quietly:

'It was my desire, is my desire, to share with you what I have that is best; and that, I take it, is not the least valuable of my possessions, such as they are! And why not? You have given to me all that makes life sweet; without which it would be unbearable. That child who came to my wife and me when I was old and she had passed her youth is all in all to us both. Had your strength and courage been for barter in the moments when my child was quivering between life and death, I would have cheerfully purchased them with not half but all! Sir, I should have given my soul! I can say this now, for gratitude is above all barter; and surely it is allowed to a father to show gratitude for the life of his child!'

This great-hearted generosity touched Harold to the quick. He could hardly speak for a few minutes. Then instinctively grasping the old man's hand he said:

'You overwhelm me. Such noble trust and generosity as you have shown me demands a return of trust. But I must think! Will you remain here and let me return to you in a little while?'

He rose quickly and slipped down the iron ladder, passing into the darkness and the mist and the flying spray.

CHAPTER-27
Age's Wisdom

Harold went to and fro on the deserted deck. All at once the course he had to pursue opened out before him. He was aware that what the noble-minded old man offered him was fortune, great fortune in any part of the world. He would have to be refused, but the refusal should be gently done. He, believing that the other had done something very wrong, had still offered to share with him his name, his honour. Such confidence demanded full confidence in return; the unwritten laws which governed the men amongst whom he had been brought up required it.

And the shape that confidence should take? He must first disabuse his new friend's mind of criminal or unworthy cause for his going away. For the sake of his own name and that of his dead father that should be done. Then he would have to suggest the real cause . . . He would in this have to trust Mr. Stonehouse's honour for secrecy. But he was worthy of trust. He would, of course, give no name, no clue; but he would put things generally in a way that he could understand.

When his mind was so far made up he wanted to finish the matter, so he turned to the wheelhouse and climbed the ladder again. It was not till he sat in the shelter by his companion that he became aware that he had become wet with the spray. The old man wishing to help him in his embarrassment said:

'Well?' Harold began at once; the straightforward habit of his life stood to him now:

'Let me say first, sir, what will I know give you pleasure.' The old man extended his hand; he had been hoping for acceptance, and this seemed like it. Harold laid his hand on it for an instant only, and then raised it as if to say 'Wait':

'You have been so good to me, so nobly generous in your wishes that I feel I owe you a certain confidence. But as it concerns not myself alone I will ask that it be kept a secret between us two. Not to be told to any other; not even your wife!'

'I will hold your secret sacred. Even from my wife; the first secret I shall have ever kept from her.'

'First, then, let me say, and this is what I know will rejoice you, that I am not leaving home and country because of any crime I have committed; not from any offence against God or man, or law. Thank God! I am free from such. I have always tried to live uprightly . . . ' Here a burst of pain overcame him, and with a dry sob he added: 'And that is what makes the terrible unfairness of it all!'

The old man laid a kindly hand on his shoulder and kept it there for a few moments.

'My poor boy! My poor boy!' was all he said. Harold shook himself as if to dislodge the bitter thoughts. Mastering himself he went on:

'There was a lady with whom I was very much thrown in contact since we were children. Her father was my father's friend. My friend too, God knows; for almost with his dying breath he gave sanction to my marrying his daughter, if it should ever be that she should care for me in that way. But he wished me to wait, and, till she was old enough to choose, to leave her free. For she is several years younger than I am; and I am not very old yet—except in heart! All this, you understand, was said in private to me; none other knew it. None knew of it even till this moment when I tell you that such a thing has been.' He paused; the other said:

'Believe me that I value your confidence, beyond all words!' Harold felt already the good effects of being able to speak of his pent-up trouble. Already this freedom from the nightmare loneliness of his own thoughts seemed to be freeing his very soul.

'I honestly kept to his wishes. Before God, I did! No man who loved a woman, honoured her, worshipped her, could have been more scrupulously careful as to leaving her free. What it was to me to so hold myself no one knows; no one ever will know. For I loved her, do love her, with every nerve and fibre of my heart. All our lives we had been friends; and I believed we loved and trusted each other. But . . . but then there came a day when I found by chance that a great trouble threatened her. Not from anything wrong that she had done; but from something perhaps foolish, harmlessly foolish except that she did not know . . . ' He stopped suddenly, fearing he might have said overmuch of Stephen's side of the affair. 'When I came to her aid, however, meaning the best, and as single-minded as a man can be, she misunderstood my words, my meaning, my very coming; and she said things which cannot be unsaid. Things . . . matters were so fixed that I could not explain; and I had to listen. She said things that I did not believe she could have said to me, to anyone. Things that I did not think she could have thought . . . I dare say she was right in some ways. I suppose I bungled in my desire to be unselfish. What she said came to me in new lights upon what I had done . . . But anyhow her statements were such that I felt I could not, should not, remain. My very presence must have been a trouble to her hereafter. There was nothing for it but to come away. There was no place for me! No hope for me! There is none on this side of the grave! . . . For I love her still, more than ever. I honour and worship her still, and ever will, and ever must! . . . I am content to forego my own happiness; but I feel there is a danger to her from what has been. That there is and must be to her unhappiness even from the fact that it was I who was the object of her wrath; and this adds to my woe. Worst of all is . . . the thought and the memory that she should have done so; she who . . . she . . . '

He turned away overcome and hid his face in his hands. The old man sat still; he knew that at such a moment silence is the best form of sympathy. But his heart glowed; the wisdom of his years told him that he had heard as yet of no absolute bar to his friend's ultimate happiness.

'I am rejoiced, my dear boy, at what you tell me of your own conduct. It would have made no difference to me had it been otherwise. But it would have meant a harder and longer climb back to the place you should hold. But it really seems that nothing is so hopeless as you think. Believe me, my dear young friend who are now as a son to my heart, that there will be bright days for you yet . . . ' He paused a moment, but mastering himself went on in a quiet voice:

'I think you are wise to go away. In the solitudes and in danger things that are little in reality will find their true perspective; and things that are worthy will appear in their constant majesty.'

He stood, and laying once again his hand on the young man's shoulder said:

'I recognise that I—that we, for my wife and little girl would be at one with me in my wish, did they know of it, must not keep you from your purpose of fighting out your trouble alone. Every man, as the Scotch proverb says, must "dree his own weird." I shall not, I must not, ask you for any promise; but I trust that if ever you do come back you will make us all glad by seeing you. And remember that what I said of myself and of all I have—all—holds good so long as I shall live!'

Before Harold could reply he had slipped down the ladder and was gone.

During the rest of the voyage, with the exception of one occasion, he did not allude to the subject again by word or implication, and Harold was grateful to him for it.

On the night before Fire Island should be sighted Harold was in the bow of the great ship looking out with eyes in which gleamed no hope. To him came through the darkness Mr. Stonehouse. He heard the footsteps and knew them; so with the instinct of courtesy, knowing that his friend would not intrude on his solitude without purpose, he turned and met him. When the American stood beside him he said, studiously avoiding looking at his companion:

'This is the last night we shall be together, and, if I may, there is one thing I would like to say to you.'

'Say all you like, sir,' said Harold as heartily as he could, 'I am sure it is well meant; and for that at any rate I shall be grateful to you.'

'You will yet be grateful, I think!' he answered gravely. 'When it comes back to you in loneliness and solitude you will, I believe, think it worth being grateful for. I don't mean that you will be grateful to me, but for the thing itself. I speak out of the wisdom of many years. At your time of life the knowledge cannot come from observation. It may my poor boy, come through pain; and if what I think is correct you will even in due time be grateful to the pain which left such golden residuum.' He paused, and Harold grew interested. There was something in the old man's manner which presaged a truth; he, at least, believed it. So the young man listened at first with his ears; and as the other spoke, his heart listened too:

'Young men are apt to think somewhat wrongly of women they love and respect. We are apt to think that such women are of a different clay from ourselves. Nay! that they are not compact of clay at all, but of some faultless, flawless material which the Almighty keeps for such fine work. It is only in middle age that men—except scamps, who learn this bad side of knowledge young—realise that women are human beings like themselves. It may be, you know, that you may have misjudged this young lady! That you have not made sufficient allowance for her youth, her nature, even the circumstances under which she spoke. You have told me that she was in some deep grief or trouble. May it not have been that this in itself unnerved her, distorted her views, aroused her passion till all within and around was tinged with the jaundice of her concern, her humiliation—whatever it was that destroyed for the time that normal self which you had known so long. May it not have been that her bitterest memory even since may be of the speaking of these very words which sent you out into the wide world to hide yourself from men. I have thought, waking and sleeping, of your position ever since you honoured me with your confidence; and with every hour the conviction has strengthened in me that there is a way out of this situation which sends a man like you into solitude with a heart hopeless and full of pain; and which leaves her perhaps in greater pain, for she has not like you the complete sense of innocence. But at present there is no way out but through time and thought. Whatever may be her ideas or wishes she is powerless. She does not know your thoughts, no matter how she may guess at them. She does not know where you are or how to reach you, no matter how complete her penitence may be. And oh! my dear young friend, remember that you are a strong man, and she is a woman. Only a woman in her passion and her weakness after all. Think this all over, my poor boy! You will have time and opportunity where you are going. God help you to judge wisely!' After a pause of a few seconds he said abruptly: 'Good night!' and moved quickly away.

* * * * *

When the time for parting came Pearl was inconsolable. Not knowing any reason why The Man should not do as she wished she was persistent in her petitions to Harold that he should come with her, and to her father and mother that they should induce him to do so. Mrs. Stonehouse would have wished him to join them if only for a time. Her husband, unable to give any hint without betraying confidence, had to content himself with trying to appease his little daughter by vague hopes rather than promises that her friend would join them at some other time.

When the *Scoriac* was warped at the pier there was a tendency on the part of the passengers to give Harold a sort of public send-off; but becoming aware of it he hurried down the gangway without waiting. Having only hand luggage, for he was to get his equipment in New York, he had cleared and passed the ring of customs officers before the most expeditious of the other passengers had collected their baggage. He had said good-bye to the Stonehouses in their own cabin. Pearl had been so much affected at saying good-bye, and his heart had so warmed to her, that at last he had said impulsively:

'Don't cry, darling. If I am spared I shall come back to you within three years. Perhaps I will write before then; but there are not many post-offices where I am going to!'

Children are easily satisfied. Their trust makes a promise a real thing; and its acceptance is the beginning of satisfaction. But for weeks after the parting she had often fits of deep depression, and at such times her tears always flowed. She took note of the date, and there was never a day that she did not think of and sigh for The Man.

And The Man, away in the wilds of Alaska, was feeling, day by day and hour by hour, the chastening and purifying influences of the wilderness. Hot passions cooled before the breath of the snowfield and the glacier. The moaning of a tortured spirit was lost in the roar of the avalanche and the scream of the cyclone. Pale sorrow and cold despair were warmed and quickened by the fierce sunlight which came suddenly and stayed only long enough to vitalise all nature.

And as the first step to understanding, The Man forgot himself.

CHAPTER-28
De Lannoy

Two years!

Not much to look back upon, but a world to look forward to. To Stephen, dowered though she was with rare personal gifts and with wealth and position accorded to but few, the hours of waiting were longer than the years that were past. Yet the time had new and startling incidents for her. Towards Christmas in the second year the Boer war had reached its climax of evil. As the news of disaster after disaster was flashed through the cable she like others felt appalled at the sacrifices that were being exacted by the God of War.

One day she casually read in The Times that the Earl de Lannoy had died in his London mansion, and further learned that he had never recovered from the shock of hearing that his two sons and his nephew had been killed. The paragraph concluded: "By his death the title passes to a distant relative. The new Lord de Lannoy is at present in India with his regiment, the 35th or 'Grey' Hussars, of which he is Colonel." She gave the matter a more than passing thought, for it was sad to find a whole family thus wiped out at a blow.

Early in February she received a telegram from her London solicitor saying that he wished to see her on an important matter. Her answer was: "Come at once"; and at tea-time Mr. Copleston arrived. He was an old friend and she greeted him warmly. She was a little chilled when he answered with what seemed unusual deference:

'I thank your Ladyship for your kindness!' She raised her eyebrows but made no comment: she was learning to be silent under surprise. When she had handed the old gentleman his tea she said:

'My aunt has chosen to remain away, thinking that you might wish to see me privately. But I take it that there is nothing which she may not share. I have no secrets from her.'

He rubbed his hands genially as he replied:

'Not at all; not at all! I should like her to be present. It will, I am sure, be a delight to us all.'

Again raised eyebrows; again silence on the subject. When a servant answered her bell she told him to ask Miss Rowly if she would kindly join them.

Aunt Laetitia and the solicitor were old cronies, and their greeting was most friendly. When the old gentlewoman had seated herself and taken her cup of tea, Mr. Copleston said to Stephen, with a sort of pomposity:

'I have to announce your succession to the Earldom de Lannoy!'

Stephen sat quite still. She knew the news was true; Mr. Copleston was not one who would jest on a business subject, and too accurate a lawyer to make an error in a matter of fact. But the fact did not seem to touch her. It was not that she was indifferent to it; few women could hear such news without a thrill. Mr. Copleston seemed at a loss. Miss Rowly rose and quietly kissed her, and saying simply, 'God bless you, my dear!' went back to her seat.

Realising that Mr. Copleston expected some acknowledgment, Stephen held out her hand to him and said quietly:

'Thank you!'

After a long pause she added quietly:

'Now, won't you tell us about it? I am in absolute ignorance; and don't understand.'

'I had better not burden you, at first, with too many details, which can come later; but give you a rough survey of the situation.'

'Your title of Countess de Lannoy comes to you through your ancestor Isobel, third and youngest daughter of the sixth Earl; Messrs Collinbrae and Jackson, knowing that my firm acted for your family, communicated with us. Lest there should be any error we followed most carefully every descendant and every branch of the family, for we thought it best not to communicate with you till your right of inheritance was beyond dispute. We arrived independently at the same result as Messrs. Collinbrae and Jackson. There is absolutely no doubt whatever of your claim. You will petition the Crown, and on reference to the House of Lords the Committee for Privileges will admit your right. May I offer my congratulations, Lady de Lannoy on your acquisition? By the way, I may say that all the estates of the Earldom, which have been from the first kept in strict entail, go with the title de Lannoy.'

During the recital Stephen was conscious of a sort of bitter comment on the tendencies of good fortune.

'Too late! too late!' something seemed to whisper, 'what delight it would have been had Father inherited . . . If Harold had not gone . . . !' All the natural joy seemed to vanish, as bubbles break into empty air.

To Aunt Laetitia the new title was a source of pride and joy, far greater than would have been the case had it come to herself. She had for so many years longed for new honours for Stephen that she had almost come to regard them as a right whose coming should not be too long delayed. Miss Rowly had never been to Lannoy; and, indeed, she knew personally nothing of the county Angleshire in which it was situated. She was naturally anxious to see the new domain; but kept her feeling concealed during the months that elapsed until Stephen's right had been conceded by the Committee for Privileges. But after that her impatience became manifest to Stephen, who said one day in a teasing, caressing way, as was sometimes her wont:

'Why, Auntie, what a hurry you are in! Lannoy will keep, won't it?'

'Oh, my dear,' she replied, shaking her head, 'I can understand your own reticence, for you don't want to seem greedy and in a hurry about your new possessions. But when people come to my age there's no time to waste. I feel I would not have complete material for happiness in the World-to-come, if there were not a remembrance of my darling in her new home!'

Stephen was much touched; she said impulsively:

'We shall go to-morrow, Auntie. No! Let us go to-day. You shall not wait an hour that I can help!' She ran to the bell; but before her hand was on the cord the other said:

'Not yet! Stephen dear. It would flurry me to start all at once; to-morrow will be time enough. And that will give you time to send word so that they will be prepared for your coming.'

How often do we look for that to-morrow which never comes? How often do we find that its looked-for rosy tints are none other than the gloom-laden grey of the present?

Before the morrow's sun was high in the heavens Stephen was hurriedly summoned to her aunt's bedside. She lay calm and peaceful; but one side of her face was alive and the other seemingly dead. In the night a paralytic stroke had seized her. The doctors said she might in time recover a little, but she would never be her old active self again. She herself, with much painful effort, managed to convey to Stephen that she knew the end was near. Stephen, knowing the wish of her heart and thinking that it might do her good to gratify her wish, asked if she should arrange that she be brought to Lannoy. Feebly and slowly, word by word, she managed to convey her idea.

'Not now, dear one. I shall see it all in time!—Soon! And I shall understand and rejoice!' For a long time she lay still, holding with her right hand, which was not paralysed, the other's hand. Then she murmured:

'You will find happiness there!' She said no more; but seemed to sleep.

From that sleep she never woke, but faded slowly, softly away.

Stephen was broken-hearted. Now, indeed, she felt alone and desolate. All were gone. Father, uncle, aunt!—And Harold. The kingdoms of the Earth which lay at her feet were of no account. One hour of the dead or departed, any of them, back again were worth them all!

Normanstand was now too utterly lonely to be endurable; so Stephen determined to go, for a time at any rate, to Lannoy. She was becoming accustomed to be called 'my lady' and 'your ladyship,' and the new loneness made her feel better prepared to take her place amongst new surroundings.

In addition, there was another spur to her going. Leonard Everard, knowing of her absolute loneliness, and feeling that in it was a possibility of renewing his old status, was beginning to make himself apparent. He had learned by experience a certain wisdom, and did not put himself forward obtrusively. But whenever they met he looked at her so meekly and so lovingly that it brought remembrances which came with blushes. So, all at once, without giving time for the news to permeate through the neighbourhood, she took her way to Lannoy with a few servants.

Stephen's life had hitherto been spent inland. She had of course now and again been for short periods to various places; but the wonder of the sea as a constant companion had been practically unknown to her.

Now at her new home its full splendour burst upon her; and so impressed itself upon her that new life seemed to open.

Lannoy was on the north-eastern coast, the castle standing at the base of a wide promontory stretching far into the North Sea. From the coast the land sloped upward to a great rolling ridge. The outlook seaward was over a mighty expanse of green sward, dotted here and there with woods and isolated clumps of trees which grew fewer and smaller as the rigour of the northern sea was borne upon them by the easterly gales.

The coast was a wild and lonely one. No habitation other than an isolated fisher's cottage was to be seen between the little fishing-port at the northern curve away to the south, where beyond a waste of sandhills and strand another tiny fishing-village nestled under a high cliff, sheltering it from northerly wind. For centuries the lords of Lannoy had kept their magnificent prospect to themselves; and though they had treated their farmers and cottagers well, none had ever been allowed to settle in the great park to seaward of the castle.

From the terrace of the castle only than one building, other than the cottage on the headland, could be seen. Far off on the very crest of the ridge was the tower of an old windmill.

CHAPTER-29

The Silver Lady

When it was known that Lady de Lannoy had come to Lannoy there was a prompt rush of such callers as the county afforded. Stephen, however, did not wish to see anyone just at present. Partly to avoid the chance meeting with strangers, and partly because she enjoyed and benefited by the exercise, she was much away from home every day. Sometimes, attended only by a groom, she rode long distances north or south along the coast; or up over the ridge behind the castle and far inland along the shaded roads through the woods; or over bleak wind-swept stretches of moorland. Sometimes she would walk, all alone, far down to the sea-road, and would sit for hours on the shore or high up on some little rocky headland where she could enjoy the luxury of solitude.

Now and again in her journeyings she made friends, most of them humble ones. She was so great a lady in her station that she could be familiar without seeming to condescend. The fishermen of the little ports to north and south came to know her, and to look gladly for her coming. Their goodwives had for her always a willing curtsy and a ready smile. As for the children, they looked on her with admiration and love, tempered with awe. She was so gentle with them, so ready to share their pleasures and interests, that after a while they came to regard her as some strange embodiment of Fairydom and Dreamland. Many a little heart was made glad by the arrival of some item of delight from the Castle; and the hearts of the sick seemed never to hope, or their eyes to look, in vain.

One friend she made who became very dear and of great import. Often she had looked up at the old windmill on the crest of the ridge and wondered who inhabited it; for that some one lived in it, or close by, was shown at times by the drifting smoke. One day she made up her mind to go and see for herself. She had a fancy not to ask anyone about it. The place was a little item of mystery; and as such to be treasured and exploited, and in due course explored. The mill itself was picturesque, and the detail at closer acquaintance sustained the far-off impression. The roadway forked on the near side of the mill, reuniting again the further side, so that the place made a sort of island—mill, out-offices and garden. As the mill was on the very top of the ridge the garden which lay seawards was sheltered by the building from the west, and from the east by a thick hedge of thorn and privet, which quite hid it from the roadway. Stephen took the lower road. Finding no entrance save a locked wooden door she followed round to the western side, where the business side of the mill had been. It was all still now and silent, and that it had long fallen into disuse was shown by the grey faded look of everything. Grass, green and luxuriant, grew untrodden between the cobble-stones with which the yard was paved. There was a sort of old-world quietude about everything which greatly appealed to Stephen.

Stephen dismounted and walked round the yard admiring everything. She did not feel as if intruding; for the gateway was wide open.

A low door in the base of the mill tower opened, and a maid appeared, a demure pretty little thing of sixteen or seventeen years, dressed in a prim strait dress and an old-fashioned Puritan cap. Seeing a stranger, she made an ejaculation and drew back hastily. Stephen called out to her:

'Don't be afraid, little girl! Will you kindly tell me who lives here?' The answer came with some hesitation:

'Sister Ruth.'

'And who is Sister Ruth?' The question came instinctively and without premeditation. The maid, embarrassed, held hard to the half-open door and shifted from foot to foot uneasily.

'I don't know!' she said at last. 'Only Sister Ruth, I suppose!' It was manifest that the matter had never afforded her anything in the nature of a problem. There was an embarrassing silence. Stephen did not wish to seem, or even to be, prying; but her curiosity was aroused. What manner of woman was this who lived so manifestly alone, and who had but a Christian name! Stephen, however, had all her life been accustomed to dominance, and at Normanstand and Norwood had made many acquaintances amongst her poorer neighbours. She was just about to ask if she might see Sister Ruth, when behind the maid in the dark of the low passage-way appeared the tall, slim figure of a silver woman. Truly a silver woman! The first flash of Stephen's thought was correct. White-haired, white-faced, white-capped, white-kerchiefed; in a plain-cut dress of light-grey silk, without adornment of any kind. The whole ensemble was as a piece of old silver. The lines of her face were very dignified, very sweet, very beautiful. Stephen felt at once that she was in the presence of no common woman. She looked an admiration which all her Quaker garments could not forbid the other to feel. She was not the first to speak; in such a noble presence the dignity of Stephen's youth imperatively demanded silence, if not humility. So she waited. The Silver Lady, for so Stephen ever after held her in her mind, said quietly, but with manifest welcome:

'Didst thou wish to see me? Wilt thou come in?' Stephen answered frankly:

'I should like to come in; if you will not think me rude. The fact is, I was struck when riding by with the beautiful situation of the mill. I thought it was only an old mill till I saw the garden hedges; and I came round to ask if I might go in.' The Silver Lady came forward at a pace that by itself expressed warmth as she said heartily:

'Indeed thou mayest. Stay! it is tea-time. Let us put thy horse in one of the sheds; there is no man here at present to do it. Then thou shalt come with me and see my beautiful view!' She was about to take the horse herself, but Stephen forestalled her with a quick: 'No, no! pray let me. I am quite accustomed.' She led the horse to a shed, and having looped the rein over a hook, patted him and ran back. The Silver Lady gave her a hand, and they entered the dark passage together.

Stephen was thinking if she ought to begin by telling her name. But the Haroun al Raschid feeling for adventure incognito is an innate principle of the sons of men. It was seldom indeed that her life had afforded her such an opportunity.

The Silver Lady on her own part also wished for silence, as she looked for the effect on her companion when the glory of the view should break upon her. When they had climbed the winding stone stair, which led up some twenty feet, there was a low wide landing with the remains of the main shaft of the mill machinery running through it. From one side rose a stone stair curving with the outer wall of the mill tower and guarded by a heavy iron rail. A dozen steps there were, and then a landing a couple of yards square; then a deep doorway cut in the thickness of the wall, round which the winding stair continued.

The Silver Lady, who had led the way, threw open the door, and motioned to her guest to enter. Stephen stood for a few moments, surprised as well as delighted, for the room before her as not like anything which she had ever seen or thought of.

It was a section of almost the whole tower, and was of considerable size, for the machinery and even the inner shaft had been removed. East and south and west the wall had been partially cut away so that great wide windows nearly the full height of the room showed the magnificent panorama. In the depths of the ample windows were little cloistered nooks where one might with a feeling of super-solitude be away from and above the world.

The room was beautifully furnished and everywhere were flowers, with leaves and sprays and branches where possible.

Even from where she stood in the doorway Stephen had a bird's-eye view of the whole countryside; not only of the coast, with which she was already familiar, and on which her windows at the Castle looked, but to the south and west, which the hill rising steep behind the castle and to southward shut out.

The Silver Lady could not but notice her guest's genuine admiration.

'Thou likest my room and my view. There is no use asking thee, I see thou dost!' Stephen answered with a little gasp.

'I think it is the quaintest and most beautiful place I have ever seen!'

'I am so glad thou likest it. I have lived here for nearly forty years; and they have been years of unutterable peace and earthly happiness! And now, thou wilt have some tea!'

Stephen left the mill that afternoon with a warmth of heart that she had been a stranger to for many a day. The two women had accepted each other simply. 'I am called Ruth,' said the Silver Lady. 'And I am Stephen,' said the Countess de Lannoy in reply. And that was all; neither had any clue to the other's identity. Stephen felt that some story lay behind that calm, sweet personality; much sorrow goes to the making of fearless quietude. The Quaker lady moved so little out of her own environment that she did not even suspect the identity of her visitor. All that she knew of change was a notice from the solicitor to the estate that, as the headship had lapsed into another branch of the possessing family, she must be prepared, if necessary, to vacate her tenancy, which was one 'at will.'

It was not long before Stephen availed herself of the permission to come again. This time she made up her mind to tell who she was, lest the concealment of her identity might lead to awkwardness. At that meeting friendship became union.

The natures of the two women expanded to each other; and after a very few meetings there was established between them a rare confidence. Even the personal austerity of Quakerdom, or the state and estate of the peeress, could not come between. Their friendship seemed to be for the life of one. To the other it would be a memory.

The Silver Lady never left the chosen routine of her own life. Whatever was the reason of her giving up the world, she kept it to herself; and Stephen respected her reticence as much as she did her confidence.

It had become a habit, early in their friendship, for Stephen to ride or walk over to the windmill in the dusk of the evening when she felt especially lonely. On one such occasion she pushed open the outer door, which was never shut, and took her way up the stone stair. She knew she would find her friend seated in the window with hands folded on lap, looking out into the silent dusk with that absorbed understanding of things which is holier than reverence, and spiritually more active than conscious prayer.

She tapped the door lightly, and stepped into the room.

With a glad exclamation, which coming through her habitual sedateness showed how much she loved the young girl, Sister Ruth started to her feet. There was something of such truth in the note she had sounded, that the lonely girl's heart went out to her in abandoned fulness. She held out her arms; and, as she came close to the other, fell rather than sank at her feet. The elder woman recognised, and knew. She made no effort to restrain her; but sinking back into her own seat laid the girl's head in her lap, and held her hands close against her breast.

'Tell me,' she whispered. 'Won't you tell me, dear child, what troubles you? Tell me! dear. It may bring peace!'

'Oh, I am miserable, miserable, miserable!' moaned Stephen in a low voice whose despair made the other's heart grow cold. The Silver Lady knew that here golden silence was the best of help; holding close the other's hands, she waited. Stephen's breast began to heave; with an impulsive motion she drew away her hands and put them before her burning face, which she pressed lower still on the other's lap. Sister Ruth knew that the trouble, whatever it was, was about to find a voice. And then came in a low shuddering whisper a voice muffled in the folds of the dress:

'I killed a man!'

In all her life the Silver Lady had never been so startled or so shocked. She had grown so to love the bright, brilliant young girl that the whispered confession cut through the silence of the dusk as a shriek of murder goes through the silent gloom of night. Her hands flew wide from her breast, and the convulsive shudder which shook her all in an instant woke Stephen through all her own deep emotion to the instinct of protection of the other.

The girl looked up, shaking her head, and said with a sadness which stilled all the other's fear:

'Ah! Don't be frightened! It is not murder that I tell you of. Perhaps if it were, the thought would be easier to bear! He would have been hurt less if it had been only his body that I slew. Well I know now that his life would have been freely given if I wished it; if it had been for my good. But it was the best of him that I killed; his soul. His noble, loving, trusting, unselfish soul. The bravest and truest soul that ever had place in a man's breast! . . . ' Her speaking ended with a sob; her body sank lower.

Sister Ruth's heart began to beat more freely. She understood now, and all the womanhood, all the wifehood, motherhood suppressed for a lifetime, awoke to the woman's need. Gently she stroked the beautiful head that lay so meekly on her lap; and as the girl sobbed with but little appearance of abatement, she said to her softly:

'Tell me, dear child. Tell me all about it! See! we are alone together. Thou and I; and God! In God's dusk; with only the silent land and sea before us! Won't thou trust me, dear one, and speak!'

And then, as the shadows fell, and far-off lights at sea began to twinkle over the waste of waters, Stephen found voice and told without reserve the secret of her shame and her remorse.

At last, when her broken voice had trailed away into gentle catchings of the breath, the older woman, knowing that the time come for comfort, took her in her strong arms, holding her face wet against her own, their tears mingling.

'Cry on, dear heart!' she said as she kissed her. 'Cry on! It will do thee good!' She was startled once again as the other seemed for an instant to grow rigid in her arms, and raising her hands cried out in a burst of almost hysterical passion:

'Cry! cry! Oh my God! my God!' Then becoming conscious of her wet face she seemed to become in an instant all limp, and sank on her knees again. There was so different a note in her voice that the other's heart leaped as she heard her say:

'God be thanked for these tears! Oh, thank God! Thank God!' Looking up she saw through the gloom the surprise in her companion's eyes and answered their query in words:

'Oh! you don't know! You can't know what it is to me! I have not cried since last I saw him pass from me in the wood!'

* * * * *

That time of confession seemed to have in some way cleared, purified and satisfied Stephen's soul. Life was now easier to bear. She was able to adapt herself, justifiably to the needs of her position; and all around her and dependent on her began to realise that amongst them was a controlling force, far-reaching sympathy, and a dominant resolution that made for good.

She began to shake off the gloom of her sorrows and to take her place in her new high station. Friends there were in many, and quondam lovers by the score. Lovers of all sorts. Fortune-hunters there were be sure, not a few. But no need was there for baseness when the lady herself was so desirable; so young, so fair, so lovable. That she was of great estate and 'richly left' made all things possible to any man who had sufficient acquisitiveness, or a good conceit of himself. In a wide circle of country were many true-lovers who would have done aught to win her praise.

And so in the East the passing of the two years of silence and gloom seemed to be the winning of something brighter to follow.

CHAPTER-30

The Lesson of The Wilderness

In the West the two years flew. Time seemed to go faster there, because life was more strenuous. Harold, being mainly alone, found endless work always before him. From daylight to dark labour never ceased; and for his own part he never wished that it should. In the wilderness, and especially under such conditions as held in Northern Alaska, labour is not merely mechanical. Every hour of the day is fraught with danger in some new form, and the head has to play its part in the strife against nature. In such a life there is not much time for thinking or brooding.

At first, when the work and his surroundings were strange to him, Harold did many useless things and ran many unnecessary risks. But his knowledge grew with experience. Privations he had in plenty; and all the fibre of his body and the strength of his resolution and endurance were now and again taxed to their utmost. But with a man of his nature and race the breaking strain is high; and endurance and resolution are qualities which develop with practice.

Gradually his mind came back to normal level; he had won seemingly through the pain that shadowed him. Without anguish he could now think, remember, look forward. Then it was that the kindly wisdom of the American came back to him, and came to stay. He began to examine himself as to his own part of the unhappy transaction; and stray moments of wonderment came as to whether the fault may not, at the very base, have his own. He began to realise that it is insufficient in this strenuous world to watch and wait; to suppress one's self; to put aside, in the wish to benefit others, all the hopes, ambitions, cravings which make for personal gain.

Thus it was that Harold's thoughts, ever circling round Stephen, came back with increasing insistence to his duty towards her. He often thought, and with a bitter feeling against himself that it came too late, of the dying trust of her father:

'Guard her and cherish her, as if you were indeed my son and she your sister . . . If it should be that you and Stephen should find that there is another affection between you remember I sanction it. But give her time! I trust that to you! She is young, and the world is all before her. Let her choose . . . And be loyal to her, if it is another! It may be a hard task; but I trust you, Harold!'

Here he would groan, as all the anguish of the past would rush back upon him; and keenest of all would be the fear, suspicion, thought which grew towards belief, that he may have betrayed that trust. . . .

At first the side of this memory personal to his own happiness was faintly emphasised; the important side was of the duty to Stephen. But as time went on the other thought became a sort of corollary; a timid, halting, blushing thought which followed sheepishly, borne down by trembling hope. No matter what adventure came to him, the thought of neglected duty returned ever afresh. Once, when he lay sick for weeks in an Indian wigwam, the idea so grew with each day of the monotony, that when he was able to crawl out by himself into the sunshine he had almost made up his mind to start back for home.

Luck is a strange thing. It seems in some mysterious way to be the divine machinery for adjusting averages. Whatever may be the measure of happiness or unhappiness, good or evil, allotted to anyone, luck is the cause or means of counter-balancing so that the main result reaches the standard set.

From the time of Harold's illness Dame Fortune seemed to change her attitude to him. The fierce frown, nay! the malignant scowl, to which he had become accustomed, changed to a smile. Hitherto everything seemed to have gone wrong with him; but now all at once all seemed to go right. He grew strong and hardy again. Indeed, he seemed by contrast to his late helplessness to be so strong and hard that it looked as if that very illness had done him good instead of harm. Game was plentiful, and he never seemed to want. Everywhere he went there were traces of gold, as though by some instinct he was tracking it to its home. He did not value gold for its own sake; but he did for the ardour of the search. Harold was essentially a man, and as a man an adventurer. To such a man of such a race adventure is the very salt of existence.

The adventurer's instinct took with it the adventurer's judgment; Harold was not content with small results. Amidst the vast primeval forces there were, he felt, vast results of their prehistoric working; and he determined to find some of them. In such a quest, purpose is much. It was hardly any wonder, then, that in time Harold found himself alone in the midst of one of the great treasure-places of the world. Only labour was needed to take from the earth riches beyond the dreams of avarice. But that labour was no easy problem; great and difficult distance had to be overcome; secrecy must be observed, for even a whisper of the existence of such a place would bring a horde of desperadoes. But all these difficulties were at least sources of interest, if not in themselves pleasures. The new Harold, seemingly freshly created by a year of danger and strenuous toil, of self-examining and humiliation, of the realisation of duty, and—though he knew it not as yet—of the dawning of hope, found delight in the thought of dangers and difficulties to be overcome. Having taken his bearings exactly so as to be safe in finding the place again, he took his specimens with him and set out to find the shortest and best route to the nearest port.

At length he came to the port and set quietly about finding men. This he did very carefully and very systematically. Finally, with the full complement, and with ample supply of stores, he started on his expedition to the new goldfields.

It is not purposed to set out here the extraordinary growth of Robinson City, for thus the mining camp soon became. Its history has long ago been told for all the world. In the early days, when everything had to be organised and protected, Harold worked like a giant, and with a system and energy which from the first established him as a master. But when the second year of his exile was coming to a close, and Robinson City was teeming with life and commerce, when banks and police and soldiers made life and property comparatively safe, he began to be restless again. This was not the life to which he had set himself. He had gone into the wilderness to be away from cities and from men; and here a city had sprung up around him and men claimed him as their chief. Moreover, with the restless feeling there began to come back to him the old thoughts and the old pain.

But he felt strong enough by this time to look forward in life as well as backward. With him now to think was to act; so much at least he had gained from his position of dominance in an upspringing city. He quietly consolidated such outlying interests as he had, placed the management of his great estate in the hands of a man he had learned to trust, and giving out that he was going to San Francisco to arrange some business, left Robinson City. He had already accumulated such a fortune that the world was before him in any way he might choose to take.

Knowing that at San Francisco, to which he had booked, he would have to run the gauntlet of certain of his friends and business connections, he made haste to leave the ship quietly at Portland, the first point she touched on her southern journey. Thence he got on the Canadian Pacific Line and took his way to Montreal.

What most arrested his attention, and in a very disconcerting way, were the glimpses of English life one sees reproduced so faithfully here and there in Canada. The whole of the past rushed back on him so overpoweringly that he was for the moment unnerved. The acute feeling of course soon became mitigated; but it was the beginning of a re-realisation of what had been, and which grew stronger with each mile as the train swept back eastward.

At first he tried to fight it; tried with all the resources of his strong nature. His mind was made up, he assured himself over and over again. The past was past, and what had been was no more to him than to any of the other passengers of the train. Destiny had long ago fulfilled itself. Stephen no doubt had by now found some one worthy of her and had married. In no dream, sleeping or waking, could he ever admit that she had married Leonard; that was the only gleam of comfort in what had grown to be remorse for his neglected duty.

And so it was that Harold An Wolf slowly drifted, though he knew it not, into something of the same intellectual position which had dominated him when he had started on his journeying and the sunset fell nightly on his despairing face. The life in the wilderness, and then in the dominance and masterdom of enterprise, had hardened and strengthened him into more self-reliant manhood, giving him greater forbearance and a more practical view of things.

When he took ship in the *Dominion*, a large cargo-boat with some passengers running to London, he had a vague purpose of visiting in secret Norcester, whence he could manage to find out how matters were at Normanstand. He would then, he felt, be in a better position to regulate his further movements. He knew that he had already a sufficient disguise in his great beard. He had nothing to fear from the tracing of him on his journey from Alaska or the interest of his fellow-passengers. He had all along been so fortunate as to be able to keep his identity concealed. The name John Robinson told nothing in itself, and the width of a whole great continent lay between him and the place of his fame. He was able to take his part freely amongst both the passengers and the officers. Even amongst the crew he soon came to be known; the men liked his geniality, and instinctively respected his enormous strength and his manifest force of character. Men who work and who know danger soon learn to recognise the forces which overcome both. And as sufficient time had not elapsed to impair his hardihood or lower his vast strength he was facile princeps. And so the crew acknowledged him; to them he was a born Captain whom to obey would be a natural duty.

After some days the weather changed. The great ship, which usually rested even-keeled on two waves, and whose bilge keels under normal conditions rendered rolling impossible, began to pitch and roll like a leviathan at play. The decks, swept by gigantic seas, were injured wherever was anything to injure. Bulwarks were torn away as though they had been compact of paper. More than once the double doors at the head of the companion stairs had been driven in. The bull's eye glasses of some of the ports were beaten from their brazen sockets. Nearly all the boats had been wrecked, broken or torn from their cranes as the great ship rolled heavily in the trough, or giant waves had struck her till she quivered like a frightened horse.

At that season she sailed on the far northern course. Driven still farther north by the gales, she came within a short way of south of Greenland. Then avoiding Moville, which should have been her place of call, she ran down the east of Britain, the wild weather still prevailing.

CHAPTER-31

The Life-Line

On the coast of Angleshire the weather in the early days of September had been stormy. With the south-west wind had come deluges of rain, not a common thing for the time of year on the east coast. Stephen, whose spirits always rose with high wind, was in a condition of prolonged excitement. She could not keep still; every day she rode long distances, and found a wonderful satisfaction in facing the strong winds. Like a true horsewoman she did not mind the wet, and had glorious gallops over the grassy ridge and down the slopes on the farther side, out on the open road or through the endless grass rides amid the pine woods.

On the Tuesday morning the storm was in full sweep, and Stephen was in wild spirits. Nothing would do her but to go out on the tower of the castle where she could walk about, and leaning on the crenellated parapet look over all the coast stretching far in front and sweeping away to the left and right. The prospect so enchanted her, and the fierce sweep of the wind so suited her exalted mood, that she remained there all the morning. The whole coast was a mass of leaping foam and flying spray, and far away to the horizon white-topped waves rolled endlessly. That day she did not even ride out, but contented herself with watching the sea and the storm from the tower. After lunch she went to her tower again; and again after tea. The storm was now furious. She made up her mind that after dinner she would ride down and see its happenings close at hand.

When she had finished dinner she went to her room to dress for her ride. The rush and roar of the storm were in her ears, and she was in wild tumultuous spirits. All her youth seemed to sweep back on her; or perhaps it was that the sickness of the last two years was swept away. Somewhere deep down in Stephen's heart, below her intention or even her consciousness, was a desire to be her old self if only for an hour. And to this end externals were of help. Without weighing the matter in her mind, and acting entirely on impulse, she told her maid to get the red habit she had not worn for years. When she was dressed she sent round to have out her white Arab; while it was getting ready she went once more to the tower to see the storm-effect in the darkening twilight. As she looked, her heart for an instant stood still. Half-way to the horizon a great ship, ablaze in the bows, was driving through the waves with all her speed. She was heading towards the little port, beyond which the shallows sent up a moving wall of white spray.

Stephen tore down the turret stair, and gave hurried directions to have beds prepared in a number of rooms, fires everywhere, and plenty of provisions. She also ordered that carriages should be sent at once to the fishing port with clothing and restoratives. There would, she felt, be need for such help before a time to be measured by minutes should have passed; and as some of her servants were as yet strange to her ways she did not leave anything to chance. One carriage was to go for the doctor who lived at Lannoy, the village over the hill, whence nothing could be seen of what was happening. She knew that others within sight or hailing would be already on their way. Work was afoot, and had she time, or thought of it, she would have chosen a more sedate garb. But in the excitement no thought of herself came to her.

In a few seconds she was in the saddle, tearing at full speed down the road that led to the port. The wind was blowing so strongly in her face that only in the lulls could she hear the hoof-strokes of the groom's horse galloping behind her.

At first the height of the road allowed her to see the ship and the port towards which she was making. But presently the road dipped, and the curving of the hill shut both from her sight; it was only when she came close that she could see either again.

Now the great ship was close at hand. The flames had gained terribly, and it was a race for life or death. There was no time do more than run her aground if life was to be saved at all. The captain, who in the gaps of the smoke could be seen upon the bridge, knew his work well. As he came near the shoal he ran a little north, and then turned sharply so as to throw the boat's head to the south of the shoal. Thus the wind would drive fire and smoke forward and leave the after part of the vessel free for a time.

The shock of her striking the sand was terrific, though the tinkle of the bell borne in on the gale showed that the engines had been slowed down. The funnels were shaken down, and the masts broke off, falling forward. A wild shriek from a hundred throats cleft the roaring of wind and wave. The mast fell, the foremast, with all its cumbering top-hamper on the bridge, which was in an instant blotted out of existence, together with the little band of gallant men who stood on it, true to their last duty. As the wind took the smoke south a man was seen to climb on the wreck of the mast aft and make fast the end of a great coil of rope which he carried. He was a huge man with a full dark beard. Two sailors working with furious haste helped him with the rope. The waves kept raising the ship a little, each time bumping her on the sand with a shock. The people on deck held frantically to the wreckage around them.

Then the bearded man, stripping to his waist and cutting off his trousers above the knee, fastened an end of the rope round his waist. The sailors stood ready one behind the other to pay it out. As a great wave rolled under the ship, he threw himself into the sea.

In the meantime the coastguard had fixed Board of Trade rocket-apparatus, and in a few seconds the prolonged roar of a rocket was heard. It flew straight towards the ship, rising at a high angle so as to fall beyond it. But the force of the wind took it up as it rose, and the gale increased so that it rose nearly vertically; and in this position the wind threw it south of its objective, and short of it. Another rocket was got ready at once, and blue lights were burned so that the course of the venturous swimmer might be noted. He swam strongly; but the great weight of the rope behind kept pulling him back, and the southern trend of the tide current and the force of the wind kept dragging him from the pier. Within the bar the waves were much less than without; but they were still so unruly that no boat in the harbour—which was not a lifeboat station—could venture out. Indeed, in the teeth of the storm it would have been a physical impossibility to have driven one seaward.

As the gathered crowd saw Stephen approach they made way for her. She had left her horse with the groom, and despite the drenching spray fought a way against the wind out on the pier. As in the glare of the blue light, which brought many things into harsh unnatural perspective, she caught sight of the set face of the swimmer rising and falling with the waves, her heart leaped. This was indeed a man! a brave man; and all the woman in her went out to him. For him, and to aid him and his work, she would have given everything, done anything; and in her heart, which beat in an ecstasy of anxiety, she prayed with that desperate conviction of hope which comes in such moments of exaltation.

But it soon became apparent that no landing could be effected. The force of the current and the wind were taking the man too far southward for him ever to win a way back. Then one of coastguards took the lead-topped cane which they use for throwing practice, and, after carefully coiling the line attached it so that it would run free, managed with a desperate effort to fling it far out. The swimmer, to whom it fell close, fought towards it frantically; and as the cord began to run through the water, managed to grasp it. A wild cheer rose from the shore and the ship. A stout line was fastened to the shore end of the cord, and the swimmer drew it out to him. He bent it on the rope which trailed behind him; then, seeing that he was himself a drag on it, with the knife which he drew from the sheath at the back of his waist, he cut himself free. One of the coastguards on the pier, helped by a host of willing hands, began drawing the end of the rope on shore. The swimmer still held the line thrown to him, and several men on the pier began to draw on it. Unhappily the thin cord broke under the strain, and within a few seconds the swimmer had drifted out of possible help. Seeing that only wild rocks lay south of the sea-wall, and that on them seas beat furiously, he turned and made out for sea. In the light beyond the glare he could see vaguely the shore bending away to the west in a deep curve of unbroken white leaping foam. There was no hope of landing there. To the south was the headland, perhaps two miles away as the crow flies. Here was the only chance for him. If he could round the headland, he might find shelter beyond; or somewhere along the farther shore some opening might present itself. Whilst the light from the blue fires still reached him he turned and made for the headland.

In the meantime on ship and on shore men worked desperately. Before long the end of the hawser was carried round on the high cliff, and pulled as taut as the force at hand could manage, and made fast. Soon endless ropes were bringing in passengers and crew as fast as place could be found for them. It became simply a race for time. If the fire, working against the wind, did not reach the hawser, and if the ship lasted the furious bumping on the sandbank, which threatened to shake her to pieces each moment, all on board might yet be saved.

Stephen's concern was now for the swimmer alone. Such a gallant soul should not perish without help, if help could be on this side of heaven. She asked the harbour-master, an old fisherman who knew every inch of the coast for miles, if anything could be done. He shook his head sadly as he answered:

'I fear no, my lady. The lifeboat from Granport is up north, no boat from here could get outside the harbour. There's never a spot in the bay where he could land, even in a less troubled sea than this. Wi' the wind ashore, there's no hope for ship or man here that cannot round the point. And a stranger is no like to do that.'

'Why not?' she asked breathlessly.

'Because, my lady, there's a wheen o' sunken rocks beyond the Head. No one that didn't know would ever think to keep out beyond them, for the cliff itself goes down sheer. He's a gallant soul yon; an' it's a sore pity he's goin' to his death. But it must be! God can save him if He wishes; but I fear none other!'

Even as he spoke rose to Stephen's mind a memory of an old churchyard with great trees and the scent of many flowers, and a child's voice that sounded harsh through the monotonous hum of bees:

'To be God, and able to do things!'

Oh; to be God, if but an hour; and able to do things! To do anything to help a brave man! A wild prayer surged up in the girl's heart:

'Oh! God, give me this man's life! Give it to me to atone for the other I destroyed! Let me but help him, and do with me as Thou wilt!'

The passion of her prayer seemed to help her, and her brain cleared. Surely something could be done! She would do what she could; but first she must understand the situation. She turned again to the old harbour-master:

'How long would it take him to reach the headland, if he can swim so far?' The answer came with a settled conviction bearing hope with it:

'The wind and tide are wi' him, an' he's a strong swimmer. Perhaps half an hour will take him there. He's all right in himself. He can swim it, sure. But alack! it's when he gets there his trouble will be, when none can warn him. Look how the waves are lashing the cliff; and mark the white water beyond! What voice can sound to him out in those deeps? How could he see if even one were there to warn?'

Here was a hope at any rate. Light and sound were the factors of safety. Some good might be effected if she could get a trumpet; and there were trumpets in the rocket-cart. Light could be had—must be had if all the fences round the headland had to be gathered for a bonfire! There was not a moment to be lost. She ran to the rocket-cart, and got a trumpet from the man in charge. Then she ran to where she had left her horse. She had plenty of escort, for by this time many gentlemen had arrived on horseback from outlying distances, and all offered their services. She thanked them and said:

'You may be useful here. When all these are ashore send on the rocket-cart, and come yourselves to the headland as quick as you can. Tell the coastguards that all those saved are to be taken to the castle. In the rocket-cart bring pitch and tar and oil, and anything that will flame. Stay!' she cried to the chief boatman. 'Give me some blue lights!' His answer chilled her:

'I'm sorry, my lady, but they are all used. There are the last of them burning now. We have burned them ever since that man began to swim ashore.'

'Then hurry on the rocket-cart!' she said as she sprang to the saddle, and swept out on the rough track that ran by the cliffs, following in bold curves the windings of the shore. The white Arab seemed to know that his speed was making for life. As he swept along, far outdistancing the groom, Stephen's heart went out in silent words which seemed to keep time to the gallop:

'Oh, to be God, and be able to do things! Give me this man's life, oh, God! Give me this man's life, to atone for that noble one which I destroyed!'

Faster and faster, over rough road, cattle track, and grassy sward; over rising and falling ground; now and again so close to the edge of the high cliff that the spume swept up the gulleys in the rocks like a snowstorm, the white Arab swept round the curve of the bay, and came out on the high headland where stood the fisher's house. On the very brink of the cliff all the fisher folk, men, women and children, stood looking at the far-off burning ship, from which the flames rose in leaping columns.

So intent were all on the cliff that they did not notice her coming; as the roar of the wind came from them to her, they could not hear her voice when she spoke from a distance. She had drawn quite close, having dismounted and hung her rein over the post of the garden paling, when one of the children saw her, and cried out:

'The lady! the lady! an' she's all in red!' The men were so intent on something that they did not seem to hear. They were peering out to the north, and were arguing in dumb show as though on something regarding which they did not agree. She drew closer, and touching the old fisherman on the shoulder, called out at his ear:

'What is it?' He answered without turning, keeping his eyes fixed:

'*I* say it's a man swimmin'. Joe and Garge here say as it's only a piece o' wood or sea-wrack. But I know I'm right. That's a man swimmin', or my old eyes have lost their power!' His words carried conviction; the seed of hope in her beating heart grew on the instant into certainty.

'It *is* a man. I saw him swim off towards here when he had taken the rope on shore. Do not turn round. Keep your eyes on him so that you may not lose sight of him in the darkness!' The old man chuckled.

'This darkness! Hee! hee! There be no differ to me between light and dark. But I'll watch him! It's you, my lady! I shan't turn round to do my reverence as you tell me to watch. But, poor soul, it'll not be for long to watch. The Skyres will have him, sure enow!'

'We can warn him!' she said, 'when he comes close enough. I have a trumpet here!' He shook his head sorrowfully:

'Ah! my lady, what trumpet could sound against that storm an' from this height?' Stephen's heart sank. But there was still hope. If the swimmer's ears could not be reached, his eyes might. Eagerly she looked back for the coming of the rocket-cart. Far off across the deep bay she could see its lamp sway as it passed over the rough ground; but alas! it would never arrive in time. With a note of despair in her voice she asked:

'How long before he reaches the rocks?' Still without turning the old man answered:

'At the rate he's going he will be in the sweep of the current through the rocks within three minutes. If he's to be saved he must turn seaward ere the stream grips him.'

'Would there be time to build a bonfire?'

'No, no! my lady. The wood couldn't catch in the time!'

For an instant a black film of despair seemed to fall on her. The surging of the blood in her head made her dizzy, and once again the prayer of the old memory rang in her brain:

'Oh to be God, and able to do things!'

On the instant an inspiration flashed through her. She, too could do things in a humble way. She could do something at any rate. If there was no time to build a fire, there was a fire already built.

The house would burn!

The two feet deep of old thatch held down with nets and battened with wreck timber would flare like a beacon. Forthwith she spoke:

'Good people, this noble man who has saved a whole shipload of others must not die without an effort. There must be light so that he can see our warning to pass beyond the rocks! The only light can be from the house. I buy it of you. It is mine; but I shall pay you for it and build you such another as you never thought of. But it must be fired at once. You have one minute to clear out all you want. In, quick and take all can. Quick! quick! for God's sake! It is for a brave man's life!'

The men and women without a word rushed into the house. They too knew the danger, and the only hope there was for a life. The assurance of the Countess took the sting from the present loss. Before the minute, which she timed watch in hand, was over, all came forth bearing armloads of their lares and penates. Then one of the younger men ran in again and out bearing a flaming stick from the fire. Stephen nodded, he held it to the northern edge of the thatch. The straw caught in a flash and the flame ran up the slope and along the edge of the roof like a quick match. The squeaking of many rats was heard and their brown bodies streamed over the roof. Before another minute had passed a great mass of flame towered into the sky and shed a red light far out over the waste of sea.

It lit up the wilderness of white water where the sea churned savagely amongst the sunken rocks; and it lit too the white face of a swimmer, now nearly spent, who rising and falling with each wave, drifted in the sea whose current bore him on towards the fatal rocks.

CHAPTER-32

'To Be God And Able To Do Things'

When the swimmer saw the light he looked up; even at the distance they could see the lift of his face; but he did not seem to realise that there was any intention in the lighting, or that it was created for his benefit. He was manifestly spent with his tremendous exertions, and with his long heavy swim in the turbulent sea. Stephen's heart went out to him in a wave of infinite pity. She tried to use the trumpet. But simple as it is, a trumpet needs skill or at least practice in its use; she could only make an unintelligible sound, and not much even of that. One of the young men said:

'Let me try it, my lady!' She handed him the trumpet and he in turn used with a will. But it was of no avail; even his strong lungs and lusty manhood availed nothing in the teeth of that furious gale. The roof and the whole house was now well alight, and the flame roared and leapt. Stephen began to make gestures bidding the swimmer, in case he might see her and understand, move round the rocks. But he made no change in his direction, and was fast approaching a point in the tide-race whence to avoid the sunken rocks would be an impossibility. The old whaler, accustomed to use all his wits in times of difficulty, said suddenly:

'How can he understand when we're all between him and the light. We are only black shadows to him; all he can see are waving arms!' His sons caught his meaning and were already dashing towards the burning house. They came back with piles of blazing wood and threw them down on the very edge of the cliff; brought more and piled them up, flinging heaps of straw on the bonfire and pouring on oil and pitch till the flames rose high. Stephen saw what was necessary and stood out of the way, but close to the old whaler, where the light fell on both of their faces as they looked in the direction of the swimmer. Stephen's red dress itself stood out like a flame.

The gale tearing up the front of the cliff had whirled away her hat; in the stress of the wind her hair was torn from its up-pinning and flew wide, itself like leaping flame.

Her gestures as she swept her right arm round, as though demonstrating the outward curve of a circle, or raising the hand above her head motioned with wide palm and spread fingers 'back! back!' seemed to have reached the swimmer's intelligence. He half rose in the water and looked about. As if seeing something that he realised, he sank back again and began swim frantically out to sea. A great throb of joy made Stephen almost faint. At last she had been able to do something to help this gallant man. In half a minute his efforts seemed to tell in his race for life. He drew sufficiently far from dangerous current for there to be a hope that he might be saved if he could last out the stress to come.

The fishermen kept watch in silent eagerness; and in their presence Stephen felt a comfort, though, like her, they could do nothing at present.

When the swimmer had passed sufficiently far out to be clear of the rocks, the fire began to lose its flame, though not its intensity. It would be fiery still for hours to come, and of great heat; but the flames ceased to leap, and in the moderated light Stephen only saw the white face for one more instant ere it faded out of her ken, when, turning, the man looked towards the light and made a gesture which she did not understand: for he put for an instant both hands before his face.

Just then there was a wild noise on the cliff. The rocket-cart drawn by sixteen splendid horses, some of them hunters, came tearing up the slope, and with it many men on horseback afoot. Many of the runners were the gentlemen who had given their horses for the good work.

As the coastguards jumped from the cart, and began to get out the rocket stand, the old whaler pointed out the direction where the swimmer's head could still be seen. Some of the sailors could see it too; though to Stephen and the laymen it was invisible. The chief boatman shook his head:

'No use throwing a line there! Even if he got it we could never drag him alive through these rocks. He would be pounded to death before twenty fathom!' Stephen's heart grew cold as she listened. Was this the end? Then with a bitter cry she wailed:

'Oh! can nothing be done? Can nothing be done? Can no boat come from the other side of the point? Must such a brave man be lost!' and her tears began to flow.

One of the young men who had just arrived, a neighbouring squire, a proved wastrel but a fine horseman, who had already regarded Stephen at the few occasions of their meeting with eyes of manifest admiration, spoke up:

'Don't cry, Lady de Lannoy. There's a chance for him yet. I'll see what I can do.'

'Bless you! oh! bless you!' she cried impulsively as she caught his hand. Then came the chill of doubt. 'But what can you do?' she added despairingly.

'Hector and I may be able to do something together.' Turning to one of the fishermen he asked:

'Is there any way down to the water in the shelter of the point?'

'Ay! ay! sir,' came the ready answer. 'There's the path as we get down by to our boats.'

'Come on, then!' he said. 'Some of you chaps show us a light on the way down. If Hector can manage the scramble there's a chance. You see,' he said, turning again to Stephen, 'Hector can swim like a fish. When he was a racer I trained him in the sea so that none of the touts could spy out his form. Many's the swim we've had together; and in rough water too, though in none so wild as this!'

'But it is a desperate chance for you!' said Stephen, woman-like drawing somewhat back from a danger she had herself evoked. The young man laughed lightly:

'What of that! I may do one good thing before I die. That fine fellow's life is worth a hundred of my wasted one! Here! some of you fellows help me with Hector. We must take him from the cart and get a girth on him instead of the saddle. We shall want something to hold on to without pulling his head down by using the bridle.'

He, followed by some others, ran to the rocket-cart where the horses stood panting, their steam rising in a white cloud in the glow of the burning house. In an incredibly short time the horse was ready with only the girth. The young squire took him by the mane and he followed eagerly; he had memories of his own. As they passed close to Stephen the squire said to one of his friends:

'Hold him a minute, Jack!' He ran over to Stephen and looked at her hard:

'Good-bye! Wish me luck; and give us light!' Tears were in her eyes and a flush on her cheek as she took his hand and clasped it hard:

'Oh, you brave man! God bless you!' He stooped suddenly and impulsively kissed the back of her hand lightly and was gone. For a fleeting moment she was angry. No man had kissed her hand before; but the thought of his liberty was swept away by another:

'Little enough when he may be going to his death!'

It was a sight to see that man and horse, surrounded by an eager crowd of helpers, scrambling down the rough zigzag, cut and worn in the very face of the cliff. They stumbled, and slipped; pebbles and broken rock fell away under their feet. Alone close to the bonfire stood Stephen, following every movement with racing blood and beating heart. The bonfire was glowing; a constant stream of men and women were dragging and hauling all sorts of material for its increase. The head of the swimmer could be seen, rising and falling amid the waves beyond the Skyres.

When about twenty feet from the water-level the path jutted out to one side left of the little beach whereon the sea now broke fiercely. This was a place where men watched, and whence at times they fished with rods; the broad rock overhung the water. The fire above, though it threw shadows, made light enough for everything. The squire held up his hand.

'Stop! We can take off this rock, if the water is deep enough. How much is it?'

'Ten fathoms sheer.'

'Good!' He motioned to them all to keep back. Then threw off all his clothes except shirt and trousers. For an instant he patted Hector and then sprang upon his back. Holding him by the mane he urged him forward with a cry. The noble animal did not hesitate an instant. He knew that grasp of the mane; that cry; that dig of the spurless heels. He sprang forward with wide dilated nostrils, and from the edge of the jutting rock jumped far out into the sea. Man and horse disappeared for a few seconds, but rose safely. The man slid from the horse's back; and, holding by the girth with one hand, swam beside him out to sea in the direction the swimmer must come on rounding the sunken rocks.

A wild cheer broke from all on the cliff above and those already scrambling back up the zigzag. Stephen kept encouraging the men to bring fuel to the bonfire:

'Bring everything you can find; the carts, the palings, the roofs, the corn, the dried fish; anything and everything that will burn. We must have light; plenty of light! Two brave men's lives are at stake now!'

The whole place was a scene of activity. Stephen stood on the edge of the cliff with the old whaler and the chief boatman and some of the women. The rest of the coastguards were by orders of their chief rigging up a whip which they thought might be necessary to hoist the men up from the water, if they could ever get close enough. One of the young men who had ridden with the rocket-cart kept tight hold of Hector's bridle; he knew it would be wanted if the horse ever had a chance of landing.

* * * * *

When Harold turned away from the dazzling blue lights on the pier, and saw the far white line of the cliffs beyond the bay, his heart sank within him. Even his great strength and hardihood, won by work and privation in the far North-West, had been already taxed in the many days of the battling with the gale when all on board who could lend a hand were taken into service. Again by the frantic struggle of the last hour or two, when the ship ran shoreward at the utmost of her speed in the last hope of beaching in time to save life. Finally in that grim struggle to draw the life-line shoreward. The cold and then the great heat, and on top of it the chill of the long swim, seemed to have struck at him. Alone on the dark sea, for soon the current and his own exertions were taking him away from the rocks, the light of the burning ship was ceasing to be effective. It was just enough to hinder his vision; looking from the patch of light which bathed the light and him he could just see far off the white water which marked the cliff fronts, and on the edge of his horizon the grim moving white wall where the waves broke on the headland.

On and on he toiled. His limbs were becoming more cramped with the cold and the terrible strain of swimming in such waves. But still the brave heart bore him up; and resolutely, sternly he forced himself afresh to the effort before him. He reasoned that where there was such a headland standing out so stark into the sea there ought to be some shelter in its lee. If he could pass it he might find calmer water and even a landing-place beyond.

Here at least was hope. He would try to round the point at any rate. Now he drew so close that the great rocks seemed to tower vast above him. He was not yet close enough to feel as though lapped in their shadow; but even the overcast sky seemed full of light above the line of the cliff. There was a strange roaring, rushing sound around him. He thought that it was not merely the waves dashing on the rocks, but that partly it came from his own ears; that his ebbing strength was feeling the frantic struggle which he was making. The end was coming, he thought; but still he kept valiantly on, set and silent, as is the way with brave men.

Suddenly from the top of the cliff a bright light flashed. He looked at it sideways as he fought his way on, and saw the light rise and fall and flicker as the flames leaped. High over him he saw fantastic figures which seemed to dance on the edge of the high cliff. They had evidently noticed him, and were making signals of some sort; but what the motions were he could not see or understand, for they were but dark silhouettes, edged with light, against the background of fire. The only thing he could think was that they meant to encourage him, and so he urged himself to further effort. It might be that help was at hand!

Several times as he turned his head sideways he saw the figures and the light, but not so clearly; it was as though the light was lessening in power. When again he looked he saw a new fire leap out on the edge of the cliff, and some figures to the right of it. They were signalling in some way. So, pausing in his swimming, he rose a little from the water and looked at them.

A thrill shot through him, and a paralysing thought that he must have gone mad. With his wet hand he cleared his eyes, though the touching them pained him terribly, and for an instant saw clearly:

There on the edge of the cliff, standing beside some men and waving her arms in a wild sweep as though motioning frantically 'Keep out! keep out!' was a woman. Instinctively he glanced to his left and saw a white waste of leaping water, through which sharp rocks rose like monstrous teeth. On the instant he saw the danger, and made out seaward, swimming frantically to clear the dangerous spot before the current would sweep him upon the rocks.

But the woman! As one remembers the last sight when the lightning has banished sight, so that vision seemed burned into his brain. A woman with a scarlet riding-habit and masses of long red hair blowing in the gale like leaping flame! Could there be two such persons in the world? No! no! It was a vision! A vision of the woman he loved, come to save him in the direst moment of great peril!

His heart beat with new hope; only the blackness of the stormy sea was before him as he strove frantically on.

Presently when he felt the current slacken, for he had been swimming across it and could feel its power, he turned and looked back. As he did so he murmured aloud:

'A dream! A vision! She came to warn me!' For as he looked all had disappeared. Cliff and coastline, dark rocks and leaping seas, blazing fire, and the warning vision of the woman he loved.

Again he looked where the waste of sea churning amongst the sunken rocks had been. He could hear the roaring of waters, the thunder of great waves beating on the iron-bound coast; but nothing could he see. He was alone on the wild sea; in the dark.

Then truly the swift shadow of despair fell upon him.

'Blind Blind!' he moaned, and for the moment, stricken with despair, sank into the trough of the waves. But the instinctive desire for life recalled him. Once more he fought his way up to the surface, and swam blindly, desperately on. Seeing nothing, he did not know which way he was going. He might have heard better had his eyes been able to help his ears; but in the sudden strange darkness all the senses were astray. In the agony of his mind he could not even feel the pain of his burnt face; the torture of his eyes had passed. But with the instinct of a strong man he kept on swimming blindly, desperately.

* * * * *

It seemed as if ages of untold agony had gone by, when he heard a voice seemingly beside him:

'Lay hold here! Catch the girth!' The voice came muffled by wind and wave. His strength was now nearly at its last.

The shock of his blindness and the agony of the moments that had passed had finished his exhaustion. But a little longer and he must have sunk into his rest. But the voice and the help it promised rallied him for a moment. He had hardly strength to speak, but he managed to gasp out:

'Where? where? Help me! I am blind!' A hand took his and guided it to a tightened girth. Instinctively his fingers closed round it, and he hung on grimly. His senses were going fast. He felt as if it was all a strange dream. A voice here in the sea! A girth! A horse; he could hear its hard breathing.

The voice came again.

'Steady! Hold on! My God! he's fainted! I must tie him on!' He heard a tearing sound, and something was wound round his wrists. Then his nerveless fingers relaxed their hold; and all passed into oblivion.

CHAPTER-33

The Queen's Room

To Stephen all that now happened seemed like a dream. She saw Hector and his gallant young master forge across the smoother water of the current whose boisterous stream had been somewhat stilled in the churning amongst the rocks, and then go north in the direction of the swimmer who, strange to say, was drifting in again towards the sunken rocks. Then she saw the swimmer's head sink under the water; and her heart grew cold. Was this to be the end! Was such a brave man to be lost after such gallant effort as he had made, and just at the moment when help was at hand!

The few seconds seemed ages. Instinctively she shut her eyes and prayed again. 'Oh! God. Give me this man's life that I may atone!'

God seemed to have heard her prayer. Nay, more! He had mercifully allowed her to be the means of averting great danger. She would never, could never, forget the look on the man's face when he saw, by the flame that she had kindled, ahead of him the danger from the sunken rocks. She had exulted at the thought. And now . . .

She was recalled by a wild cheer beside her. Opening her eyes she saw that the man's head had risen again from the water. He was swimming furiously, this time seaward. But close at hand were the heads of the swimming horse and man . . . She saw the young squire seize the man . . .

And then the rush of her tears blinded her. When she could see again the horse had turned and was making back again to the shelter of the point. The squire had his arm stretched across the horse's back; he was holding up the sailor's head, which seemed to roll helplessly with every motion of the cumbering sea.

For a little she thought he was dead, but the voice of the old whaler reassured her:

'He was just in time! The poor chap was done!' And so with beating heart and eyes that did not flinch now she watched the slow progress to the shelter of the point. The coastguards and fishermen had made up their minds where the landing could be made, and were ready; on the rocky shelf, whence Hector had at jumped, they stood by with lines. When the squire had steered and encouraged the horse, whose snorting could be heard from the sheltered water, till he was just below the rocks, they lowered a noosed rope. This he fastened round the senseless man below his shoulders. One strong, careful pull, and he was safe on land; and soon was being borne up the steep zigzag on the shoulders of the willing crowd.

In the meantime other ropes were passed down to the squire. One he placed round his own waist; two others he fastened one on each side of the horse's girth. Then his friend lowered the bridle, and he managed to put it on the horse and attached a rope to it. The fishermen took the lines, and, paying out as they went so as to leave plenty of slack line, got on the rocks just above the little beach whereon, sheltered though it was, the seas broke heavily. There they waited, ready to pull the horse through the surf when he should have come close enough.

Stephen did not see the rescue of the horse; for just then a tall grave man spoke to her:

'Pardon me, Lady de Lannoy, but is the man to be brought up to the Castle? I am told you have given orders that all the rescued shall be taken there.' She answered unhesitatingly:

'Certainly! I gave orders before coming out that preparation was to be made for them.'

'I am Mr. Hilton. I have just come down to do lacum tenens for Dr. Winter at Lannoch Port. I rode over on hearing there was a wreck, and came here with the rocket-cart. I shall take charge of the man and bring him up. He will doubtless want some special care.'

'If you will be so good!' she answered, feeling a diffidence which was new to her. At that moment the crowd carrying the senseless man began to appear over the cliff, coming up the zig-zag. The Doctor hurried towards him; she followed at a little distance, fearing lest she should hamper him. Under his orders they laid the patient on the weather side of the bonfire so that the smoke would not reach him. The Doctor knelt by his side.

An instant after he looked up and said:

'He is alive; his heart is beating, though faintly. He had better be taken away at once. There is no means here of shelter.'

'Bring him in the rocket-cart; it is the only conveyance here,' cried Stephen. 'And bring Mr. Hepburn too. He also will need some care after his gallant service. I shall ride on and advise my household of your coming. And you good people come all to the Castle. You are to be my guests if you will so honour me. No! No! Really I should prefer to ride alone!'

She said this impulsively, seeing that several of the gentlemen were running for their horses to accompany her. 'I shall not wait to thank that valiant young gentleman. I shall see him at Lannoy.'

As she was speaking she had taken the bridle of her horse. One of the young men stooped and held his hand; she bowed, put her foot in it and sprang to the saddle. In an instant she was flying across country at full speed, in the dark. A wild mood was on her, reaction from the prolonged agony of apprehension. There was little which she would not have done just then.

The gale whistled round her and now and again she shouted with pure joy. It seemed as if God Himself had answered her prayer and given her the returning life!

By the time she had reached the Castle the wild ride had done its soothing work. She was calm again, comparatively; her wits and feelings were her own.

There was plenty to keep her occupied, mind and body. The train of persons saved from the wreck were arriving in all sorts of vehicles, and as clothes had to be found for them as well as food and shelter there was no end to the exertions necessary. She felt as though the world were not wide enough for the welcome she wished to extend. Its exercise was a sort of reward of her exertions; a thank-offering for the response to her prayer. She moved amongst her guests, forgetful of herself; of her strange attire; of the state of dishevelment and grime in which she was, the result of the storm, her long ride over rough ground with its share of marshes and pools, and the smoke from the bonfire and the blazing house. The strangers wondered at first, till they came to understand that she was the Lady Bountiful who had stretched her helpful hands to them. Those who could, made themselves useful with the new batches of arrivals. The whole Castle was lit from cellar to tower. The kitchens were making lordly provision, the servants were carrying piles of clothes of all sorts, and helping to fit those who came still wet from their passage through or over the heavy sea.

In the general disposition of chambers Stephen ordered to be set apart for the rescued swimmer the Royal Chamber where Queen Elizabeth had lain; and for Mr. Hepburn that which had been occupied by the Second George. She had a sort of idea that the stranger was God's guest who was coming to her house; and that nothing could be too good for him. As she waited for his coming, even though she swept to and fro in her ministrations to others, she felt as though she trod on air. Some great weight seemed to have been removed from her. Her soul was free again!

At last the rocket-cart arrived, and with it many horsemen and such men and women as could run across country with equal speed to the horses labouring by the longer road.

The rescued man was still senseless, but that alone did not seem to cause anxiety to the Doctor, who hurried him at once into the prepared room. When, assisted by some of the other men, he had undressed him, rubbed him down and put him to bed, and had seen some of the others who had been rescued from the wreck, he sought out Lady de Lannoy. He told her that his anxiety was for the man's sight; an announcement which blanched his hearer's cheeks. She had so made up her mind as to his perfect safety that the knowledge of any kind of ill came like a cruel shock. She questioned Mr. Hilton closely; so closely that he thought it well to tell her at once all that he surmised and feared:

'That fine young fellow who swam out with his horse to him, tells me that when he neared him he cried out that he was blind. I have made some inquiries from those on the ship, and they tell me that he was a passenger, named Robinson. Not only was he not blind then, but he was the strongest and most alert man on the ship. If it be blindness it must have come on during that long swim. It may be that before leaving the ship he received some special injury—indeed he has several cuts and burns and bruises—and that the irritation of the sea-water increased it. I can do nothing till he wakes. At present he is in such a state that nothing can be done for him. Later I shall if necessary give him a hypodermic to ensure sleep. In the morning when I come again I shall examine him fully.'

'But you are not going away to-night!' said Stephen in dismay. 'Can't you manage to stay here? Indeed you must! Look at all these people, some of whom may need special attention or perhaps treatment. We do not know yet if any may be injured.' He answered at once:

'Of course I shall stay if you wish it. But there are two other doctors here already. I must go over to my own place to get some necessary instruments for the examination of this special patient. But that I can do in the early morning.'

'Can I not send for what you want; the whole household are at your service. All that can be done for that gallant man must be done. You can send to London for special help if you wish. If that man is blind, or in danger of blindness, we must have the best oculist in the world for him.'

'All shall be done that is possible,' said he earnestly. 'But till I examine him in the morning we can do nothing. I am myself an oculist; that is my department in St. Stephen's Hospital. I have an idea of what is wrong, but I cannot diagnose exactly until I can use the ophthalmoscope.' His words gave Stephen confidence. Laying her hand on his arm unconsciously in the extremity of pity she said earnestly:

'Oh, do what you can for him. He must be a noble creature; and all that is possible must be done. I shall never rest happily if through any failing on my part he suffers as you fear.'

'I shall do all I can,' he said with equal earnestness, touched with her eager pity. 'And I shall not trust myself alone, if any other can be of service. Depend upon it, Lady de Lannoy, all shall be as you wish.'

There was little sleep in the Castle that night till late. Mr. Hilton slept on a sofa in the Queen's Room after he had administered a narcotic to his patient.

As soon as the eastern sky began to quicken, he rode, as he had arranged during the evening, to Dr. Winter's house at Lannoch Port where he was staying. After selecting such instruments and drugs as he required, he came back in the dogcart.

It was still early morning when he regained the Castle. He found Lady de Lannoy up and looking anxiously for him. Her concern was somewhat abated when he was able to tell her that his patient still slept.

It was a painful scene for Mr. Hilton when his patient woke. Fortunately some of the after-effects of the narcotic remained, for his despair at realising that he was blind was terrible. It was not that he was violent; to be so under his present circumstances would have been foreign to Harold's nature. But there was a despair which was infinitely more sad to witness than passion. He simply moaned to himself:

'Blind! Blind!' and again in every phase of horrified amazement, as though he could not realise the truth: 'Blind! Blind!' The Doctor laid his hand on his breast and said very gently:

'My poor fellow, it is a dreadful thing to face, to think of. But as yet I have not been able to come to any conclusion; unable even to examine you. I do not wish to encourage hopes that may be false, but there are cases when injury is not vital and perhaps only temporary. In such case your best chance, indeed your only chance, is to keep quiet. You must not even think if possible of anything that may excite you. I am now about to examine you with the ophthalmoscope. You are a man; none of us who saw your splendid feat last night can doubt your pluck. Now I want you to use some of it to help us both. You, for your recovery, if such is possible; me, to help me in my work. I have asked some of your late companions who tell me that on shipboard you were not only well and of good sight, but that you were remarkable even amongst strong men. Whatever it is you suffer from must have come on quickly. Tell me all you can remember of it.'

The Doctor listened attentively whilst Harold told all he could remember of his sufferings. When he spoke of the return of old rheumatic pains his hearer said involuntarily: 'Good!' Harold paused; but went on at once. The Doctor recognised that he had rightly appraised his remark, and by it judged that he was a well-educated man. Something in the method of speaking struck him, and he said, as nonchalantly as he could:

'By the way, which was your University?'

'Cambridge. Trinity.' He spoke without thinking, and the instant he had done so stopped. The sense of his blindness rushed back on him. He could not see; and his ears were not yet trained to take the place of his eyes. He must guard himself. Thenceforward he was so cautious in his replies that Mr. Hilton felt convinced there was some purpose in his reticence. He therefore stopped asking questions, and began to examine him. He was unable to come to much result; his opinion was shown in his report to Lady de Lannoy:

'I am unable to say anything definite as yet. The case is a most interesting one; as a case and quite apart from the splendid fellow who is the subject of it. I have hopes that within a few days I may be able to know more. I need not trouble you with surgical terms; but later on if the diagnosis supports the supposition at present in my mind I shall be able to speak more fully. In the meantime I shall, with your permission, wait here so that I may watch him myself.'

'Oh you are good. Thank you! Thank you!' said Stephen. She had so taken the man under her own care that she was grateful for any kindness shown to him.

'Not at all,' said Mr. Hilton. 'Any man who behaved as that fellow did has a claim on any of us who may help him. No time of mine could be better spent.'

When he went back to the patient's room he entered softly, for he thought he might be asleep. The room was, according to his instructions, quite dark, and as it was unfamiliar to him he felt his way cautiously. Harold, however, heard the small noise he made and said quietly:

'Who is there?'

'It is I; Hilton.'

'Are you alone?'

'Yes.'

'Look round the room and see. Then lock the door and come and talk to me if you will. You will pity a poor blind fellow, I know. The darkness has come down upon me so quickly that I am not accustomed to it!' There was a break in his voice which moved the other. He lit a candle, feeling that the doing so would impress his patient, and went round the room; not with catlike movement this time—he wanted the other to hear him. When he had turned the key in the lock, as sharply as he could, he came to the bedside and sat down. Harold spoke again after a short pause:

'Is that candle still lit?'

'Yes! Would you like it put out?'

'If you don't mind! Again I say pity me and pardon me. But I want to ask you something privately, between our two selves; and I will feel more of equality than if you were looking at me, whilst I cannot see you.' Mr Hilton blew out the candle.

'There! We are equal now.'

'Thank you!' A long pause; then he went on:

'When a man becomes suddenly blind is there usually, or even occasionally, any sort of odd sight? . . . Does he see anything like a dream, a vision?'

'Not that I know of. I have never heard of such a case. As a rule people struck blind by lightning, which is the most common cause, sometimes remember with extraordinary accuracy the last thing they have seen. Just as though it were photographed on the retina!'

'Thank you! Is such usually the recurrence of any old dream or anything they have much thought of?'

'Not that I know of. It would be unusual!' Harold waited a long time before he spoke again. When he did so it was in a different voice; a constrained voice. The Doctor, accustomed to take enlightenment from trivial details, noted it:

'Now tell me, Mr. Hilton, something about what has happened. Where am I?'

'In Lannoy Castle.'

'Where is it?'

'In Angleshire!'

'Who does it belong to?'

'Lady de Lannoy. The Countess de Lannoy; they tell me she is a Countess in her own right.'

'It is very good of her to have me here. Is she an old lady?'

'No! A young one. Young and very beautiful.' After a pause before his query:

'What's she like? Describe her to me!'

'She is young, a little over twenty. Tall and of a very fine figure. She has eyes like black diamonds, and hair like a flame!' For a long time Harold remained still. Then he said:

'Tell me all you know or have learned of this whole affair. How was I rescued, and by whom?' So the Doctor proceeded to give him every detail he knew of. When he was quite through, the other again lay still for a long time. The silence was broken by a gentle tap at the door. The Doctor lit a candle. He turned the key softly, so that no one would notice that the door was locked. Something was said in a low whisper. Then the door was gently closed, and the Doctor returning said:

'Lady Lannoy wants, if it will not disturb you, to ask how you are. Ordinarily I should not let anyone see you. But she is not only your hostess, but, as I have just told you, it was her ride to the headland, where she burned the house to give you light, which was the beginning of your rescue. Still if you think it better not . . . !'

'I hardly like anybody to see me like this!' said Harold, feebly seeking an excuse.

'My dear man,' said the other, 'you may be easy in your mind, she won't see much of you. You are all bandages and beard. She'll have to wait a while before she sees you.'

'Didn't she see me last night?'

'Not she! Whilst we were trying to restore you she was rushing back to the Castle to see that all was ready for you, and for the others from the wreck.' This vaguely soothed Harold.

If his surmise was correct, and if she had not seen him then, it was well that he was bandaged now. He felt that it would not do to refuse to let her see him; it might look suspicious. So after pausing a short while he said in a low voice:

'I suppose she had better come now. We must not keep her waiting!' When the Doctor brought her to his bedside Stephen felt in a measure awed. His bandaged face and head and his great beard, singed in patches, looked to her in the dim light rather awesome. In a very gentle voice she said kind things to the sick man, who acknowledged them in a feeble whisper. The Doctor, a keen observer, noticed the change in his voice, and determined to understand more. Stephen spoke of his bravery, and of how it was due to him that all on the ship were saved; and as she spoke her emotion moved her so much that her sweet voice shook and quivered. To the ears of the man who had now only sound to guide him, it was music of the sweetest he had ever heard. Fearing lest his voice should betray him, he whispered his own thanks feebly and in few words.

When Stephen went away the Doctor went with her; it was more than an hour before he returned. He found his patient in what he considered a state of suppressed excitement; for, though his thoughts were manifestly collected and his words were calm, he was restless and excited in other ways. He had evidently been thinking of his own condition; for shortly after the Doctor came in he said:

'Are we alone?'

'Quite!'

'I want you to arrange that there shall not be any nurse with me.'

'My dear sir! Don't handicap me, and yourself, with such a restriction. It is for your own good that you should have regular and constant attention.'

'But I don't wish it. Not for the present at all events. I am not accustomed to a nurse, and shall not feel comfortable. In a few days perhaps . . . ' The decided tone of his voice struck the other. Keeping his own thoughts and intentions in abeyance, even to himself, he answered heartily:

'All right! I shall not have any nurse, at present.'

'Thanks!' There was relief in the tone which seemed undue, and Mr. Hilton again took mental note. Presently he asked a question, but in such a tone that the Doctor pricked up his ears. There was a premeditated self-suppression, a gravity of restraint, which implied some falsity; some intention other than the words conveyed:

'It must have been a job to carry me up those stairs.' The Doctor was doubting everything, but as the safest attitude he stuck to literal truth so far as his words conveyed it:

'Yes. You are no light weight!' To himself he mused:

'How did he know there were stairs? He cannot know it; he was senseless! Therefore he must be guessing or inquiring!' Harold went on:

'I suppose the Castle is on high ground. Can you see far from the windows? I suppose we are up a good height?'

'From the windows you can see all round the promontory. But we are not high up; that is, the room is not high from the ground, though the Castle is from the sea.' Harold asked again, his voice vibrating in the note of gladness:

'Are we on the ground floor then?'

'Yes.'

'And I suppose the gardens are below us?'

'Yes.' The answer was given quickly, for a thought was floating through him: Why did this strong brave man, suddenly stricken blind, wish to know whether his windows were at a height? He was not surprised when his patient reaching out a hand rested it on his arm and said in an imploring tone:

'It should be moonlight; full moon two nights ago. Won't you pull up the blind and describe to me all you see? . . . Tell me fully . . . Remember, I am blind!'

This somehow fixed the Doctor's thought:

'Suicide! But I must convey the inutility of such effort by inference, not falsity.'

Accordingly he began to describe the scene, from the very base of the wall, where below the balcony the great border was glorious with a mass of foliage plants, away to the distant sea, now bathed in the flood of moonlight. Harold asked question after question; the Doctor replying accurately till he felt that the patient was building up a concrete idea of his surroundings near and far. Then he left him. He stood for a long time out in the passage thinking. He said to himself as he moved away:

'The poor fellow has some grim intention in his mind. I must not let him know that I suspect; but to-night I will watch without his knowing it!'

CHAPTER-34
Waiting

Mr. Hilton telegraphed at once countermanding, for the present, the nurse for whom he had sent.

That night, when the household had all retired, he came quietly to his patient's room, and entering noiselessly, sat silent in a far corner. There was no artificial right; the patient had to be kept in darkness. There was, however, a bright moonlight; sufficient light stole in through the edges of the blinds to allow him, when his eyes grew accustomed, to see what might happen.

Harold lay quite still till the house was quiet. He had been thinking, ever since he had ascertained the identity of Stephen. In his weakness and the paralysing despair of his blindness all his former grief and apprehension had come bank upon him in a great wave; veritably the tide of circumstances seemed to run hard against him. He had had no idea of forcing himself upon Stephen; and yet here he was a guest in her house, without her knowledge or his own. She had saved his life by her energy and resource. Fortunately she did not as yet know him; the bandages, and his act in suppressing his voice, had so far protected him. But such could not last for long. He could not see to protect himself, and take precautions as need arose. And he knew well that Stephen's nature would not allow her to be satisfied without doing all that was possible to help one who had under her eyes made a great effort on behalf of others, and to whom there was the added bond that his life was due to her. In but a little time she must find out to whom she ministered.

What then would happen? Her kindness was such that when she realised the blindness of her old friend she might so pity him that out of the depths of her pity she would forgive. She would take back all the past; and now that she knew of his old love for her, would perhaps be willing to marry him. Back flooded the old memory of her independence and her theory of sexual equality. If out of any selfish or mistaken idea she did not hesitate to ask a man to marry her, would it be likely that when the nobler and more heroic side of her nature spoke she would hesitate to a similar act in pursuance of her self-sacrifice?

So it might be that she would either find herself once again flouted, or else married to a man she did not love.

Such a catastrophe should not happen, whatever the cost to him. He would, blind as he was, steal away in the night and take himself out of her life; this time for ever. Better the ingratitude of an unknown man, the saving of whose life was due to her, than the long dull routine of a spoiled life, which would otherwise be her unhappy lot.

When once this idea had taken root in his mind he had taken such steps as had been open to him without endangering the secrecy of his motive. Thanks to his subtle questioning of the Doctor, he now knew that his room was close to the ground, so that he would easily drop from the window and steal away with out immediate danger of any restraining accident. If he could once get away he would be all right. There was a large sum to his credit in each of two London banks. He would manage somehow to find his way to London; even if he had to walk and beg his way.

He felt that now in the silence of the night the time had come. Quietly he rose and felt his way to the door, now and again stumbling and knocking against unknown obstacles in the manner of the recently blind. After each such noise he paused and listened. He felt as if the very walls had ears. When he reached the door he turned the key softly. Then he breathed more freely. He felt that he was at last alone and free to move without suspicion.

Then began a great and arduous search; one that was infinitely difficult and exasperating; and full of pathos to the sympathetic man who watched him in silence. Mr. Hilton could not understand his movements as he felt his way about the room, opening drawers and armoires, now and again stooping down and feeling along the floor. He did not betray his presence, however, but moved noiselessly away as the other approached. It was a hideously real game of blindman's-buff, with perhaps a life as the forfeit.

Harold went all over the room, and at last sat down on the edge of his bed with a hollow suppressed groan that was full of pain. He had found his clothes, but realised that they were now but rags. He put on the clothes, and then for a long time sat quiet, rocking gently to and fro as one in pain, a figure of infinite woe. At last he roused himself. His mind was made up; the time for action had come. He groped his way towards the window looking south. The Doctor, who had taken off his shoes, followed him with catlike stealthiness.

He easily threw open the window, for it was already partly open for ventilation.

When Mr. Hilton saw him sit on the rail of the balcony and begin to raise his feet, getting ready to drop over, he rushed forward and seized him. Harold instinctively grappled with him; the habit of his Alaskan life amidst continual danger made in such a case action swift as thought. Mr. Hilton, with the single desire to prevent him from killing himself, threw himself backward and pulled Harold with him to the stone floor.

Harold, as he held him in a grip of iron, thundered out, forgetful in the excitement of the moment the hushed voice to which he had limited himself:

'What do you want? who are you?'

'H-s-s-sh! I am Mr. Hilton.' Harold relaxed the rigour of his grasp but still held him firmly:

'How did you come here? I locked my door!'

'I have been in the room a long time. I suspected something, and came to watch; to prevent your rash act.'

'Rash act! How?'

'Why, man, if you didn't kill, you would at least cripple yourself.'

'How can I cripple myself when the flower-bed is only a few feet below?'

'There are other dangers for a man who—a man in your sad state. And, besides, have I no duty to prevent a suicide!' Here a brilliant idea struck Harold. This man had evidently got some wrong impression; but it would serve to shield his real purpose. He would therefore encourage it. For the moment, of course, his purpose to escape unnoticed was foiled; but he would wait, and in due time seize another opportunity. In a harder and more determined tone than he had yet used he said:

'I don't see what right you have to interfere. I shall kill myself if I like.'

'Not whilst you are in my care!' This was spoken with a resolution equal to his own. Then Mr. Hilton went on, more softly and with infinite compassion: 'Moreover, I want to have a talk with you which may alter your views.' Harold interrupted, still playing the game of hiding his real purpose:

'I shall do as I wish; as I intend.'

'You are injuring yourself even now by standing in the draught of that open window. Your eyes will feel it before long . . . Are you mad . . . ?'

Harold felt a prick like a pin in his neck; and turned to seize his companion. He could not find him, and for a few moments stumbled through the dark, raging . . .

It seemed a long time before he remembered anything. He had a sense of time lapsed; of dreamland thoughts and visions. Then gradually recollection came back. He tried to move; but found it impossible. His arms and legs were extended wide and were tied; he could feel the cord hurting his wrists and ankles as he moved. To him it was awful to be thus blind and helpless; and anger began to surge up. He heard the voice of Mr. Hilton close by him speaking in a calm, grave, sympathetic tone:

'My poor fellow, I hated to take such a step; but it was really necessary for your own safety. You are a man, and a brave one. Won't you listen to me for a few minutes? When you have heard what I have to say I shall release you. In the meantime I apologise for the outrage, as I dare say you consider it!' Harold was reasonable; and he was now blind and helpless. Moreover, there was something in the Doctor's voice that carried a sense of power with it.

'Go on! I shall listen!' He compelled himself to quietude. The Doctor saw, and realised that he was master of himself. There were some snips of scissors, and he was free.

'See! all I want is calm for a short time, and you have it. May I go on?'

'Go on!' said Harold, not without respect. The Doctor after a pause spoke:

'My poor fellow, I want you to understand that I wish to help you, to do all in my power to restore to you that which you seem to have lost! I can sympathise with your desire to quit life altogether now that the best part of it, sight, seems gone. I do not pretend to judge the actions of my fellows; and if you determine to carry out your purpose I shall not be able to prevent you for ever. I shall not try to. But you certainly shall not do so till you know what I know! I had wished to wait till I could be a little more certain before I took you into confidence with regard to my guessing as to the future. But your desire to destroy yourself forces my hand. Now let me tell you that there is a possibility of the removal of the cause of your purpose.'

'What do you mean?' gasped Harold. He was afraid to think outright and to the full what the other's words seemed to imply.

'I mean,' said the other solemnly, 'that there is a possibility, more than a possibility, that you may recover your sight!' As he spoke there was a little break in his voice. He too was somewhat unnerved at the situation.

Harold lay still. The whole universe seemed to sway, and then whirl round him in chaotic mass. Through it at length he seemed to hear the calm voice:

'At first I could not be sure of my surmise, for when I used the ophthalmoscope your suffering was too recent to disclose the cause I looked for. Now I am fairly sure of it. What I have since heard from you has convinced me; your having suffered from rheumatic fever, and the recrudescence of the rheumatic pain after your terrible experience of the fire and that long chilling swim with so seemingly hopeless an end to it; the symptoms which I have since noticed, though they have not been as enlightening to me as they might be. Your disease, as I have diagnosed it, is an obscure one and not common. I have not before been able to study a case. All these things give me great hopes.'

'Thank God! Thank God!' the voice from the bed was now a whisper.

'Thank God! say I too. This that you suffer from is an acute form of inflammation of the optic nerve. It may of course end badly; in permanent loss of sight. But I hope—I believe, that in your case it will not be so. You are young, and you are immensely strong; not merely muscularly, but in constitution. I can see that you have been an athlete, and no mean one either. All this will stand to you. But it will take time. It will need all your own help; all the calm restraint of your body and your mind. I am doing all that science knows; you must do the rest!' He waited, giving time to the other to realise his ideas. Harold lay still for a long time before he spoke:

'Doctor.' The voice was so strangely different that the other was more hopeful at once. He had feared opposition, or conflict of some kind. He answered as cheerily as he could:

'Yes! I am listening.'

'You are a good fellow; and I am grateful to you, both for what you have done and what you have told me. I cannot say how grateful just yet; hope unmans me at present. But I think you deserve that I should tell you the truth!' The other nodded; he forgot that the speaker could not see.

'I was not intending to commit suicide. Such an idea didn't even enter my head. To me, suicide is the resource of a coward. I have been in too many tight places to ever fear that.'

'Then in the name of goodness why were you trying to get out of that window?'

'I wanted to escape; to get away!'

'In your shirt and trousers; and they are not over much! Without even slippers!' A faint smile curled round the lips of the injured man. Hope was beginning to help already.

'Even that way!'

'But man alive! you were going to your death. How could you expect to get away in such an outfit without being discovered? When you were missed the whole countryside would have been up, and even before the hue-and-cry the first person who saw you would have taken charge of you.'

'I know! I know! I had thought of it all. But I was willing to chance it. I had my own reasons!' He was silent a while. The Doctor was silent too. Each man was thinking in his own way. Presently the Doctor spoke:

'Look here, old chap! I don't want to pry into your secrets; but, won't you let me help you? I can hold my tongue. I want to help you. You have earned that wish from any man, and woman too, who saw the burning ship and what you did to save those on board. There is nothing I would not do for you. Nothing! I don't ask you to tell me all; only enough for me to understand and help. I can see that you have some overpowering wish to get away. Some reason that I cannot fathom, certainly without a clue. You may trust me, I assure you. If you could look into my face, my eyes, you would understand. But—There! take my hand. It may tell you something!'

Harold took the hand placed in his, and held it close. He pressed his other hand over it also, as though the effect of the two hands would bring him double knowledge. It was infinitely pathetic to see him trying to make his untrained fingers do the duty of his trained eyes. But, trained or not, his hands had their instinct. Laying down gently the hand he held he said, turning his bandaged eyes in the direction of his companion:

'I shall trust you! Are we alone; absolutely alone?'

'Absolutely!'

'Have I your solemn promise that anything I say shall never go beyond yourself?'

'I promise. I can swear, if it will make your mind more easy in the matter.'

'What do you hold most sacred in the world?' Harold had an odd thought; his question was its result.

'All told, I should think my profession! Perhaps it doesn't seem to you much to swear by; but it is all my world! But I have been brought up in honour, and you may trust my promise—as much as anything I could swear.'

'All right! My reason for wanting to get away was because I knew Lady de Lannoy!'

'What!' Then after a pause: 'I should have thought that was a reason for wanting to stay. She seems not only one of the most beautiful, but the sweetest woman I ever met.'

'She is all that! And a thousand times more!'

'Then why—Pardon me!'

'I cannot tell you all; but you must take it that my need to get away is imperative.' After pondering a while Mr. Hilton said suddenly:

'I must ask your pardon again. Are you sure there is no mistake. Lady de Lannoy is not married; has not been. She is Countess in her own right. It is quite a romance. She inherited from some old branch of more than three hundred years ago.' Again Harold smiled; he quite saw what the other meant.

He answered gravely

'I understand. But it does not alter my opinion; my purpose. It is needful—absolutely and imperatively needful that I get away without her recognising me, or knowing who I am.'

'She does not know you now. She has not seen you yet.'

'That is why I hoped to get away in time; before she should recognise me. If I stay quiet and do all you wish, will you help me?'

'I will! And what then?'

'When I am well, if it should be so, I shall steal away, this time clothed, and disappear out of her life without her knowing. She may think it ungrateful that one whom she has treated so well should behave so badly. But that can't be helped. It is the lesser evil of the two.'

'And I must abet you? All right! I will do it; though you must forgive me if you should ever hear that I have abused you and said bad things of you. It will have to be all in the day's work if I am not ultimately to give you away. I must take steps at once to keep her from seeing you. I shall have to invent some story; some new kind of dangerous disease, perhaps. I shall stay here and nurse you myself!' Harold spoke in joyful gratitude:

'Oh, you *are* good. But can you spare the time? How long will it all take?'

'Some weeks! Perhaps!' He paused as if thinking. 'Perhaps in a month's time I shall unbandage your eyes. You will then see; or . . . '

'I understand! I shall be patient!'

In the morning Mr. Hilton in reporting to Lady de Lannoy told her that he considered it would be necessary to keep his patient very quiet, both in mind and body. In the course of the conversation he said:

'Anything which might upset him must be studiously avoided. He is not an easy patient to deal with; he doesn't like people to go near him. I think, therefore, it will be well if even you do not see him. He seems to have an odd distrust of people, especially of women. It may be that he is fretful in his blindness, which is in itself so trying to a strong man. But besides, the treatment is not calculated to have a very buoyant effect. It is apt to make a man fretful to lie in the dark, and know that he has to do so for indefinite weeks. Pilocarpin, and salicylate of soda, and mercury do not tend towards cheerfulness. Nor do blisters on the forehead add to the content of life!'

'I quite understand,' said Stephen, 'and I will be careful not to go near him till he is well. Please God! it may bring him back his sight. Thank you a thousand times for your determination to stay with him.'

So it was that for more than two weeks Harold was kept all alone. No one attended him but the Doctor. He slept in the patient's room for the whole of the first week, and never had him out of sight for more than a few minutes at a time. He was then able to leave him alone for longer periods, and settled himself in the bedroom next to him. Every hour or two he would visit him. Occasionally he would be away for half a day, but never for more. Stephen rigidly observed the Doctor's advice herself, and gave strict orders that his instructions were to be obeyed.

Harold himself went through a period of mental suffering. It was agony to him to think of Stephen being so near at hand, and yet not to be able to see her, or even to hear her voice. All the pain of his loss of her affection seemed to crowd back on him, and with it the new need of escaping from her unknown. More than ever he felt it would not do that she should ever learn his identity. Her pity for him, and possibly her woman's regard for a man's effort in time of stress, might lead through the gates of her own self-sacrifice to his restoration to his old place in her affections. Nay! it could not be his old place; for at the close of those days she had learned of his love for her.

CHAPTER-35
A Cry

The third week had nearly elapsed, and as yet no one was allowed to see the patient.

For a time Stephen was inclined to be chagrined. It is not pleasant to have even the most generous and benevolent intentions thwarted; and she had set her mind on making much of this man whom fate and his own bravery had thrown athwart her life. But in these days Stephen was in some ways a changed woman. She had so much that she wished to forget and that she would have given worlds to recall, that she could not bear even to think of any militant or even questioning attitude. She even began to take herself to task more seriously than she had ever done with regard to social and conventional duties. When she found her house full of so many and so varied guests, it was borne in upon her that such a position as her own, with such consequent duties, called for the presence of some elder person of her own sex and of her own class.

No better proof of Stephen's intellectual process and its result could be adduced than her first act of recognition: she summoned an elderly lady to live with her and matronise her house. This lady, the widow of a distant relation, complied with all the charted requirements of respectability, and had what to Stephen's eyes was a positive gift: that of minding her own business and not interfering in any matter whatever. Lady de Lannoy, she felt, was her own master and quite able to take care of herself. Her own presence was all that convention required. So she limited herself to this duty, with admirable result to all, herself included. After a few days Stephen would almost forget that she was present.

Mr. Hilton kept bravely to his undertaking. He never gave even a hint of his hopes of the restoration of sight; and he was so assiduous in his attention that there arose no opportunity of accidental discovery of the secret. He knew that when the time did come he would find himself in a very unpleasant situation. Want of confidence, and even of intentional deceit, might be attributed to him; and he would not be able to deny nor explain. He was, however; determined to stick to his word. If he could but save his patient's sight he would be satisfied.

But to Stephen all the mystery seemed to grow out of its first shadowy importance into something real. There was coming to her a vague idea that she would do well not to manifest any concern, any anxiety, any curiosity. Instinct was at work; she was content to trust it, and wait.

One forenoon she received by messenger a letter which interested her much. So much that at first she was unwilling to show it to anyone, and took it to her own boudoir to read over again in privacy. She had a sort of feeling of expectancy with regard to it; such as sensitive natures feel before a thunderstorm. The letter was natural enough in itself. It was dated that morning from Varilands, a neighbouring estate which marched with Lannoy to the south.

> 'My Dear Madam,—Will you pardon me a great liberty, and allow my little girl and me to come to see you to-day? I shall explain when we meet. When I say that we are Americans and have come seven thousand miles for the purpose, you will, I am sure, understand that it is no common interest which has brought us, and it will be the excuse for our eagerness. I should write you more fully, but as the matter is a confidential one I thought it would be better to speak. We shall be doubly grateful if you will have the kindness to see us alone. I write as a mother in making this appeal to your kindness; for my child—she is only a little over eight years old—has the matter so deeply in her heart that any disappointment or undue delay would I fear affect her health. We presume to take your kindness for granted and will call a little before twelve o'clock.
>
> 'I may perhaps say (in case you should feel any hesitation as to my *bona fides*) that my husband purchased some years ago this estate. We were to have come here to live in the early summer, but were kept in the West by some important business of his.
>
> 'Believe me, yours sincerely,
> 'Alice Stonehouse.'

Stephen had, of course, no hesitation as to receiving the lady. Even had there been objection, the curiosity she had in common with her kind would have swept difficulties aside. She gave orders that when Mrs. Stonehouse arrived with her daughter they were to be shown at once into the Mandarin drawing-room. That they would probably stay for lunch. She would see them alone.

A little before twelve o'clock Mrs. Stonehouse and Pearl arrived, and were shown into the room where Lady de Lannoy awaited them. The high sun, streaming in from the side, shone on her beautiful hair, making it look like living gold. When the Americans came in they were for an instant entranced by her beauty. One glance at Mrs. Stonehouse's sweet sympathetic face was enough to establish her in Stephen's good graces forever. As for Pearl, she was like one who has unexpectedly seen a fairy or a goddess. She had been keeping guardedly behind her mother, but on the instant she came out fearlessly into the open.

Stephen advanced quickly and shook hands with Mrs. Stonehouse, saying heartily:

'I am so glad you have come. I am honoured in being trusted.'

'Thank you so much, Lady de Lannoy. I felt that you would not mind, especially when you know why we came. Indeed I had no choice. Pearl insisted on it; and when Pearl is urgent—we who love her have all to give way. This is Pearl!'

In an instant Stephen was on her knees by the beautiful child.

The red rosebud of a mouth was raised to her kiss, and the little arms went lovingly round her neck and clung to her. As the mother looked on delighted she thought she had never seen a more beautiful sight. The two faces so different, and yet with so much in common. The red hair and the flaxen, both tints of gold. The fine colour of each heightened to a bright flush in their eagerness. Stephen was so little used to children, and yet loved them so, that all the womanhood in her, which is possible motherhood, went out in an instant to the lovely eager child. She felt the keenest pleasure when the little thing, having rubbed her silk-gloved palms over her face, and then holding her away so that she could see her many beauties, whispered in her ear:

'How pretty you are!'

'You darling!' whispered Stephen in reply. 'We must love each other very much, you and I!'

When the two ladies had sat down, Stephen holding Pearl in her lap, Mrs. Stonehouse said:

'I suppose you have wondered, Lady de Lannoy, what has brought us here?'

'Indeed I was very much interested.'

'Then I had better tell you all from the beginning so that you may understand.' She proceeded to give the details of the meeting with Mr. Robinson on the *Scoriac*. Of how Pearl took to him and insisted on making him her special friend; of the terrible incident of her being swept overboard, and of the gallant rescue. Mrs. Stonehouse was much moved as she spoke. All that fearful time, of which the minutes had seemed years of agony, came back to her so vividly at times that she could hardly speak. Pearl listened too; all eagerness, but without fear. Stephen was greatly moved and held Pearl close to her all the time, as though protecting her. When the mother spoke of her feeling when she saw the brave man struggling up and down the giant waves, and now and again losing sight of him in the trough of the sea, she put out one hand and held the mother's with a grasp which vibrated in sympathy, whilst the great tears welled over in her eyes and ran down her cheeks. Pearl, watching her keenly, said nothing, but taking her tiny cambric handkerchief from her pocket silently wiped the tears away, and clung all the tighter. It was her turn to protect now!

Pearl's own time for tears came when her mother began to tell this new and sympathetic friend of how she became so much attached to her rescuer that when she knew he would not be coming to the West with them, but going off to the wildest region of the far North, her health became impaired; and that it was only when Mr. Robinson promised to come back to see her within three years that she was at all comforted. And how, ever since, she had held the man in her heart and thought of him every day; sleeping as well as waking, for he was a factor in her dreams!

Stephen was more than ever moved, for the child's constancy touched her as well as her grief. She strained the little thing in her strong young arms, as though the fervency of her grasp would bring belief and comfort; as it did. She in her turn dried the others' eyes. Then Mrs. Stonehouse went on with her story:

'We were at Banff, high up in the Rockies, when we read of the burning and wrecking of the *Dominion*. It is, as you know, a Montreal boat of the Allan Line; so that naturally there was a full telegraphic report in all the Canadian papers. When we read of the brave man who swam ashore with the line and who was unable to reach the port but swam out across the bay, Pearl took it for granted that it must have been "The Man," as she always called Mr. Robinson. When by the next paper we learned that the man's name *was* Robinson nothing would convince her that it was not *her* Mr. Robinson. My husband, I may tell you, had firmly come to the same conclusion. He had ever since the rescue of our child always looked for any news from Alaska, whither he knew Mr. Robinson had gone. He learned that up away in the very far North a new goldfield had been discovered by a man of the same name; and that a new town, Robinson City, began to grow up in the wilderness, where the condition of life from the cold was a new experience to even the most hardy gold miners. Then we began to think that the young hero who had so gallantly saved our darling was meeting some of his reward . . . !'

She paused, her voice breaking. Stephen was in a glow of holy feeling. Gladness, joy, gratitude, enthusiasm; she knew not which. It all seemed like a noble dream which was coming true. Mrs. Stonehouse went on:-

'From Californian papers of last month we learned that Robinson, of Robinson City, had sailed for San Francisco, but had disappeared when the ship touched at Portland; and then the whole chain of his identity seemed complete. Nothing would satisfy Pearl but that we should come at once to England and see "The Man," who was wounded and blind, and do what we could for him. Her father could not then come himself; he had important work on hand which he could not leave without some preparation. But he is following us and may be here at any time.

'And now, we want you to help us, Lady de Lannoy. We are not sure yet of the identity of Mr. Robinson, but we shall know the instant we see him, or hear his voice. We have learned that he is still here. Won't you let us? Do let us see him as soon as ever you can!' There was a pleading tone in her voice which alone would have moved Stephen, even had she not been wrought up already by the glowing fervour of her new friend.

But she paused. She did not know what to say; how to tell them that as yet she herself knew nothing. She, too, in the depths of her own heart knew—*knew*—that it was the same Robinson. And she also knew that both identities were one with another. The beating of her heart and the wild surging of her blood told her all. She was afraid to speak lest her voice should betray her.

She could not even think. She would have to be alone for that.

Mrs. Stonehouse, with the wisdom and power of age, waited, suspending judgment. But Pearl was in a fever of anxiety; she could imagine nothing which could keep her away from The Man. But she saw that there was some difficulty, some cause of delay. So she too added her pleading. Putting her mouth close to Lady de Lannoy's ear she whispered very faintly, very caressingly:

'What is your name? Your own name? Your very own name?'

'Stephen, my darling!'

'Oh, won't you let us see The Man, Stephen; dear Stephen! I love him so; and I do *so* want to see him. It is ages till I see him! Won't you let me? I shall be so good—Stephen!' And she strained her closer in her little arms and kissed her all over face, cheeks and forehead and eyes and mouth wooingly. Stephen returned the embrace and the kisses, but remained silent a little longer. Then she found voice:

'I hardly know what to say. Believe me, I should—I shall, do all I can; but the fact is that I am not in authority. The Doctor has taken him in charge and will not let anyone go near him: He will not even have a nurse, but watches and attends to him himself. He says it might be fatal if anything should occur to agitate him. Why, even I am not allowed to see him!'

'Haven't you seen him yet at all; ever, ever, Stephen?' asked Pearl, all her timidity gone. Stephen smiled—a wan smile it was, as she answered:

'I saw him in the water, but it was too far away to distinguish. And it was only by firelight.'

'Oh yes, I know,' said Pearl; 'Mother and Daddy told me how you had burned the house down to give him light. Didn't you want to see him more after that? I should!' Stephen drew the impulsive child closer as she answered:

'Indeed I did, dear. But I had to think of what was good for him. I went to his room the next day when he was awake, and the Doctor let me come in for only a moment.'

'Well! What did you see. Didn't you know him?' She forgot that the other did not know him from her point of view. But the question went through Stephen's heart like a sword. What would she not have given to have known him! What would she not give to know him now! . . . She spoke mechanically:

'The room was quite dark. It is necessary, the Doctor says, that he be kept in the dark. I saw only a big beard, partly burned away by the fire; and a great bandage which covered his eyes!' Pearl's hold relaxed, she slipped like an eel to the floor and ran over to her mother. Her new friend was all very well, but no one would do as well as mother when she was in trouble.

'Oh mother, mother! My Robinson had no beard!' Her mother stroked her face comfortingly as she answered:

'But, my dear, it is more than two years since you saw him. Two years and three months, for it was in June that we crossed.' How the date thrilled Stephen. It verified her assumption.

Mrs. Stonehouse did not notice, but went on:

'His beard would have grown. Men wear beards up in the cold place where he was.' Pearl kissed her; there was no need for words. Throwing herself again on Stephen's knees she went on with her questioning:

'But didn't you hear him?'

'I heard very little, darling. He was very weak. It was only the morning after the wreck, and he spoke in a whisper!' Then with an instinct of self-preservation she added: 'But how could I learn anything by hearing him when he was a stranger to me? I had never even heard of Mr. Robinson!'

As she was speaking she found her own ideas, the proofs of her own conviction growing. This was surely another link in the chain of proving that all three men were but one. But in such case Harold must know; must have tried to hide his identity!

She feared, with keen eyes upon her, to pursue the thought. But her blood began to grow cold and her brain to swim. With an effort she went on:

'Even since then I have not been allowed to go near him. Of course I must obey orders. I am waiting as patiently as I can. But we must ask the Doctor if he thinks his patient will see you—will let you see him—though he will not let me.' This she added with a touch of what she felt: regret rather than bitter ness. There was no room for bitterness in her full heart where Harold was concerned.

'Will you ask the Doctor now?' Pearl did not let grass grow under her feet. For answer Stephen rang the bell, and when a servant appeared asked:

'Is Mr. Hilton in the house?'

'I think not, your Ladyship. He said he was going over to Port Lannoch. Shall I inquire if he left word at what time he would be back?'

'If you please!' The man returned in a few minutes with the butler, who said:

'Mr. Hilton said, your Ladyship, that he expected to be back by one o'clock at latest.'

'Please ask him on his arrival if he will kindly come here at once. Do not let us be disturbed until then.' The butler bowed and withdrew.

'Now,' said Stephen, 'as we have to wait till our tyrant comes, won't you tell me all that went on after The Man had left you?' Pearl brightened up at once. Stephen would have given anything to get away even for a while. Beliefs and hopes and fears were surging up, till she felt choking. But the habit of her life, especially her life of the last two years, gave her self-control. And so she waited, trying with all her might to follow the child's prattle.

After a long wait Pearl exclaimed: 'Oh! I do wish that Doctor would come. I want to see The Man!' She was so restless, marching about the room, that Stephen said:

'Would you like to go out on the balcony, darling; of course if Mother will let you? It is quite safe, I assure you, Mrs. Stonehouse. It is wide and open and is just above the flower-borders, with a stone tail. You can see the road from it by which Mr. Hilton comes from Port Lannoch. He will be riding.' Pearl yielded at once to the diversion. It would at any rate be something to do, to watch. Stephen opened the French window and the child ran out on the balcony.

When Stephen came back to her seat Mrs. Stonehouse said quietly:

'I am glad she is away for a few minutes. She has been over wrought, and I am always afraid for her. She is so sensitive. And after all she is only a baby!'

'She is a darling!' said Stephen impulsively; and she meant it. Mrs. Stonehouse smiled gratefully as she went on:

'I suppose you noticed what a hold on her imagination that episode of Mollie Watford at the bank had. Mr. Stonehouse is, as perhaps you know, a very rich man. He has made his fortune himself, and most honourably; and we are all very proud of him, and of it. So Pearl does not think of the money for itself. But the feeling was everything; she really loves Mr. Robinson; as indeed she ought! He has done so much for us that it would be a pride and a privilege for us to show our gratitude. My husband, between ourselves, wanted to make him his partner. He tells me that, quite independent of our feeling towards him, he is just the man he wanted. And if indeed it was he who discovered the Alaskan goldfield and organised and ruled Robinson City, it is a proof that Mr. Stonehouse's judgment was sound. Now he is injured, and blind; and our little Pearl loves him. If indeed he be the man we believe he is, then we may be able to do something which all his millions cannot buy. He will come to us, and be as a son to us, and a brother to Pearl. We will be his eyes; and nothing but love and patience will guide his footsteps!' She paused, her mouth quivering; then she went on:

'If it is not our Mr. Robinson, then it will be our pleasure to do all that is necessary for his comfort. If he is a poor man he will never want . . . It will be a privilege to save so gallant a man from hardship . . . ' Here she came to a stop.

Stephen too was glad of the pause, for the emotion which the words and their remembrances evoked was choking her. Had not Harold been as her own father's son. As her own brother! . . . She turned away, fearing lest her face should betray her.

All at once Mrs. Stonehouse started to her feet, her face suddenly white with fear; for a cry had come to their ears. A cry which even Stephen knew as Pearl's. The mother ran to the window.

The balcony was empty. She came back into the room, and, ran to the door.

But on the instant a voice that both women knew was heard from without:

'Help there! Help, I say! The child has fainted. Is there no one there? And I am blind!'

CHAPTER-36
Light

Harold had been in a state of increasing restlessness. The month of waiting which Dr. Hilton had laid down for him seemed to wear away with extraordinary slowness; this was increased by the lack of companionship, and further by the cutting off of even the little episodes usual to daily life. His patience, great as it was naturally and trained as it had been by the years of self-repression, was beginning to give way. Often and often there came over him a wild desire to tear off the irksome bandages and try for himself whether the hopes held out to him were being even partially justified. He was restrained only by the fear of perpetual blindness, which came over him in a sort of cold wave at each reaction. Time, too, added to his fear of discovery; but he could not but think that his self-sought isolation must be a challenge to the curiosity of each and all who knew of it. And with all these disturbing causes came the main one, which never lessened but always grew: that whatever might happen Stephen would be further from him than ever. Look at the matter how he would; turn it round in whatsoever possible or impossible way, he could see no relief to this gloomy conclusion.

For it is in the nature of love that it creates or enlarges its own pain. If troubles or difficulties there be from natural causes, then it will exaggerate them into nightmare proportions. But if there be none, it will create them. Love is in fact the most serious thing that comes to man; where it exists all else seem as phantoms, or at best as actualities of lesser degree. During the better part of two years his troubles had but slept; and as nothing wakes the pangs of old love better than the sound of a voice, all the old acute pain of love and the agony that followed its denial were back with him. Surely he could never, never believe that Stephen did not mean what she had said to him that morning in the beech grove. All his new resolution not to hamper her with the burden of a blind and lonely-hearted man was back to the full.

In such mood had he been that morning. He was additionally disturbed because the Doctor had gone early to Port Lannoch; and as he was the only person with whom he could talk, he clung to him with something of the helpless feeling of a frightened child to its nurse.

The day being full of sunshine the window was open, and only the dark-green blind which crackled and rustled with every passing breeze made the darkness of the room. Harold was dressed and lay on a sofa placed back in the room, where the few rays of light thus entering could not reach him. His eyes and forehead were bandaged as ever. For some days the Doctor, who had his own reasons and his own purpose, had not taken them off; so the feeling of blind helplessness was doubly upon him. He knew he was blind; and he knew also that if he were not he could not in his present condition see.

All at once he started up awake. His hearing had in the weeks of darkness grown abnormally acute, and some trifling sound had recalled him to himself. It might have been inspiration, but he seemed to be conscious of some presence in the room.

As he rose from the sofa, with the violent motion of a strong man startled into unconscious activity, he sent a shock of fear to the eager child who had strayed into the room through the open window. Had he presented a normal appearance, she would not have been frightened. She would have recognised his identity despite the changes, and have sprung to him so impulsively that she would have been in his arms before she had time to think. But now all she saw was a great beard topped with a mass of linen and lint, which obscured all the rest of the face and seemed in the gloom like a gigantic and ominous turban.

In her fright she screamed out. He in turn, forgetful for the moment of his intention of silence, called aloud:

'Who is that?' Pearl, who had been instinctively backing towards the window by which she had entered, and whose thoughts in her fright had gone back to her mother—refuge in time of danger—cried out:

'Mother, Mother! It is him! It is The Man!' She would have run towards him in spite of his forbidding appearance; but the shock had been too much for her. The little knees trembled and gave way; the brain reeled; and with a moan she sank on the floor in a swoon.

Harold knew the voice the instant she spoke; there was no need for the enlightening words

'Pearl! Pearl!' he cried. 'Come to me, darling!' But as he spoke he heard her moan, and the soft thud of her little body on the thick carpet. He guessed the truth and groped his way towards where the sound had been, for he feared lest he might trample upon her in too great eagerness. Kneeling by her he touched her little feet, and then felt his way to her face. And as he did so, such is the double action of the mind, even in the midst of his care the remembrance swept across his mind of how he had once knelt in just such manner in an old church by another little senseless form. In his confusion of mind he lost the direction of the door, and coming to the window pushed forward the flapping blind and went out on the balcony. He knew from the freshness of the air and the distant sounds that he was in the open. This disturbed him, as he wished to find someone who could attend to the fainting child. But as he had lost the way back to the room now, he groped along the wall of the Castle with one hand, whilst he held Pearl securely in the other. As he went he called out for help.

When he came opposite the window of the Mandarin room Mrs. Stonehouse saw him; she ran to him and caught Pearl in her arms. She was so agitated, so lost in concern for the child that she never even thought to speak to the man whom she had come so far to seek. She wailed over the child:

'Pearl! Pearl! What is it, darling? It is Mother!' She laid the girl on the sofa, and taking the flowers out of a glass began to sprinkle water on the child's face. Harold knew her voice and waited in patience. Presently the child sighed; the mother, relieved, thought of other things at last and looked around her.

There was yet another trouble. There on the floor, where she had slipped down, lay Lady de Lannoy in a swoon. She called out instinctively, forgetting for the moment that the man was blind, but feeling all the old confidence which he had won in her heart:

'Oh! Mr. Robinson, help me! Lady de Lannoy has fainted too, and I do not know what to do!' As she spoke she looked up at him and remembered his blindness. But she had no time to alter her words; the instant she had spoken Harold, who had been leaning against the window-sash, and whose mind was calmer since with his acute hearing he too had heard Pearl sigh, seemed to leap into the room.

'Where is she? Where is she? Oh, God, now am I blind indeed!'

It gave her a pang to hear him and to see him turn helplessly with his arms and hands outstretched as though he would feel for her in the air.

Without pause, and under an instinctive and uncontrollable impulse, he tore the bandages from his eyes. The sun was streaming in. As he met it his eyes blinked and a cry burst from him; a wild cry whose joy and surprise pierced even through the shut portals of the swooning woman's brain. Not for worlds would she ever after have lost the memory of that sound:

'Light! light! Oh, God! Oh, God! I am not blind!'

But he looked round him still in terrified wonder:

'Where is she? Where is she? I cannot see her! Stephen! Stephen! where are you?' Mrs. Stonehouse, bewildered, pointed where Stephen's snow-white face and brilliant hair seemed in the streaming sunlight like ivory and gold:

'There! There!' He caught her arm mechanically, and putting his eyes to her wrist, tried to look along her pointed finger. In an instant he dropped her arm moaning.

'I cannot see her! What is it that is over me? This is worse than to be blind!' He covered his face with his hands and sobbed.

He felt light strong fingers on his forehead and hands; fingers whose touch he would have known had they been laid on him were he no longer quick. A voice whose music he had heard in his dreams for two long years said softly:

'I am here, Harold! I am here! Oh! do not sob like that; it breaks my heart to hear you!' He took his hands from his face and held hers in them, staring intently at her as though his passionate gaze would win through every obstacle.

That moment he never forgot. Never could forget! He saw the room all rich in yellow. He saw Pearl, pale but glad-eyed, lying on a sofa holding the hand of her mother, who stood beside her. He saw the great high window open, the lines of the covered stone balcony without, the stretch of green sward all vivid in the sunshine, and beyond it the blue quivering sea. He saw all but that for which his very soul longed; without to see which sight itself was valueless . . . But still he looked, and looked; and Stephen saw in his dark eyes, though he could not see her, that which made her own eyes fill and the warm red glow on her face again . . . Then she raised her eyes again, and the gladness of her beating heart seemed the answer to his own.

For as he looked he saw, as though emerging from a mist whose obscurity melted with each instant, what was to him the one face in all the world. He did not think then of its beauty—that would come later; and besides no beauty of one born of woman could outmatch the memorised beauty which had so long held his heart. But that he had so schooled himself in long months of gloomy despair, he would have taken her in his arms there and then; and, heedless of the presence of others, have poured out his full heart to her.

Mrs. Stonehouse saw and understood. So too Pearl, who though a child was a woman-child; softly they rose up to steal away. But Stephen saw them; her own instincts, too, told her that her hour had not come. What she hoped for must come alone! So she called to her guests:

'Don't go! Don't go, Mrs. Stonehouse. You know now that Harold and I are old friends, though neither of us knew it—till this moment. We were brought up as . . . almost as brother and sister. Pearl, isn't it lovely to see your friend . . . to see The Man again?'

She was so happy that she could only express herself, with dignity, through the happiness of others.

Pearl actually shrieked with joy as she rushed across the room and flung herself into Harold's arms as he stooped to her. He raised her; and she kissed him again and again, and put her little hands all over his face and stroked, very, very gently, his eyes, and said:

'Oh, I am so glad! And so glad your poor eyes are unbind again! May I call you Harold, too?'

'You darling!' was all he could say as he kissed her, and holding her in one arm went across and shook hands with Mrs. Stonehouse, who wrung his hand hard.

There was a little awkwardness in the group, for none of them knew what would be best to do next. In the midst of it there came a light knock at the door, and Mr. Hilton entered saying:

"They told me you wished to see me at once—Hulloa!' He rushed across the room and took Harold by the shoulders, turning his face to the light. He looked in his eyes long and earnestly, the others holding their breaths. Presently he said, without relaxing his gaze:

'Did you see mistily at first?'

'Yes.'

'Seeing at the periphery; but the centre being opaque?'

'Yes! How did you know? Why, I couldn't see'—see pointing to Stephen—'Lady de Lannoy; though her face was right in front of me!'

Dr. Hilton took his hands from his patient's shoulders and shook him warmly by both hands:-

'I am glad, old fellow! It was worth waiting for, wasn't it? But I say, it was a dangerous thing to take off those bandages before I permitted. However, it has done no harm! But it was lucky that I mistrusted your patience and put the time for the experiment a week later than I thought necessary... What is it?' He turned from one to the other questioningly; there was a look on Harold's face that he did not quite comprehend.

'H-s-h,' said the latter warningly, 'I'll tell you all about it . . . some time!'

The awkward pause was broken by Pearl, who came to the Doctor and said:

'I must kiss you, you know. It was you who saved The Man's eyes. Stephen has told me how you watched him!' The Doctor was somewhat taken aback; as yet he was ignorant of Pearl's existence. However, he raised the child in his arms and kissed her, saying:

'Thank you, my dear! I did all I could. But he helped much himself; except at the very last. Don't you ever go and take off bandages, if you should ever have the misfortune to have them on, without the doctor's permission!' Pearl nodded her head wisely and then wriggled out of his arms and came again to Harold, looking up at him protectingly and saying in an old-fashioned way:

'How are you feeling now? None the worse, I hope, *Harold*!'

The Man lifted her up and kissed her again. When he set her down she came over to Lady de Lannoy and held up her arms to be lifted:

'And I must kiss you again too, Stephen!' If Lady de Lannoy hadn't loved the sweet little thing already she would have loved her for that!

The door was opened, and the butler announced:

'Luncheon is served, your Ladyship.'

* * * * *

After a few days Harold went over to Varilands to stay for a while with the Stonehouses. Mr. Stonehouse had arrived, and both men were rejoiced to meet again. The elder never betrayed by word or sign that he recognised the identity of the other person of the drama of whom he had told him and who had come so accidentally into his life; and the younger was grateful to him for it. Harold went almost every day to Lannoy, and sometimes the Stonehouses went with him; at other times Stephen paid flying visits to Varilands. She did not make any effort to detain Harold; she would not for worlds have made a sign which might influence him. She was full now of that diffidence which every woman has who loves. She felt that she must wait; must wait even if the waiting lasted to her grave. She felt, as every woman does who really loves, that she had found her Master.

And Harold, to whom something of the same diffidence was an old story, got the idea that her reticence was a part of the same feeling whose violent expression had sent him out into the wilderness. And with the thought came the idea of his duty, implied in her father's dying trust: 'Give her time! . . . Let her choose!' For him the clock seemed to have stopped for two whole years, and he was back at the time when the guardianship of his boy life was beginning to yield to the larger and more selfish guardianship of manhood.

Stephen, noticing that he did not come near her as closely as she felt he might, and not realising his true reason—for when did love ever realise the true reason of the bashfulness of love?—felt a chillness which in turn reacted on her own manner.

And so these two ardent souls, who yearned for each other's love and the full expression of it, seemed as if they might end after all in drifting apart. Each thought that their secret was concealed. But both secrets were already known to Mrs. Stonehouse, who knew nothing; and to Mr. Stonehouse, who knew everything. Even Pearl had her own ideas, as was once shown in a confidence when they were alone in Stephen's bedroom after helping her to finish her dressing, just as Stephen herself had at a similar age helped her Uncle Gilbert. After some coy leading up to the subject of pretty dresses, the child putting her little mouth to the other's ear whispered:

'May I be your bridesmaid, Stephen?' The woman was taken aback; but she had to speak at once, for the child's eyes were on her:

'Of course you will, darling. But I—I may never be married.'

'You! You must! I know someone who will make you!' Stephen's heart beat hard and rapidly. The child's talk, though sweet and dear, was more than embarrassing. With, however, the desire to play with fire, which is a part of the nature of women, she answered:

'You have some queer ideas, little one, in that pretty knowledge-box of yours.'

'Oh! he never told me. But I know it all the same! And you know it too, Stephen!' This was getting too close to be without danger; so she tried to divert the thought from herself:

'My darling, you may guess about other people, though I don't say you ought; but you must not guess about me!'

'All right!' then she held up her arms to be lifted on the other's knee and said:

'I want to whisper to you!' Her voice and manner were so full of feeling that somehow the other was moved. She bent her head, and Pearl taking her neck in her little palms, said:

'I thought, oh! long ago, that I would marry him myself. But you knew him first . . . And he only saved me . . . But you saved him!' . . . And then she laid her head down on the throbbing bosom, and sobbed . . .

And Stephen sobbed too.

Before they left the room, Stephen said to her, very gravely, for the issue might be one of great concern:

'Of course, Pearl dear, our secrets are all between ourselves!' Pearl crossed her two forefingers and kissed them. But she said nothing; she had sworn! Stephen went on:

'And, darling, you will remember too that one must never speak or even think if they can help it about anyone's marrying anyone else till they say so themselves! What is it, dear, that you are smiling at?'

'I know, Stephen! I musn't take off the bandage till the Doctor says so!'

Stephen smiled and kissed her. Hand in hand, Pearl chattering merrily, they went down to the drawing-room.

CHAPTER-37
Golden Silence

Each day that passed seemed to add to the trouble in the heart of these young people; to widen the difficulty of expressing themselves. To Stephen, who had accepted the new condition of things and whose whole nature had bloomed again under the sunshine of hope, it was the less intolerable. She had set herself to wait, as had countless thousands of women before her; and as due proportion will, till the final cataclysm abolishes earthly unions. But Harold felt the growth, both positive and negative, as a new torture; and he began to feel that he would be unable to go through with it. In his heart was the constant struggle of hope; and in opposition to it the seeming realisation of every new fancy of evil. That bitter hour, when the whole of creation was for him turned upside down, was having its sad effect at last. Had it not been for that horrid remembrance he would have come to believe enough in himself to put his future to the test. He would have made an opportunity at which Stephen and himself would have with the fires of their mutual love burned away the encircling mist. There are times when a single minute of commonsense would turn sorrow into joy; and yet that minute, our own natures being the opposing forces, will be allowed to pass.

Those who loved these young people were much concerned about them. Mrs. Stonehouse took their trouble so much to heart that she spoke to her husband about it, seriously advising that one or other of them should make an effort to bring things in the right way for their happiness. The woman was sure of the woman's feeling. It is from men, not women, that women hide their love. By side-glances and unthinking moments women note and learn. The man knew already, from his own lips, of the man's passion. But his lips were sealed by his loyalty; and he said earnestly:

'My dear, we must not interfere. Not now, at any rate; we might cause them great trouble. I am as sure as you are that they really love each other. But they must win happiness by themselves and through themselves alone.

Otherwise it would never be to them what it ought to be; what it might be; what it will be!'

So these friends were silent, and the little tragedy developed. Harold's patience began to give way under the constant strain of self-suppression. Stephen tried to hide her love and fear, under the mask of a gracious calm. This the other took for indifference.

At last there came an hour which was full of new, hopeless agony to Stephen. She heard Harold, in a fragment of conversation, speak to Mr. Stonehouse of the need of returning to Alaska. That sounded like a word of doom. In her inmost heart she knew that Harold loved her; and had she been free she would have herself spoken the words which would have drawn the full truth to them both. But how could she do so, having the remembrance of that other episode; when, without the reality of love, she had declared herself? . . . Oh! the shame of it . . . The folly! . . . And Harold knew it all! How could he ever believe that it was real this time! . . .

By the exercise of that self-restraint which long suffering had taught her, Stephen so managed to control herself that none of her guests realised what a blow she had received from a casual word. She bore herself gallantly till the last moment. After the old fashion of her youth, she had from the Castle steps seen their departure. Then she took her way to her own room, and locked herself in. She did not often, in these days, give way to tears; when she did cry it was as a luxury, and not from poignant cause. Her deep emotion was dry-eyed as of old. Now, she did not cry, she sat still, her hands clasped below her knees, with set white face gazing out on the far-off sea. For hours she sat there lonely; staring fixedly all the time, though her thoughts were whirling wildly. At first she had some vague purpose, which she hoped might eventually work out into a plan. But thought would not come. Everywhere there was the same beginning: a wild, burning desire to let Harold understand her feeling towards him; to blot out, with the conviction of trust and love, those bitter moments when in the madness of her overstrung passion she had heaped such insult upon him. Everywhere the same end: an impasse. He seemingly could not, would not, understand. She knew now that the man had diffidences, forbearances, self-judgments and self-denials which made for the suppression, in what he considered to be her interest, of his own desires. This was tragedy indeed! Again and again came back the remembrance of that bitter regret of her Aunt Laetitia, which no happiness and no pain of her own had ever been able to efface:

'To love; and be helpless! To wait, and wait, and wait; with heart all aflame! To hope, and hope; till time seemed to have passed away, and all the world to stand still on your hopeless misery! To know that a word might open up Heaven; and yet to have to remain mute! To keep back the glances that could enlighten, to modulate the tones that might betray! To see all you hoped for passing away . . . !'

At last she seemed to understand the true force of pride; which has in it a thousand forces of its own, positive, negative, restrainful. Oh! how blind she had been! How little she had learned from the miseries that the other woman whom she loved had suffered! How unsympathetic she had been; how self-engrossed; how callous to the sensibilities of others! And now to her, in her turn, had come the same suffering; the same galling of the iron fetters of pride, and of convention which is its original expression! Must it be that the very salt of youth must lose its savour, before the joys of youth could be won! What, after all, was youth if out of its own inherent power it must work its own destruction! If youth was so, why not then trust the wisdom of age? If youth could not act for its own redemption . . .

Here the rudiment of a thought struck her and changed the current of her reason. A thought so winged with hope that she dared not even try to complete it! . . . She thought, and thought till the long autumn shadows fell around her. But the misty purpose had become real.

After dinner she went up alone to the mill. It was late for a visit, for the Silver Lady kept early hours. But she found her friend as usual in her room, whose windows swept the course of the sun. Seeing that her visitor was in a state of mental disturbance such as she had once before exhibited, she blew out the candles and took the same seat in the eastern window she had occupied on the night which they both so well remembered.

Stephen understood both acts, and was grateful afresh. The darkness would be a help to her in what she had to say; and the resumption of the old seat and attitude did away with the awkwardness of new confidence. During the weeks that had passed Stephen had kept her friend informed of the rescue and progress of the injured man. Since the discovery of Harold's identity she had allowed her to infer her feeling towards him.

Shyly she had conveyed her hopes that all the bitter part of the past might be wiped out. To the woman who already knew of the love that had always been, but had only awakened to consciousness in the absence of its object, a hint was sufficient to build upon. She had noticed the gloom that had of late been creeping over the girl's happiness; and she had been much troubled about it. But she had thought it wiser to be silent; she well knew that should unhappily the time for comfort come, it must be precluded by new and more explicit confidence. So she too had been anxiously waiting the progress of events. Now; as she put her arms round the girl she said softly; not in the whisper which implies doubt of some kind, but in the soft voices which conveys sympathy and trust:

'Tell me, dear child!'

And then in broken words shyly spoken, and spoken in such a way that the silences were more eloquent than the words, the girl conveyed what was in her heart. The other listened, now and again stroking the beautiful hair. When all was said, there was a brief pause. The Silver Lady spoke no word; but the pressure of her delicate hand conveyed sympathy.

In but a half-conscious way, in words that came so shrinkingly through the darkness that they hardly reached the ear bent low to catch them, came Stephen's murmured thought:

'Oh, if he only knew! And I can't tell him; I can't! dare not! I must not. How could I dishonour him by bearing myself towards him as to that other . . . worthless . . . ! Oh! the happy, happy girls, who have mothers . . . !' All the muscles of her body seemed to shrink and collapse, till she was like an inert mass at the Silver Lady's feet.

But the other understood!

After a long, long pause; when Stephen's sobbing had died away; when each muscle of her body had become rigid on its return to normal calm; the Silver Lady began to talk of other matters, and conversation became normal. Stephen's courage seemed somehow to be restored, and she talked brightly.

Before they parted the Silver Lady made a request. She said in her natural voice:

'Couldst thou bring that gallant man who saved so many lives, and to whom the Lord was so good in the restoration of his sight, to see me? Thou knowest I have made a resolution not to go forth from this calm place whilst I may remain. But I should like to see him before he returns to that far North where he has done such wonders. He is evidently a man of kind heart; perhaps he will not mind coming to see a lonely woman who is no longer young. There is much I should like to ask him of that land of which nothing was known in my own youth. Perhaps he will not mind seeing me alone.' Stephen's heart beat furiously. She felt suffocating with new hope, for what could be but good from Harold's meeting with that sweet woman who had already brought so much comfort into her own life? She was abashed, and yet radiant; she seemed to tread on air as she stood beside her friend saying farewell. She did not wish to speak. So the two women kissed and parted.

It had been arranged that two days hence the Stonehouse party were to spend the day at Lannoy, coming before lunch and staying the night, as they wanted in the afternoon to return a visit at some distance to the north of Lannoy. Harold was to ride over with them.

When the Varilands party arrived, Stephen told them of Sister Ruth's wish to see Harold. Pearl at once proffered a request that she also should be taken at some other time to see the Silver Lady. Harold acquiesced heartily; and it was agreed that some time in the late afternoon he should pay the visit. Stephen would bring him.

Strangely enough, she felt no awkwardness, no trepidation, as they rode up the steep road to the Mill.

When the introduction had been effected, and half an hour had been consumed in conventional small talk, Stephen, obedience to a look from the Silver Lady, rose. She said in they most natural way she could:

'Now Sister Ruth, I will leave you two alone, if you do not mind. Harold can tell you all you want to know about Alaska; and perhaps, if you are very good, he will tell some of his adventures! Good afternoon, dear. I wish you were to be with us to-night; but I know your rule. I go for my ride. Sultan has had no exercise for five days; and he looked at me quite reproachfully when we met this morning. Au revoir, Harold. We shall meet at dinner!'

When she had gone Harold came back from the door, and stood in the window looking east. The Silver Lady came and stood beside him. She did not seem to notice his face, but in the mysterious way of women she watched him keenly. She wished to satisfy her own mind before she undertook her self-appointed task.

Her eyes were turned towards the headland towards which Stephen on her white Arab was galloping at breakneck speed. He was too good a horseman himself, and he knew her prowess on horseback too well to have any anxiety regarding such a rider at Stephen. It was not fear, then, that made his face so white, and his eyes to have such an illimitable sadness.

The Silver Lady made up her mind. All her instincts were to trust him. She recognised a noble nature, with which truth would be her surest force.

'Come,' she said, 'sit here, friend; where another friend has often sat with me. From this you can see all the coastline, and all that thou wilt!' Harold put a chair beside the one she pointed out; and when she was seated he sat also. She began at once with a desperate courage:

'I have wanted much to see thee. I have heard much of thee, before thy coming.' There was something in the tone of her voice which arrested his attention, and he looked keenly at her. Here, in the full light, her face looked sadly white and he noticed that her lips trembled. He said with all the kindliness of his nature, for from the first moment he had seen her he had taken to her, her purity and earnestness and sweetness appealing to some aspiration within him:

'You are pale! I fear you are not well! May I call your maid? Can I do anything for you?' She waved her hand gently:

'Nay! It is nothing. It is but the result of a sleepless night and much thought.'

'Oh! I wish I had known! I could have put off my visit; and I could have come any other time to suit you.' She smiled gently:

'I fear that would have availed but little. It was of thy coming that I was concerned.' Seeing his look of amazement, she went on quickly, her voice becoming more steady as she lost sight of herself in her task:

'Be patient a little with me. I am an old woman; and until recently it has been many and many years since the calm which I sought here has been ruffled. I had come to believe that for me earthly troubles were no more. But there has come into my life a new concern. I have heard so much of thee, and before thy coming.' The recurrence of the phrase struck him. He would have asked how such could be, but he deemed it better to wait. She went on:

'I have been wishful to ask thy advice. But why should not I tell thee outright that which troubles me? I am not used, at least for these many years, to dissemble. I can but trust thee in all; and lean on thy man's mercy to understand, and to aid me!'

'I shall do all in my power, believe me!' said Harold simply. 'Speak freely!' She pointed out of the window, where Stephen's white horse seemed on the mighty sweep of green sward like a little dot.

'It is of her that I would speak to thee!' Harold's heart began to beat hard; he felt that something was coming. The Silver Lady went on:

'Why thinkest thou that she rideth at such speed? It is her habit!' He waited. She continued:

'Doth it not seem to thee that such reckless movement is the result of much trouble; that she seeketh forgetfulness?' He knew that she was speaking truly; and somehow the conviction was borne upon him that she knew his secret heart, and was appealing to it. If it was about Stephen!

If her disquiet was about her; then God bless her! He would be patient and grateful. The Quaker's voice seemed to come through his thought, as though she had continued speaking whilst he had paused:

'We have all our own secrets. I have had mine; and I doubt not that thou hast had, may still have, thine own. Stephen hath hers! May I speak to thee of her?'

'I shall be proud! Oh! madam, I thank you with all my heart for your sweet kindness to her. I cannot say what I feel; for she has always been very dear to me!' In the pause before she spoke again the beating of his own heart seemed to re-echo the quick sounds of Stephen's galloping horse. He was surprised at the method of her speech when it did come; for she forgot her Quaker idiom, and spoke in the phrasing of her youth:

'Do you love her still?'

'With all my soul! More than ever!'

'Then, God be thanked; for it is in your power to do much good. To rescue a poor, human, grieving soul from despair!' Her words conveyed joy greater than she knew. Harold did not himself know why the air seemed filled with sounds that seemed to answer every doubt of his life. He felt, understood, with that understanding which is quicker than thought. The Silver Lady went on now with a rush:

'See, I have trusted you indeed! I have given away another woman's secret; but I do it without fear. I can see that you also are troubled; and when I look back on my own life and remember the trouble that sent me out of the world; a lonely recluse here in this spot far from the stress of life, I rejoice that any act of mine can save such another tragedy as my own. I see that I need not go into detail. You know that I am speaking truth. It was before you came so heroically on this new scene that she told me her secret. At a time when nothing was known of you except that you had disappeared. When she laid bare her poor bleeding heart to me, she did it in such wise that for an instant I feared that it was a murder which she had committed. Indeed, she called it so! You understand that I know all your secret; all her part in it at least. And I know that you understand what loving duty lies before you. I see it in your eyes; your brave, true eyes! Go! and the Lord be with thee!' Her accustomed idiom had returned with prayer. She turned her head away, and, standing up, leaned against the window. Bending over, he took her hand and said simply:

'God bless you! I shall come back to thank you either to-night or to-morrow; and I hope that she will be with me.'

He went quickly out of the room. The woman stood for long looking out of the window, and following with tear-dimmed eyes the movement of his great black horse as he swept across country straight as the crow flies, towards the headland whither Stephen had gone.

* * * * *

Stephen passed over the wide expanse without thought; certainly without memory of it. Never in her after-life could she recall any thought that had passed through her mind from the time she left the open gate of the windmill yard till she pulled up her smoking, panting horse beside the ruin of the fisher's house.

Stephen was not unhappy! She was not happy in any conscious form. She was satisfied rather than dissatisfied. She was a woman! A woman who waited the coming of a man!

For a while she stood at the edge of the cliff, and looked at the turmoil of the tide churning on the rocks below. Her heart went out in a great burst of thankfulness that it was her hand which had been privileged to aid in rescuing so dear a life. Then she looked around her. Ostensibly it was to survey the ruined house; but in reality to search, even then under her lashes, the whole green expanse sloping up to the windmill for some moving figure. She saw that which made her throat swell and her ears to hear celestial music. But she would not allow herself to think, of that at all events. She was all woman now; all-patient, and all-submissive. She waited the man; and the man was coming!

For a few minutes she walked round the house as though looking at it critically for some after-purpose. After the wreck Stephen had suggested to Trinity House that there should be a lighthouse on the point; and offered to bear the expense of building it. She was awaiting the answer of the Brethren; and of course nothing would be done in clearing the ground for any purpose till the answer had come. She felt now that if that reply was negative, she would herself build there a pleasure-house of her own.

Then she went to the edge of the cliff, and went down the zigzag by which the man and horse had gone to their gallant task. At the edge of the flat rock she sat and thought.

And through all her thoughts passed the rider who even now was thundering over the green sward on his way to her. In her fancy at first, and later in her ears, she could hear the sound of his sweeping gallop.

It was thus that a man should come to a woman!

She had no doubts now. Her quietude was a hymn of grateful praise!

The sound stopped. With all her ears she listened, her heart now beginning to beat furiously. The sea before her, all lines and furrows with the passing tide, was dark under the shadow of the cliff; and the edge of the shadow was marked with the golden hue of sunset.

And then she saw suddenly a pillar of shadow beyond the line of the cliff. It rested but a moment, moved swiftly along the edge, and then was lost to her eyes.

But to another sense there was greater comfort: she heard the clatter of rolling pebbles and the scramble of eager feet. Harold was hastening down the zigzag.

Oh! the music of that sound! It woke all the finer instincts of the woman. All the dross and thought of self passed away. Nature, sweet and simple and true, reigned alone. Instinctively she rose and came towards him. In the simple nobility of her self-surrender and her purpose, which were at one with the grandeur of nature around her, to be negative was to be false.

Since he had spoken with the Silver Lady Harold had swept through the air; the rush of his foaming horse over the sward had been but a slow physical progress, which mocked the on-sweep of his mind. In is rapid ride he too had been finding himself. By the reading of his own soul he knew now that love needs a voice; that a man's love, to be welcomed to the full, should be dominant and self-believing.

When the two saw each other's eyes there was no need for words. Harold came close, opening wide his arms, Stephen flew to them.

In that divine moment, when their mouths met, both knew that their souls were one.

* * *

www.ingramcontent.com/pod-product-compliance
Ingram Content Group UK Ltd.
Pitfield, Milton Keynes, MK11 3LW, UK
UKHW040232290926
15471UKWH00002B/134

9 789355 841001